1995

# Teaching AT THE Middle Level

## A PROFESSIONAL'S HANDBOOK

SANDRA L. SCHURR, University of South Florida, Tampa, Florida

JULIA THOMASON, Appalachian State University, Boone, North Carolina

MAX THOMPSON, Appalachian State University, Boone, North Carolina

JOHN H. LOUNSBURY, EDITOR
EDITORIAL COORDINATION: The National Resource Center for Middle Grades Education, University of South Florida, Tampa, Florida

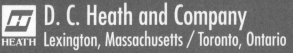 D. C. Heath and Company
HEATH Lexington, Massachusetts / Toronto, Ontario

# Table of Contents

# MODULE 6:

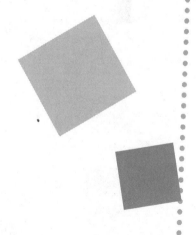

# About the Authors

## SANDRA L. SCHURR

Sandra Schurr, Ed. D., is the Director of the National Resource Center for Middle Grades/High School Education located at the University of South Florida in Tampa. She is also a tenured faculty member in the Secondary Education Department with primary responsibility for the graduate programs in middle level education.

She has authored several books, including *The Definitive Middle School Guide*; *Tools, Treasures, and Measures for Middle Grade Educators*; *Dynamite in the Classroom*, *How to Evaluate Your Middle School Program*; and *ABC's of Classroom Evaluation*.

Sandra Schurr is also a national and international consultant in the areas of authentic assessment, restructuring of middle level/high schools, and alternative delivery systems for classroom instruction.

## JULIA THOMASON

Julia Thomason, Ph. D., is Professor of Education in the Curriculum and Instruction Department of Appalachian State University in Boone, North Carolina. She has authored and co-authored a number of publications for the National Middle School Association on young adolescent development and its implications for middle school curriculum and instruction. Her most well-known titles are "Middle School and Beyond" (with Paul George) and "We Who Laugh, Last!" (with Walt Grebing).

Julia Thomason has been a consultant and evaluator for over 300 schools and school districts throughout the United States and Canada in the areas of middle school education, reorganization, and reform. In addition, she has been a speaker for a number of national organizations related to education.

## MAX THOMPSON

Max Thompson, Ed. D., is Professor of Curriculum and Instruction at Appalachian State University in Boone, North Carolina. He specializes in cognitive instructional strategies, integrated curriculum development, and authentic/performance assessment. He has authored numerous articles, chapters, and teachers' handbooks and guides in his areas of specialty, as well as delivered presentations and workshops.

Max Thompson has been a national and international consultant for several years in the areas of school restructuring, curriculum development and evaluation, teaching at-risk students, and designing middle school programs for learning.

# MODULE 1

# The Developmental Characteristics of Young Adolescents

**M**iddle school students are neither elementary nor secondary students; they are members of a unique third tier in education. These ten- to fourteen-year-olds have their own set of developmental characteristics and needs that must be recognized and addressed. The more genuine knowledge we have about middle grade learners, the better the chances are that our decisions will result in success for both our students and ourselves.

What are these developmental characteristics, competencies, and needs? Since the beginning of the middle school movement over thirty years ago, attention has centered on the cognitive, emotional, physical, and social aspects of middle school students' development. Recently, character development has come in for its share of study and discussion. This module explores all of these developmental issues and suggests ways teachers and administrators can make and implement decisions that promote students' self-acceptance and continued growth.

# Contents

# Topic 1 · COGNITIVE DEVELOPMENT

## ▶ What is it?

The term *cognitive development* is gradually replacing what educators used to call intellectual development (in contrast to the emotional, or affective, side of learning). At the same time, new information on cognitive growth and development has caused a shift in focus from the student as the product of teacher efforts to learning as the product—with the student as the worker who produces that learning. The old educational paradigm looked like this:

STUDENT AS PRODUCT

TEACHER AS WORKER

ADMINISTRATOR AS MANAGER

The new paradigm, which focuses on cognitive development, is as follows:

LEARNING AS PRODUCT

STUDENT AS WORKER

TEACHER AS MANAGER

There are several cognitive characteristics of young adolescents that teachers should take into account as they begin to create an environment in which learning is the product and the student is the worker.

## Cognitive Characteristics of Young Adolescents

■ **Intense curiosity, especially about the things that interest them**
Middle grade students have intense interests, many of which are very short-lived. These interests can move from topic to topic with the speed of light. (Remember the dinosaur period followed immediately by the devotion to the cello?)

- **A wide range of intellectual abilities, from concrete to abstract** Students at this age are often developing on two different cognitive levels simultaneously. In one subject, students might function at the level of concrete operations while in another they may exercise abstract thinking or even formal operational thinking. Those who are capable of formal operations will probably not exercise this kind of thinking spontaneously or consistently, and this very inconsistency marks the young adolescent as fairly normal.

- **Increasing metacognition (the ability to understand and articulate how they know the things they know)** If you ask students at this stage to name their state capital, they not only can give you the correct answer but also can explain how they know that answer is correct. They are beginning to know *how* they know.

- **Willingness to learn material they consider useful and relevant** Every teacher has probably heard the dreaded question, "Why do we have to know this, and when will we ever use it?" When the answer is acceptable, learning takes place; when it is not acceptable, students may go through the motions of learning while assimilating and understanding very little.

- **Egocentricism and difficulty in seeing events and intentions from another's point of view** Much of young adolescents' time and energy are spent on attempting to understand exactly how ideas, events, rules, and actions affect them personally. With this constant attention to self, seeing things from another point of view is very difficult for them. While they are not as egocentric as smaller children who have little awareness of the outside world, they are still very introspective. They tend to assume that if they themselves have not actually experienced whatever is being considered, it can't be very important. Further, they have difficulty understanding why someone would act differently from the way they would in a similar situation.

- **Shift in creative abilities toward the cognitive** In younger children, creative activities such as drawing, singing, or dancing are not necessarily thoughtful actions. They tend to be spontaneous and, for the most part, clearly affective. In young adolescents, however, these creative actions tend to be more practiced, thought-out, and rule oriented, and, therefore, more cognitive.

# ► How do we address students' cognitive needs?

As you begin to plan your lessons with a focus on learning as the product and the student as the worker, you need to consider and resolve for yourself three critical issues.

**Issue 1:** Are you comfortable with the idea that, for the most part, middle school students learn more like elementary students than like secondary students? They may look like high school students, but we have come to realize that cognitively they process and retain information more like students in the earlier grades. This issue is important to consider as you develop lessons, instructional strategies, materials, schedules, and assessments.

**Issue 2:** Are you comfortable with the idea that young adolescents learn best in cooperative, decentralized settings where they are constantly interacting with materials and with one another? Classrooms where this philosophy has been adopted appear less systematic and somewhat less orderly than traditional classrooms. Students move about and go where they need to go to find information. Teachers function more as facilitators than as centers of instruction. Depending on how you resolve this issue, student and teacher roles may be redefined, and the appearance of the classroom may be significantly altered.

**Issue 3:** Are you comfortable with the idea that learning takes *time?* In many classrooms, if you were to ask a student, "Didn't anyone ever teach you that?" the student would be justified in answering, "No. But someone did mention it to me once, I think." There is little doubt that facilitating true cognition takes more time than that needed to simply convey information. While providing adequate time for learning may result in less content coverage, it can significantly enhance learning.

Once you have resolved these three issues, you are ready to start designing developmentally appropriate curriculum and instruction. The following are some quick-start suggestions for making your expectations, lessons, and assignments responsive to the cognitive characteristics of young adolescents:

## 1. Begin lessons with the concrete.

Wherever your students operate cognitively is where lessons should begin. Students can then develop schema and scaffolds that provide a base for information and concepts they encounter subsequently. If this strategy seems too elementary, remember Issue 1.

## 2. Create lessons that are brief but fairly intense.

Middle grade students have short but intense attention spans. In fact, there is a growing belief that their attention spans equal a minute for each year of their chronological age, plus one. If that is the case, then the most effective lessons consist of several short bites.

## 3. Allow students to interact with one another and with materials.

We all have stories to tell about times when we, as teachers, explained and explained a concept to no avail. Then one student said just three words to another student, and the concept was revealed to everyone in a virtual epiphany. If this seems unaccountable, remember Issue 2.

## 4. Ask exploratory questions that require higher-level thinking.

A great deal has been written about questioning strategies. Wait time, random-response patterns, impulsive versus reflective responders, and Bloom's taxonomy have all received a great deal of press. Are there any magic questions that cause students to pursue an idea and explore the answers? Of course, the answer is no. However, there are five questions that, when fully incorporated into lessons and discussions, seem to help students think more deeply and thoroughly.

- **"What if . . . ?"** While this may sound at first like a question more suited for kindergarten than for middle school, it has considerable merit for middle grade students. *What if a nuclear waste dump were proposed for your area? What if the driving age were raised to 18? What if your school went year round? What if . . . ?*

  How do *What if* questions differ from *What* questions? Consider these examples. A classic *What* question is, *What were the causes of the American Civil War? What* questions require mere recall of information. A classic *What if* question is, *What if we had a civil war in 1994? What might be the causes? What if* questions require knowledge, comprehension, synthesis, analysis, evaluation, generalization, and prediction.

- **"How do you know?"** This question requires students to practice their newly developing metacognitive abilities—thinking about their own thinking and knowing how they know. In practice it might work this way.

> TEACHER: What is the capital of North Carolina?
>
> STUDENT: Raleigh.
>
> TEACHER: How do you know?
>
> STUDENT: The governor lives there, the legislature meets there, we saw the capitol building on our fifth-grade field trip, and there is a star on the state map at Raleigh.

That's knowing how you know.

- **"Are you sure?"** Asking students to justify their answers requires them to substantiate their choices, to argue, and to persuade others to their points of view. All this needs to be done orally; middle school students are masters at nodding affirmatively even when they don't have a clue. By asking them to voice their reasons for being sure, you can help them think more deeply and express themselves more effectively.

- **"Will you think out loud please?"** (or, **"Let me hear you think out loud."**) Students who give only visual feedback to a question—a nod, a smile, a gesture—may or may not have any idea of what is going on. The only way for you to be certain is to listen to them think through their answers. Verbalization can be difficult for young adolescents—they have had so little practice. Listening to their thinking allows you to adjust or correct their reasoning when appropriate.

- **"Of what value is this information to you?"** Those of us who have taught for more than twenty minutes have had to answer the question, "Why do we have to learn this stuff?" In other words, "Of what value is this information to me as a student?" If we agree that young adolescents are willing to learn things they consider useful and relevant to them *now*, it stands to reason that we should help them start to answer this question for themselves. When they begin to make what are essentially evaluative judgments about the material to be learned, they can begin to internalize their personal need for that information.

## 5. Be prepared for off-the-track responses.

When students are learning new concepts and pushing themselves to think at ever higher levels, they often generate ideas that seem brilliant initially but are in fact off the track. Then it is your job to guide, probe, lead, and cue, while protecting fragile egos.

## 6. Leave some loose ends, and leave some questions unanswered.

Much of the traditional curriculum for the middle grades is designed to be vertical: a question is allotted one, and only one, answer. We know that in life, however, most questions have multiple answers and resolving an issue becomes a matter of selecting the best or most suitable ones. Furthermore, as adults we know that some questions do not have answers. Middle school students are developing their capacity to deal with ambiguity; you can give them chances to practice.

## 7. Create an environment where taking risks and chances is safe.

Many students are so afraid of making mistakes and of being wrong that they won't take chances. The "good students" are often the least likely to risk being wrong. Let them see you venture and risk. On those occasions when you are hasty or careless in your thinking, admit it. You will help them see that taking chances in class discussions is not a life-threatening prospect.

## 8. Create authentic lesson presentations, demonstrations, and experiences.

Because middle grade students lack a sophisticated time and space perspective, they live for the moment. We have already noted their eagerness to learn information and skills they consider relevant. If you consider these characteristics in relation to their desire to act, rather than sit passively, it becomes apparent that they need teacher demonstrations at the very minimum and actual experiential learning whenever and wherever possible.

## 9. Use visual aids.

Young adolescents are probably the most media-literate members of our society. If time spent on a task—in this case, the task of watching and viewing—counts, we have many experts in every class. You can address this talent for accessing information visually by using graphics, overheads, charts, and illustrations in your classroom.

## 10. Provide opportunities for students to explore materials for themselves—both individually and with others.

Cooperative learning may not be the only solution, but it is a significant one. When learners interact with one another and with the materials in a meaningful and investigative manner, their learning is likely to be considerably enhanced.

## 11. Utilize a wide variety of teaching techniques.

Young adolescents are moment-to-moment creatures. Unpredictable as they are, they *can* be counted on to respond to variety. A lecture/recitation format does not adequately address this need. Variety does.

## 12. Ensure opportunities to rehearse and practice key concepts.

With curriculum content so broad and time so short, teachers are often reduced to *mentioning* rather than *teaching* some key concepts. In order for thorough learning to occur, students need time to practice. There is little doubt, for example, that lab-oriented science produces more long-term learning, application, and transfer than lecture-oriented science does.

# ▶ Where do we go for more information?

Thomason, J. 1988. Six steps to clearer thinking. *Oasis* 3: 16–19.
Considers the developmental characteristics of young adolescents and the implications of these characteristics for thinking. Promotes the idea that middle grade students learn more like elementary students and therefore need more active hands-on experiences. Offers a list of questions that promote higher level thinking, greater student investigation, more connectedness among content areas, and more substantive teacher-student and student-student conversations.

Sousa, D. 1992. Helping students remember what you teach. *Middle School Journal* 23: 21–23.
Investigates real, authentic learning as opposed to content coverage and "mentioning." Includes discussion of factors that affect content retention, comprehension strategies, verbal cues, image cues, spacing effect, rehearsal and practice, organization of new information, and influence of information in memory. Suggests eight important strategies for teachers that can improve students' retention of learning, including teachers' linking new knowledge with previously mastered content, using a variety of techniques, and organizing the new materials so that students can classify information and put it in long-term memory.

## *References*

George, P., and Lawrence, G. 1982. *Handbook for middle school teaching*. Glenview, IL: Scott, Foresman and Company.

# Topic 2  EMOTIONAL DEVELOPMENT

> ## ▶ What is it?

No one knows better than teachers and parents how erratic and inconsistent young adolescents can be. We know their periods of anxiety and fear contrast with periods of almost intolerable bravado. The term *mood swings* takes on added meaning for people who interact with middle grade students.

We tend to think of young adolescence as a time of psychological turmoil equaled at no other time in human development. But the truth probably is that most middle grade students are basically optimistic and hopeful. When they ask the question, "Am I normal?" the answer is almost always yes. When they ask, "Who am I?" we recognize a healthy search to form a conscious sense of their own individuality and uniqueness.

The middle years can, however, become a negative turning point in the development of a sense of self. Perhaps the most powerful risk is the "big lie" that young adolescents are frequently told and come to believe, the lie that they are inadequate (Van Hoose and Strahan, 1988). Some manage to let go of the big lie during this emotionally stressful time and form a sense of themselves as competent human beings. Others carry a feeling of inadequacy throughout their adult lives. As a teacher, you can make a positive difference. You have a significant and profound influence on the young people with whom you work. To a considerable degree, consciously or unconsciously, you are helping young adolescents answer the age-old question, "Who am I, and is that enough?"

What should teachers and administrators know about young adolescents in order to have the most positive effect possible on how students come to answer this question? What characteristics, needs, and competencies of this age group must be addressed?

> **"*I*ndividual variability is the norm because they are developing so idiosyncratically during early adolescence.**"
>
> (Stevenson, 1992)

# Emotional Characteristics of Young Adolescents

- **Chemical and hormonal imbalances** During puberty, body changes that are a normal part of physical development have a considerable impact on students' emotional development as well. You might think of adolescence as a time when the hormones say Yes! Yes! while parents and teachers say No! No! The next section of this module explores these physical changes in more detail.

- **Idealism** Young adolescents want everyone around them to be totally above reproach. When an idol or hero falls from grace in the eyes of a thirteen-year-old, the fall is total and the disappointment complete.

- **A closer resemblance to children than to adults** While your students may look like adults in many cases, they are still very childlike emotionally. Like children, their highs are the highest and their lows are "the pits."

- **A need for personal as well as for family security** Maslow cites physical safety as a major need of humans. Middle grade students also have a considerable need to believe that their family members are safe and that the family as a unit is secure.

- **Increasing awareness of themselves as individuals, especially in comparison with others** If we think that middle grade students use school for cognitive and intellectual growth, we deceive ourselves. They use school to measure themselves constantly against their peers. How the peer group acts and develops serves as their barometer for normalcy. At the same time, they are measuring themselves against the models they are constantly exposed to in the media.

- **A tendency to be unrealistically self-critical** Ask the students you consider the most talented, healthy, skilled, artistic, and wholesome in your school whether they are happy with themselves. Their answers will almost assuredly consist of a hundred things they believe are weird, unacceptable, barely adequate, or just plain wrong about themselves. Young adolescents are almost universally dissatisfied with themselves at the very time they are forming their adult sense of self—the sense of self they will carry for life.

Young adolescents are

- Able to trust others even when that trust may sometimes be violated and undervalued

- Able to take and accept criticism and, to some extent, rejection

- Capable of great love for their families while at the same time recognizing family dysfunction

- Becoming more comfortable with their growing sense of intimacy with others

- Becoming better able to deal with hatred and anger

- **A tendency to be easily offended** Adolescents can misconstrue almost any statement as a bitter attack directed at some imagined personal shortcoming.

- **Need for privacy** Middle grade students need time to be alone to think through events and feelings. It is the time when they learn about the new persons they are becoming.

- **Vulnerability to naive arguments and difficulty in seeing more than one side to any discussion** These qualities are related to adolescent egocentrism and inability to see things from another's point of view. Your challenge is to bear these qualities in mind during classroom discussions, where they will inevitably surface.

- **An emerging sense of humor** Since laughter is an emotional release, adolescence is a developmentally appropriate time to sharpen the sense of humor. Young adolescents are terrified of laughing at themselves, however, and their attempts at humor are almost always directed toward others; sometimes toward peers, sometimes toward people less fortunate than they, and many times toward teachers. (Teasing behavior is perfectly normal, and adults should probably, for the most part, ignore it.)

- **A basic optimism and hopefulness** In addition to the "big lie" of adolescents' inadequacy, a second great lie emerged a few years ago—the lie that all middle grade students are miserable, unhappy, despondent people who hate their parents and are likely to be suicidal. Joan Lipsitz, in *Successful Schools for Young Adolescents* (1984), maintains that while far too many of our students are indeed unhappy and despondent, the vast majority are normal, well-adjusted, happy people.

# ► How do we address students' emotional needs?

Before exploring how we can use our considerable influence as teachers and administrators to ensure positive emotional growth in our students, we should consider two critical concepts.

**Concept 1:** Many developmentalists are coming to believe that adults are pretty much the same people they were when they were twelve to fourteen years old. If that is the case, middle school teachers are present at the creation of human beings who are developing the patterns that will characterize them for the rest of their lives. Attending to a young adolescent's emotional growth becomes critically important.

**Concept 2:** A second idea gaining support by those who study emotional development holds that we are to a great extent the people others have told us we are. External forces have a powerful effect on our personal sense of self. If parents and teachers are supportive and encouraging, we tend to think positively about ourselves. If they are not, we have feelings of inadequacy, inferiority, and guilt. As the saying goes, "You are not who you think you are. You are not who I think you are. You are who you think I think you are."

Once you and your team members have discussed these concepts, the next step is to look at some nurturing policies and practices that you can implement immediately, whatever your school's curriculum or organizational structure.

## 1. Know thyself.

This precept is especially significant in relation to your role in fostering the emotional development of your students. You may find it difficult to effect the suggestions that follow if you have not yet dealt personally with the issues involved.

## 2. Understand and accept the typical behaviors of the age group.

Almost invariably, when someone says, "I wish that child would act her age," the child already is. Mood swings are normal, anger is normal, doubt is normal, errors in judgment are normal. When young people are trying on different emotional personalities, they are going to make a few mistakes. In most circumstances, your job is to minimize those mistakes by assuring students that they are perfectly normal and that all the world is really not looking at them. The imaginary spotlight and imaginary audience of David Elkind (1984) are all too real to young adolescents.

### 3. Be an honest, available role model.

Perhaps there is no other time students need you more. They need a reliable sounding board for their newly forming thoughts and ideas about themselves and the world around them. The advisor/advisee program as a structured time for adult availability is discussed in a later module. For now, it is enough to recognize that your time with your students is often the best part of their day and that you as middle school teachers play a significant part in their growing up. You need to be there for them and to be there willingly and enthusiastically.

### 4. Be a good, attentive listener.

Along with simply being there, you will want to hear and attend to what students are telling you. In many cases, students don't want to hear what you have to say; they want to hear what they have to say. Often they don't know what they are thinking until they hear themselves saying it.

### 5. Avoid sarcasm.

Young adolescents are highly sensitive to imagined criticism, and we adults are often the unconscious cause of their hurt feelings. We need to make things right again in a way that is appropriate to the original "offense." Embarrassing students in public and apologizing in private is not the way to deal with the problem.

### 6. Help students to feel skilled and competent.

Genuine praise, not a false sense of accomplishment, contributes significantly to the young adolescent's sense of self-worth and authentic growth. Success with one task enhances the student's desire to try something more difficult.

### 7. Provide praise and reinforcement in appropriate ways.

Middle grade students like to know that someone is proud of them and appreciates their efforts. For many young adolescents, however, the need to be one of the group is more important than the joy of being singled out by the teacher. Consequently, you may often want to provide praise and reinforcement in private or in some low-key way.

## 8. Create an environment in which students can experience acceptance by peers.

Middle grade students need to combine their peer association with their need to feel (and be) skilled and competent. They need to feel that they have something to offer the group. One way for students to answer the question, "Am I normal and like everyone else?" is for them to work and associate with many different peer role models. And one of the best ways for them to be accepted by their peers is to be considered good at something. You as a teacher can structure productive peer associations in the classroom as well as help individual students identify their areas of strength and expertise.

## 9. Help students feel acceptance by adults.

During this time of emotional growth, middle grade students experience a dichotomy between wanting adult acceptance and needing desperately to separate from those same adults. If you compare students with each other, even when the comparison is positive, you may create a sense that you are not accepting them for what they are, that "just being me" is not enough. Alienation and anonymity are harsh emotions, and adolescents frequently experience them.

**TIPS FOR TEACHERS AND TEAMS**

There are appropriate and inappropriate ways to show empathy and compassion. Remember, you can share feelings without shouldering blame.

Don't confuse physical size with emotional maturity. Some of the most emotionally confused students look like adults.

## ► Where do we go for more information?

Van Hoose, J., and Strahan, D. 1988. *Young adolescent development and school practices: Promoting harmony.* Columbus, OH: National Middle School Association.
A small but information-rich monograph. Provides considerable insight into the emotional development of young adolescents. Suggests what teachers can expect as well as what they can do to help students through this sometimes turbulent period. Includes interviews and vignettes of students relating real-life situations in their own words.

Elkind, D. 1984. *All grown up and no place to go.* Reading, MA: Addison-Wesley Publishing Company.
A well-known and near-classic book with a powerful statement about rushed childhood and hurried adolescence. Argues that too much is expected too soon for most children and that when children are asked to cope too early with adult emotional and social situations, they are almost certain to experience failure and self-doubt. Suggests a delayed entry into the adult world and supports the premise that middle schools are not and should not be emotional and social rehearsal stages for high school and adulthood.

# References

Lipsitz, J. 1984. *Successful schools for young adolescents*. New Brunswick, NJ: Transaction Books.

Stevenson, C. 1992. *Teaching the ten to fourteen year old*. White Plains, NY: Longman Press.

# PHYSICAL DEVELOPMENT

## ▶ What is it?

**G**rowth and development rates affect middle grade students in many more ways than we might commonly think. Young adolescents are in a period of rapid change physically, cognitively, emotionally, and socially. Physical development, to some extent, runs the entire process.

This period of maturation is characterized by rapid growth spurts, awkwardness, developing motor skills, and increased strength and endurance—or it isn't! There is no guarantee for young adolescents that reaching the age of thirteen will automatically initiate their eagerly anticipated growth spurt. For some, the process begins at nine or ten; for others, there is no evidence of physical maturation until the late teens. And, within this range, each individual child is different.

If there are no givens and no absolutes, how *can* we characterize young adolescents physically? How do they behave? What are their vulnerabilities? What are their competencies and needs?

### Physical Characteristics of Young Adolescents

- **Uneven growth spurts** Middle grade students experience accelerated physical development marked by increases in weight, height, heart size, lung capacity, and muscular strength.

- **A tendency toward poor motor coordination** As a group, middle grade students are not particularly physically fit or well coordinated. Many have poor levels of endurance, strength, and flexibility. They may be more overweight and less healthy than at other times in their development.

> **"E**arly adolescence is characterized by periods of pronounced and accelerated growth. It is perhaps the most dynamic growth period that humans experience with the exception of the fetal and prenatal period.**"**
>
> (McEwin & Thomason, 1989)

- **Muscular development and changes in body contour** Rapid changes in adolescence can result in a disproportionate body framework. Hands and feet seem too big, noses stick out, and nothing ever seems to fit.

- **Sexual development** This occurs earlier, for the most part, among girls than among boys. As a group, however, middle grade students experience biological sexual development several years sooner than adolescents of a century ago did. Increased hormonal secretions have a major impact on middle grade students' reactions to the opposite sex. Boys and girls notice each other in a new way.

- **Mood swings** We cannot anticipate who will come in the classroom door each day. When the hormones are a positive force, life is good; when they are not, the day can be far from joyful!

- **Abrupt transitions from alertness and excessive energy to fatigue and lethargy** Within minutes the student who has been the life of the party can almost literally drop off to sleep. Adults can mistake these swings for deliberate acts rather than normal consequences of this stage of physical development.

- **Increased nutritional demands and unpredictable food preferences** Anyone who has fed hungry teenagers knows that their energy level requires great quantities of calories to support their activities. Planning a diet that pleases them, however, can be a gamble.

- **Need for plenty of rest and sleep** The rate of growth and development for young adolescents takes a great deal of energy and stamina. Middle grade students, somewhat like young infants, need sleep to store up energy for the significant growth spurt they are now experiencing.

- **Need for frequent and somewhat continuous movement** Bundles of energy one minute and lethargic creatures the next, young adolescents have a seemingly contradictory amount of energy. But their need to move about, change positions, and basically wiggle is standard behavior.

# ► How do we address students' physical needs?

The Carnegie Council on Adolescent Development gives considerable emphasis to the need for attention to young adolescents' health and physical fitness (*Fateful Choices*, 1988). Cognitive success alone is not a sufficient goal. Addressing the physical needs of students, however, requires a commitment from the entire administrative and teaching staff.

## 1. Design a comprehensive health and physical fitness program that is relevant to the specific needs and capabilities of young adolescents.

Responsibility for such a program should not belong entirely to the physical education teachers and coaches; everyone benefits from healthy students. Your program should include supervised exercise regimens conducted by trained leaders, instruction in personal hygiene, access to accurate information and facts, and opportunities for students to ask questions and get straight answers about their physical development.

## 2. Plan opportunities for all students to experience physical success.

Every student needs the chance to demonstrate competence in a sport, game, or dance activity. Create and support intramural programs that ensure that the less physically gifted, talented, and skilled have their chance to participate.

## 3. Provide for adequate nutrition.

About the time young adolescents need more food to sustain their growth, they enter the "thin is in" phase and begin to diet and exercise frequently, generally ignoring their nutritional needs. Schools can attend to this behavior by building nutritional information and counseling into the health curriculum. In addition, students' dietary needs, along with their healthy food aversions, should be considered when school lunches are planned.

## 4. Vary the pace of lessons.

Plan short breaks, and build in activities that allow students to interact with their peers and physically stretch and move around. Keep in mind that their restlessness results from real physical needs.

## PHYSICAL COMPETENCIES

For the most part, young adolescents

- Can perform increasingly complex motor activities

- Demonstrate increasing flexibility

- Do heavier work as well as run faster and longer

- Play and participate in increasingly more "physical" activities. Some have the talents and skills for field games, court games, racket sports, and gymnastics.

- Enjoy athletic achievement and increasing levels of physical performance

- Become more interested in physical fitness

## 5. Help students come to terms with their personal talents, skills, proficiencies, and inadequacies.

This can include helping students face responsibility for sexual behavior, which is often based on feelings that have developed before full emotional and social maturity are present. It should also include helping students come to terms with the temporary condition of their bodies—their lack of coordination and proportion.

# ▶ Where do we go for more information?

Irvin, J., ed. 1992. *Transforming middle level education: Perspectives and possibilities*. Needham, MA: Allyn and Bacon.
A very complete volume of articles on a number of middle level issues. Includes a brief but thorough section on physical characteristics and the tremendous effect and potential consequences that physical development involves ("A Portrait of Diversity: The Middle Level Student," by Joel Milgram of the University of Cincinnati).

Muth, K., and Alvermann, D. 1992. *Teaching and learning in the middle school*. Needham, MA: Allyn and Bacon.
Provides case studies of students whose stories demonstrate the relationships between cognitive, social, emotional, and physical development. Examines the effects of puberty, problems in physical development, self-concept, and the psychological and social effects of physical development (Chapter Two, "Young Adolescent Development").

# References

Carnegie Council on Adolescent Development. 1992. *Fateful choices: Healthy youth for the 21st century*. New York: Carnegie Corporation of New York.

Lipsitz, J. 1984. *Successful schools for young adolescents*. New Brunswick, NJ: Transaction Books.

McEwin, K., and Thomason, J. 1989. *Who they are: How we teach*. Columbus, OH: National Middle School Association.

Rickard, L., and Woods, A. 1993. Curriculum and pedagogy in middle school physical education. *Middle School Journal* 24(4): 51–55.

# Topic 4 · SOCIAL DEVELOPMENT

## ▶ What is it?

**B**asically, social development occurs as young adolescents become aware of themselves not only as individuals but also collectively as members of society. During this period of their development, middle grade students are ready to take a broader view. They become increasingly aware that they need a more comprehensive and global sense of themselves as participants in the family, peer group, community, nation, and world. They are beginning to come to terms with society's expectations for them and to develop their social skills. They are ready to begin contributing to society.

In this section, we will consider the social characteristics of young adolescents, what teachers can reasonably expect of them, and what they need from teachers and other adult role models to help them become socially successful.

### Social Characteristics of Young Adolescents

- **Peer-group orientation and motivation** Middle grade students are shifting from a family-oriented structure for making decisions toward a more peer-centered model. Their mirror of social acceptability is their peer group and their barometer of social success is controlled by their friends and developmental age mates. Conformity to peer pressure is to be expected.

- **Failure to adapt and flourish in uncompromising settings** While adults may have learned the art of social compromise, young adolescents are much more likely to shut down and turn off than to attempt to make the best of a situation.

- **Argumentativeness** They can be counted on to take sides in any major or minor socially relevant debate. To some degree they seem "bound to bicker."

## FIVE SOCIAL MYTHS

1. All young adolescents are estranged from their parents.

2. This period of development is necessarily turbulent.

3. There is one typical pattern of adolescent development and behavior.

4. Young adolescence is a subculture of age rather than of race, ethnicity, cultural heritage, or occupation.

5. Peers are the end-all and be-all of social relationships.

(George & Lawrence, 1982)

# SOCIAL COMPETENCIES

**Young adolescents are capable, to some extent, of**

- **Originating and maintaining opposite-sex relationships**
- **Demonstrating autonomous and assertive behaviors**
- **Shifting their social focus from family to peers**
- **Valuing adults as reliable resources**
- **Being optimistic and selfless**

- **Flashes of social consciousness punctuating egocentricity** For the most part, middle grade students are interested primarily in how society is going to work for them personally and only secondarily in how they can work for the good of others.

- **Social self-consciousness** They seem totally absorbed in what others will think of them. As David Elkind (1984) has pointed out, they are victims of the imaginary-spotlight and imaginary-audience syndrome. They believe that if they make even the smallest mistake, *everyone* will know. The slightest social blunder or even social unease can feel to them like a major disaster.

- **Rejection of adult standards and adult viewpoints on many social issues** This is the appropriate time for young adolescents to break away from their total dependence on parents and other adults and assume a new role. That act almost always entails rejecting previous points of view.

- **Social fads** If there was ever a group for whom the words *slave to fashion* are appropriate, that group is young adolescents. They often worry to the extreme about what is socially in and out and follow fads doggedly.

- **Exaggerated responses** They can usually be counted on to over-act. They can almost *always* be counted on to *overreact*.

- **Extreme social shyness or social extroversion beyond their years** We have all experienced social situations where one young person could not be dragged into the conversation and another could not be dragged from the room. (Frequently the middle grade students with the strongest social skills also have strong cognitive, physical, and emotional skills as well.)

- **Need for supportive and stable home environments** Though their definitions of *home* may differ, young adolescents express a consistent need for stability. In discussions with ten- to fourteen-year-olds, the need for family security and a personally stable life are often mentioned. With much of their lives in turmoil, they have an enhanced need for something to be dependable and reliable. For many, these qualities are part of what *home* means.

# ► How do we address students' social needs?

As adults, teachers, and role models, you have many opportunities to influence students' social development and especially to decrease any sense of social alienation and anonymity. You can structure activities and create an atmosphere that encourages young adolescents to truly become a part of society and to contribute to its causes.

## 1. Design and participate in school-based social activities.

Create opportunities for students to interact with peers in adult settings. Students need a social practice field that provides the opportunity to exercise their social skills with minimal risk and without undue pressure to be perfect. Teachers are frequently very good at helping students recognize and focus on what is expected and what is acceptable.

## 2. Encourage and participate in intramural programs.

Make sure that these activities emphasize the social aspects of competition and of winning and losing.

## 3. Help students feel acceptance by adults, as well as by their peers.

Middle graders are somewhat like toddlers in that they take three steps forward and then look back to see how well they are doing. As well as needing acceptance by their peers, they often need assurance that they are doing well by adult standards. We might not think they care much about what we think, but that is only because they are often excellent actors.

## 4. Help students see how they fit into the complex roles society expects of them.

Although society has become much more conscious of gender inequality, society's expectations for men and women are still somewhat different. Understanding the roles and responsibilities that society expects and values helps students develop a sense of who they are and how they will deal with these expectations.

## TIPS FOR TEACHERS AND TEAMS

Use extensive peer teaching.

Involve community members.

Engage in frequent social and ethical discussions with students.

Emphasize critical as well as creative thinking in dealing with social questions and situations.

### 5. Allow students to work in groups and to teach one another.

Experiences such as these increase social interaction and foster greater understanding among the smaller social groups represented in the total group.

### 6. Provide opportunities for students to work and interact with others from socially different walks of life.

Schools help students develop a sense of what is normal behavior. One additional responsibility of the school is to expand the student's sense of what is "normal." Expanding this awareness comes about when students have the chance to see, be with, and work with all types of people representing different races, ethnic groups, cultures, and abilities.

### 7. Provide for community involvement.

The marked increase in community and service learning projects around the country supports our awareness that young adolescents are both interested in and quite capable of giving something back to their towns, cities, and communities. For the first time in their lives they are ready to affect the outer world. One way to do this is to provide students meaningful community involvement.

### 8. Attend to and respect students' constant need for social self-definition.

Young adolescents continually measure themselves against others to determine whether they are normal.

## References

Elkind, D. 1984. *All grown up and no place to go.* Reading, MA: Addison-Wesley Publishing Company.

George, P., and Lawrence, G. 1982. *Handbook for middle school teaching.* Glenview, IL: Scott, Foresman and Company.

# ▶ What is it?

The last several decades have seen a running debate on whether or not schools should teach morals, ethics, and values. The advocates have claimed that these were not being taught elsewhere and that schools should therefore take responsibility for them. The opponents have maintained that accountability for values and morals belongs to the home and family and that schools, insofar as possible, should be "values free."

The debate is ongoing, and it has serious implications for the complete development of our youth. Have we created a valueless society? Should only certain values be included in a school curriculum and the rest be ignored or left to the family? Should our schools aspire to be models of democratic morals, ethics, and values? If so, should these be taught in order for children to see and accept their worth?

We believe that middle schools should be models of a moral democracy. Further, we believe that young adolescents share certain characteristics, competencies, and needs where morals, ethics, and values are concerned. Finally, we believe that there are things you as a teacher and as a member of a team can do to enhance character development in your students.

As a working term, we prefer *character development* to *values clarification* or *moral development*. Perhaps there will be less debate over whether young adolescents need to develop character than over whose morals and ethics should be modeled, taught, and learned. We trust that *character development* is a less value-laden term and therefore less controversial and more useful in discussion.

## CHARACTER DEVELOPMENT COMPETENCIES

Middle grade students are becoming more

- PURPOSEFUL in their thoughts and actions

- PRODUCTIVE members of a community and society

- CRITICAL in their thinking about morals and ethics

# Character Development Characteristics of Young Adolescents

- **Idealism**  Middle grade students are almost adamant about fairness. "You're not fair" is the worst rebuke a twelve-year-old can hurl at a teacher. "You're hard but you're fair" is a high compliment. Middle grade students also have definite ideas about what adults should be and do. Idols fly high. Any disappointment results in a steep and decided fall from grace, and there is practically nothing a fallen idol can do to be rehabilitated.

- **A tendency to pose large, usually unanswerable, questions**  Young adolescents crave to know the meaning of life and to discover the role society expects them to play. They seem to realize that adults don't have all the answers, but they are considerably offended when their questions are trivialized or treated lightly.

- **Reflectiveness and introspection about their newly developing consciences**  As they begin to confront new and more sophisticated situations requiring moral and ethical decisions, young adolescents look inward for answers and reasons. Remember that when thirteen-year-olds come to you to discuss an issue, they often want just to hear themselves talk and need you simply to listen.

- **Confrontation of difficult moral and ethical questions**  As much as we might try to protect our youth from the hard realities connected with growing up, their middle grade years are filled with weighty events and decisions. In fact, the actions and consequences faced by previous generations may have been quite mild in comparison. Many of us have no idea how difficult life is for some of our students. If we did, perhaps we would more fully reward their courage in even coming to school.

- **A need for support**  If we rely primarily on the home and church to influence moral and ethical development, we may seriously compromise students who do not have home and church as resources. At the very time when young adolescents need to confront issues presented to them personally and through the media, they may have little adult support to guide their thinking and reasoning. Without this support, many middle grade students are going to reach whatever conclusions they finally reach about morals and ethics very much by themselves and in isolation. The adults in their schools must be willing and able to help them examine their newly developing senses of right and wrong.

■ **A longing for conformity that may result in less than desirable moral and ethical role models**  Social approval may supersede moral convictions. Self-esteem, so important at this time in a young adolescent's life, may come from being accepted by the "wrong crowd" if the need for acceptance is greater than the urge toward high moral principles.

# ▶ How do we address students' needs?

You can begin integrating character development issues now in your current relationship with middle grade students, as well as begin accommodating these issues as you rethink curriculum and organizational designs.

1. Act as caregivers, models, and mentors.

2. Create a positive moral climate throughout the school community (in the classroom, within the team, and throughout the school).

3. Model moral discipline.

4. Plan for and create democratic situations within classrooms and within teams.

5. Teach values through a curriculum that is consistent with the community's expectation of its schools.

6. Use cooperative discussion groups and learning situations to allow students to hear how they and their peers are dealing with ethical issues.

7. Encourage students' moral reflection (which may or may not be shared with the teacher or with other students).

8. Teach conflict resolution as a vehicle for settling disputes which might otherwise result in violence, injury, or some other form of personal hurt.

9. Promote care beyond the classroom.

10. Respect students' personal environments.

11. Recruit parents and community members to be in the school as role models and to become partners in character education.

## ▶ TIPS FOR TEACHERS AND TEAMS

Teachers who are concerned about morals, ethics, values, and character development in young adolescents

- Present clear, consistent, and sincere messages

- Don't "pull rank" and aren't dictatorial

- Communicate high standards and high expectations

- Really listen to their students

- Communicate their commitment through actions

- Earn respect and respect others

## ▶ Where do we go for more information?

*Educational Leadership.* 1993, November.
An entire issue devoted to character education. Presents a great deal of information about the development of character within schools, including the theory of character development. Cites concrete examples of programs that have been successful in schools. (While this issue is not specific to middle schools nor to young adolescents, almost all of the material is applicable to them.)

### References

Kohlberg, L. 1969. Stage and sequence: The cognitive developmental approach to socialization. In *Handbook of socialization theory and research,* ed. D. Goslin. Chicago: Rand McNally and Company.

Williams, M. M. 1993. Actions speak louder than words: What students think. *Educational Leadership* (November)51(3): 22–23.

# K - W - L: Developmental Characteristics of Young Adolescents

The K-W-L strategy helps you think about what you already know, what you think you want to learn more about, and then later to think about what you have learned.

**K**   First list what you *know* about the characteristics, competencies, and needs of middle grade students.

**W**   Now list what you *want to know* more about.

**L**   Later, after reading and working through this module, you may want to return to the information in the first two columns and add what you *have learned* about these topics.

| What do you know? | What do you want to know? | What have you learned? |
| --- | --- | --- |
| | | |

# 2 Making the Transition to a Middle School

If young adolescents are unique, should their schools reflect that uniqueness? We would probably agree that neither the high school model nor the elementary model is appropriate for twelve- to fourteen-year-olds. What seems to be needed are schools that bridge the gap, schools that are neither elementary nor secondary, but instead are independent and developmentally appropriate.

In this module, we will consider some of the larger issues involved in making the transition to a fully realized middle school. How might a school, a district, or even a group of interested teachers within a school redesign their programs and strategies to make them more learner-centered? How can educators maximize students' strengths and respond to their needs? How much time does such a transition take? What about staff development? Where do you start? These are some of the questions this module attempts to answer.

# Contents

# Topic 1    YOUNG ADOLESCENTS: A REFRESHER

## ▶ Who are they?

If the cornerstone of a true middle school is its learner-centered responsiveness, what do we need to know about those learners? In the previous module, we considered five important dimensions of young adolescent development and suggested ways teachers and schools might respond to middle grade students' abilities and needs. Here we will take a brief look at some generalizations about the age group. Later in this module, we will examine how these generalizations can serve as the foundation for setting goals, generating philosophy statements, and developing effective leaders and teachers.

First of all, young adolescents are in process: they are getting somewhere, but they *aren't there yet*. A significant degree of consensus has emerged among specialists in adolescent development as they describe this stage of the process of growing up. Let's look at how some of these experts have formulated the needs of middle grade students.

In *Beyond Customs*, Charity James described, some twenty years ago, twelve personal needs of young adolescents (James 1974). The timeliness of her description may surprise you. We have taken the liberty of pairing and rephrasing her statements in order to point out the contradictory but complementary nature of the young adolescent's need for

- Looking inward and responding to their outer world
- Intensity and for routine
- Fact and for myth and legend
- Physical activity and for stillness
- Belonging and for separateness
- Needing and for being needed

Gayle Dorman (1984) describes their basic needs for

- Competence and achievement
- Self-exploration that leads to self-definition

## YOUNG ADOLESCENTS CAN USUALLY BE COUNTED ON TO

- **Learn more like elementary students than like high school students**

- **Begin to develop a capacity for higher level thinking**

- **Constantly ask "Am I normal?" "Do I fit?" and "Am I like everyone else?"**

- **Try on various emotional types and roles**

- **Rehearse for various social settings**

- **Begin to develop a conscience and a moral code**

- **Learn to master their developing physical bodies**

- Social interaction with peers and adults
- Physical activity
- Meaningful participation in school and community
- Routine, limits, and structure
- Diversity

More recently, Claire Cole (1988) states that young adolescents need to

- Develop a personal identity independent of adults
- Cope with the emotional, physical, and social changes that occur between childhood and true adolescence
- Explore their interests and capabilities along with the relationship of these interests and capabilities to future education, work, and leisure
- Understand the relationship between themselves and their peer group
- Make decisions and accept responsibility for themselves

Even more recently, James Beane (1993) identifies the need of young adolescents to

- Begin to see how their social, emotional, cognitive, and physical characteristics will fit into their life-span development and to understand the implications of these characteristics for their personal and social lives
- Develop a sense of personal identity, including positive self-esteem and a clear self-concept
- Explore their questions about values, morals, and ethics
- Find a secure place and some level of status in the peer group
- Come to terms with their growing need for independence and with their continued dependence on adults for various kinds of security
- Deal with commercial pressures, such as those related to fashion, music, and leisure activities
- Balance and reconcile the different expectations of home, school, peer group, and other everyday-life settings
- Begin to develop commitments to people and causes in order to foster their personal sense of self-worth, achievement, and affiliation

# ▶ How do we address students' needs?

The first task is to accept middle grade students for who they really are rather than wishing they were more like little children or more like grown-ups. Once this principle is firmly established, you can go about creating an environment that supports young adolescents and provides the foundation for their development by

1. **Knowing thyself.** Middle grade students need teachers who are secure, dependable, and stable.

2. **Accepting responsibility for developing relationships.** Middle grade students need teachers who are particularly responsive to them and who care about them as people.

3. **Creating mutual trust.** Middle grade students are quick to sense any breech of trust from either their peers or their teachers. They need to know that adults are trustworthy and reliable.

4. **Protecting fragile egos.** At this vulnerable emotional stage, young adolescents are supersensitive to any real or imagined insult. They are quick to feel hurt and slow to recover and forgive. They need teachers who are aware of the pain a careless or sarcastic remark can cause.

5. **Having high but reasonable expectations.** Generally, middle grade students are far more capable than adults think, although less able than some adults want to believe.

6. **Recognizing the uniqueness of young adolescents.** They are neither elementary nor secondary students. They are unique unto themselves—and all the more interesting because of it.

# ▶ Where do we go for more information?

George, P., Stevenson, C., Thomason, J., and Beane, J. 1992. *The middle school and beyond*. Alexandria, VA: Association for Supervision and Curriculum Development.
A look at teachers and students, their relationships with one another, and the results of those associations. Includes a section that deals with middle school organization and the developmental needs and the philosophical values that underlie school practices. Contains useful sections on curriculum and leadership issues.

Van Hoose, J., and Strahan, D. 1988. *Young adolescent development and school practices: Promoting harmony*. Columbus, OH: National Middle School Association.
A detailed but very readable small book on the cognitive, social, emotional, and physical development of ten- to fourteen-year-olds. Illustrates the domains of development with real stories about students who exemplify those characteristics. Provides a great deal of information for teachers who want to become more developmentally responsive.

## References

Beane, J. (1993). *A middle school curriculum: From rhetoric to reality*. Columbus, OH: National Middle School Association.

Cole, C. (1988). *Guidance in the middle level schools: Everyone's responsibility*. Columbus, OH: National Middle School Association.

Dorman, G. (1984). *Middle grades assessment program*. Carboro, NC: Center for Early Adolescence.

James, C. (1974). *Beyond customs*. NY: Agathon Press, Inc.

# Topic 2  TURNING POINTS AND RECOMMENDATIONS

## ▶ What are they?

In 1989, the Carnegie Foundation Task Force on Education of Young Adolescents released a groundbreaking study titled *Turning Points*. The study, which characterizes early adolescence as a major turning point in life, gave validity, credibility, and considerable visibility to the cause of middle school education.

*Turning Points* echoed the work of middle level educators who had been envisioning the ideal middle school for over three decades. It filled a serious gap in available reports on education for the young adolescent.

The report of the Carnegie study characterizes early adolescence as an important turning point in life. In addition, a turning point occurs when a district, school, teacher group, or board of education realizes that it is time to direct major attention and resources to improving middle level education. This turning point requires educators to explore ways to be more developmentally responsive to the needs of young adolescents, to reorganize and reconceptualize schools in the middle school, to make learning the focus of curriculum and instruction, and to create a more learner-centered environment.

Sometimes this turning point is the result of declining enrollment. Sometimes it results from fiscal concerns or physical changes: an elementary building may be running out of space or a high school building may have space that is underutilized. Sometimes the turning point is the result of political pressure. Sometimes it comes as educators recognize that it is time to upgrade, update, and move forward as best practice and current research suggest. Increasingly, a turning point is reached when teachers and building leaders are ready to make significant changes in organization and in philosophy because they recognize that the current program is not meeting the needs of the students.

Whatever the reasons, there comes a time to study recommended practices and successful programs, engage in meaningful staff development, and reorganize the middle grades. When the time is right, that is truly a turning point.

> **"Most young adolescents attend massive, impersonal schools, learn from unconnected and seemingly irrelevant curricula, know well and trust few adults in school, and lack access to health care and counseling. Millions of these young people fail to receive the guidance and attention they need to become healthy, thoughtful, and productive adults."**
>
> (*Turning Points,* 1989)

In this section we will consider some of the recommendations of the Carnegie study about best practices for the middle grades. Later in this module, we will look at the experiences of some schools that have successfully made the transition from traditional programs to exemplary schools for young adolescents.

## Recommendations

*Turning Points* contains specific recommendations, not only for schools, but for families, communities, and other agencies as well. It helps spell out a plan for transforming a school ready to rethink and reorganize education for ten- to fourteen-year-olds. The following are some recommendations cited in this report:

- Create small communities for learning.

    – Organize houses, teams, or schools within schools.

    – Form teams of teachers and students.

    – Create a climate of belonging in a community through an advisory program.

- Teach a core curriculum of common knowledge.

    – Teach students to think critically.

    – Guide them to adopt healthful lifestyles.

    – Incorporate socially conscious and socially active projects.

    – Integrate thematic units and interdisciplinary approaches.

    – Determine to teach and test learner-centered information in developmentally responsive ways.

    – Provide core curriculum opportunities and access for every student in the school.

- Ensure success for all students.

    – Use cooperative learning and peer tutoring.

    – Eliminate tracking and ability grouping.

    – Expand opportunities to learn for all students.

- Empower teachers and administrators.

    – Decentralize decision making about curriculum, schedules, budgets, student grouping, materials, and the like; put those decisions close to the students rather than in the principal's office (or even further away).

    – Set up site-based decision-making bodies, such as program improvement councils and governance committees of teachers, students, administrators, support staff, parents, and community members.

    – Designate leaders for each house, team, or shareholder group; include secretarial as well as professional staff.

- Staff schools with experts in teaching young adolescents.

  - Hire selectively from those specifically prepared for middle school or decidedly committed to young adolescents.
  - Update professional credentials through university study.
  - Establish ongoing staff development in the field.

- Improve academic performance through fostering better health and fitness.

  - Ensure access to health services.
  - Provide school-linked or school-based clinics.
  - Make the school a health-promoting environment.

- Re-engage families in the education of young adolescents.

  - Enlist families to play meaningful roles in the school.
  - Inform families through frequent newsletters and calls.
  - Provide not just for parent involvement but for a definite family role in the learning process.

- Connect schools with communities.

  - Provide opportunities for students to serve their communities.
  - Establish community-wide study places, tutoring, homework hot lines, and alternative programs for dropouts.
  - Expand career guidance for students through mentoring and apprenticeships.
  - Ensure students' access to community services.

# ► How do we get started?

Making the transition to a middle school and creating an environment, a curriculum, and an organization that meet the unique needs of young adolescents are collaborative tasks involving administrative and support staff. You might begin to assess where your school is now and set goals for the future using the Taking Stock Checklist found at the end of this section. The checklist is based on the Carnegie task force recommendations and the experiences of other middle schools.

> "*The success of the transformed middle school will stand or fall on the willingness of teachers and other staff to invest their efforts in the young adolescent student. Teachers must understand and want to teach young adolescents and find the middle grade schools a rewarding place to work.*"
>
> (*Turning Points,* 1989)

# ► Where do we go for more information?

Carnegie Council on Adolescent Development. 1989. *Turning points: Preparing American youth for the 21st century*. NY: Carnegie Corporation of New York.

Produced by a task force that included federal, state, and local government officials, education experts, teachers, and administrators. Speaks to the urgency for new approaches and structures within middle grade schools. States clear, concise, and specific recommendations for improving the educational experiences of all middle grade students. Examines the conditions of early adolescence. Acknowledges that many young adolescents have certain advantages and are guided to make choices that prepare them socially, academically, and emotionally to become productive and well-adjusted adults. Calls for schools that will benefit those students who have in the past not received guidance and attention appropriate to their specific needs (the students we refer to as "at risk" because they lack skills and higher level thinking abilities to solve problems and determine the behaviors most beneficial to them). Advocates transforming middle grade schools to benefit all students.

Frances K. K. (1992). A new paradigm of schooling: Connecting school, home and community. In *Transforming middle level education: Perspectives and possibilities*, ed. J. Irvin, 63–71. Needham, MA: Allyn & Bacon.

Looks at the needs of young adolescents broadly in terms of their culture and at how schools can respond to cultural circumstances. Examines the social changes that have impacted our students and our schools. Suggests a new way to organize schools that is appropriate for our rapidly changing society. Stresses the need for developing strong connections and building a greater sense of community within our schools.

## *References*

Carnegie Council on Adolescent Development. 1989. *Turning points: Preparing American youth for the 21st century*. NY: Carnegie Corporation of New York.

# Taking Stock Checklist

**School Improvement Council**

_____ Council functions as an ongoing school governance committee.

_____ It is made up of teachers, administrators, school support staff, parents, students, and representatives from businesses, youth service organizations, and the community.

_____ It participates in all operations of the school.

**Small Communities of Learners**

_____ A personal learning environment has been created.

_____ All students have a meaningful relationship with at least one adult through an advisor/advisee program or similar student support program.

_____ A strong recognition/reward program supports all students.

_____ The school organization consists of teams of students and teachers forming together a "house" within the school.

_____ Teachers and students stay together within their "house" throughout a student's middle school career.

_____ Teams consist of teachers licensed in a rich variety of subject areas.

_____ A designated team leader is recognized and compensated.

_____ Time is made available within the school day for team planning as well as for individual teacher planning.

_____ Each team is empowered to make decisions concerning the management of its "house," including budgeting, space allocation, curriculum and methods, scheduling, and discipline policies.

_____ Flexible or block scheduling has been implemented to facilitate interdisciplinary learning fully.

## Core Curriculum

_____ Content and instruction are developmentally appropriate; they are organized around the needs and concerns of young adolescents.

_____ The curriculum consists of interdisciplinary units in which traditionally separate subjects (math, social studies, language arts, science, fine arts, music, physical education, industrial arts, home economics, etc.) blend into integrated lessons as they relate to a central theme or issue of interest and importance to students.

_____ Instructional methods are developmentally appropriate in that they actively engage students in learning; lesson plans are inquiry-oriented; students participate actively in communicating ideas; and teachers are facilitators, not lecturers or conveyors of facts.

_____ Cooperative learning, peer teaching/tutoring, and hands-on activities are the primary teaching methods.

_____ A community service component included in the curriculum inspires students to develop good citizenship and a sense of social responsibility and values.

## Authentic Assessment

_____ Assessment reflects the purposes of instruction and requires students to demonstrate a range of thinking skills.

_____ Students have many opportunities to demonstrate achievement and ability rather than one or two high-stakes measurements such as unit tests or final exams.

_____ Portfolios of student work developed over periods of time play a significant role; other developmentally appropriate methods, such as hands-on labs and creative projects, are major parts of assessment.

_____ Assessments challenge all students to high levels of critical thinking, not mere recall of memorized facts.

**Success for All Students**

_____ Heterogeneous grouping is used advantageously in cooperative learning groups, cross-age tutoring, and peer teaching.

_____ Tracking has been eliminated; students move in and out of flexible groups according to current and ever-changing needs and interests.

_____ Students of all ability levels are equal members of each "house."

_____ Developing and enhancing each student's self-esteem are given primary importance.

_____ High-level content, high-level thinking, and high expectations are afforded to every student in order to promote positive mental health, validation of personal competence, and achievement of the greatest level of academic competence possible.

_____ The school environment promotes acceptance and respect of self and others.

_____ Students feel safe from violence, drug-related activity, and all types of abuse.

_____ Discipline programs are proactive, not reactive; rewards are emphasized over punishments; corporal punishment is not practiced.

_____ Students are readily recognized for a variety of achievements and accomplishments, not just those that are academic or sports-related; everyone has the opportunity to feel like a winner.

_____ A rich diversity of clubs and extracurricular opportunities provides every student with opportunities to explore his/her interests.

_____ A variety of intramural recreational activities are available so that every student can enjoy physical exercise and fitness; there is no emphasis on creating future high school athletes or sports stars.

_____ A counseling component emphasizing prevention, such as the Indiana Department of Education's Developmental Guidance Program, is in place and emphasizes maintenance of mental health and career/vocational guidance.

## Community Connections

_____ Students participate as valued members of the community through a service component within the curriculum.

_____ Community members, parents, family members, and business leaders are considered school and classroom resources.

_____ Available programs link students with community resources and family service agencies; students can easily access these resources from the school.

_____ Businesses, churches, and youth service organizations are part of the school improvement council.

## Teachers as Lifelong Learners

_____ Staff is dedicated to middle level students and strategies; their training and certification process is tied to knowledge of the developmental characteristics and needs of young adolescents.

_____ Staff development programs are used for continual improvement of staff and their movement toward long-range school goals.

_____ A recognition structure motivates and rewards exemplary teachers.

_____ All staff value and participate in ongoing professional development.

# Topic 3 · THE TRANSITION PROCESS

## ► What is it?

Once a school or district has reached a turning point, whatever the motivation, it is time to begin the process of transition. The transition process here refers not only to wholesale change, such as transforming a junior high school into a middle school, but to other, smaller changes as well. Any school or district that is interested in making changes in areas such as curriculum, grouping, scheduling, or assessment will find that many of the same principles hold true, whatever the degree of change.

The first issue to consider is often the human one. Administrators and teachers will be very interested in how their professional lives will change with the implementation of a new organization. Central office staff may be expected to perform new roles, and they will want to know what those roles and responsibilities are. Parents will be very interested in how the change will affect their children in particular.

Time is another critical factor. Throughout the last three decades, when districts have attempted to change too quickly, the transition has been very rocky. Quite often the concept of middle school (rather than the inadequate preparation of the shareholders) was blamed for the problems.

Because thousands of districts have now made the change to the predominant grade 6–8 middle school, we now have considerable cumulative experience in how to get the best results with the fewest headaches. We have learned that the three essential principles for any successful transition process are

*INFORM EVERYONE*

*INVOLVE EVERYONE*

*SAY EXACTLY THE SAME THINGS TO EVERYONE*

When *everyone* is *informed* and informed often, and when everyone is told the *same things*, there is less chance that rumors will win out over the truth. When everyone is informed about the same things, trust develops.

# ► How do we get started?

Paul George (1993) proposes six steps for an effective transition. Each step is equal to roughly a year.

## Step 1: NEED

Planners determine that a move to middle school may meet one or more important needs manifested by students or schools in the district.

## Step 2: STUDY

Planners study the middle school concept and its implications for the district.

## Step 3: PLAN

Specific guidelines, programs, and action plans are developed to translate the middle school concept into real school programs.

## Step 4: OPEN

New middle school programs are implemented and evaluated formatively.

## Step 5: FIX

Leaders make certain that mistakes are reviewed and corrected so as to bring the original intentions to fruition.

## Step 6: EVALUATE

Summative evaluations determine the extent to which the new middle school programs are producing the desired outcomes.

Jim Garvin (1990) suggests a two-year plan with a slightly different focus. His "getting started" plan includes the following steps:

**Year 1** Gather data, form working committees, report results, develop recommendations, gain board approval.

**Year 2** Develop plans for faculty and parents based on (1) understanding young adolescents' characteristics and needs and (2) understanding the middle school concept.

*Fall:* Organize. Possibilities include teaming, advisory programs, expanded exploratories, and scheduling. Select core team members for the staff and adopt a schedule.

*Winter:* Select remainder of staff and implement intensive training for teams and advisors.

*Spring:* Assign students and develop the student orientation process.

These two models for transition assume a wholesale reorganization within a district or a change from some other organizational model to a middle school. But what about a single school that finds itself at a turning point and needs to make a different kind of transition? Where might you start in that case?

Bob Spear (1992) suggests an approach to school-based transition that would seem to work regardless of what type of transition is being proposed. He used this approach in his own school, Powder Mill Middle in Southwick, Massachusetts.

1. Have the staff identify areas of perceived strength and areas that need change.

2. Generate a "needs improvement" list.

3. Prioritize the list into a regrouped needs list.

4. Set up a developmental plan for the change.

5. Establish a time line.

6. Plan for evaluation.

No matter which planning guide best suits the needs of your particular situation, several points remain constant:

- The more people involved in the plan, the more input there is.
- Successful change takes time.
- Staff development is an integral part of transition.
- People who are committed to the change need to see it through to the end.
- Evaluation will prove that the transition was worth it.

## BOARD OF EDUCATION ROLE IN TRANSITION

Create community and media awareness.

Serve on steering committee.

Provide financial support.

## ADMINISTRATIVE STAFF ROLE IN TRANSITION

Create community and staff awareness.

Serve on steering committee.

Provide knowledge base.

Facilitate in-house communication.

## LEAD TEACHERS' ROLE IN TRANSITION

Serve on steering committee.

Provide knowledge base.

Demonstrate exemplary teaching.

## ▶ Where do we go for more information?

Irvin, J., ed. 1992. *Transforming middle level education: Perspectives and possibilities*. Needham, MA: Allyn & Bacon.
Contains chapters on climate and culture, developing a sense of mission, the process of change, and maintaining middle schools (Part Two: Developing a Sense of Responsiveness).

## *References*

Garvin, J. 1990. *Sane transition to the middle school program*. Newburyport, MA: Garvin Consulting Services.

George, P., and Alexander, W. 1993. *The exemplary middle school*. Orlando, FL: Holt, Rinehart and Winston, Inc.

Spear, R. 1992. The process of change: Developing effective middle school programs. In *Transforming middle level education: Perspectives and possibilities*, ed. J. Irvin. Needham, MA: Allyn & Bacon.

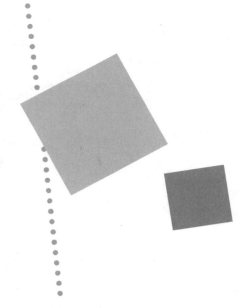

# Steps Toward Implementing Effective Middle Schools

FROM *Ten Steps Toward Implementing Effective Middle Schools*
 by Paul S. George

As thousands of school leaders search for effective ways to carry out broad mandates for new middle schools, a study of successes and failures permits the development of a series of guidelines. Experiences of the last decade may help lead educators to successful implementation.

*Step One:*    **Clarification and Disclosure of Motivation**

Begin by laying out all the reasons for the move to middle school. Integration and declining enrollment can be used as effective levers for bringing about an opportunity for change. Have a completely open agenda for change from the beginning.

*Step Two:*    **Exploration and Commitment by Central Administration**

The greater the understanding and commitment from the central office, the longer time available for advance planning and the larger the sums committed to the process.

*Step Three:*    **Exploration and Commitment of Supervisory, Building Level Leadership, and School Board Personnel**

Key district leaders and school board members who are brought in at this point can usually be counted on to provide greater verbal and financial support for the changes and requisite staff development programs which must follow. Failure to orient the school board at an early date may later be construed by these policy makers as a usurpation of their role and authority.

**Step Four:    Selection and Appointment of Project Coordinator**

The coordinator should, when possible, have had an in-depth exposure to the middle school movement either through graduate study or via experience. Failing this, the appointee should be someone with a background of training and experience which includes both elementary and secondary levels. Ideally, this appointment should occur two years prior to the opening of the reorganized schools, allowing for a properly paced unfolding of the necessary processes.

**Step Five:    Formation of a Reorganization Steering Committee**

A planning group of professionals and community representatives must be in on all policy decisions made from this point. It is this group which should be given the tasks of preparing a philosophical statement and rationale to support the reorganization and of identifying a public time line for the consideration of local issues and the completion of tasks on which consensus is eventually reached. The steering committee should be led by the coordinator through a process of orientation to the middle school concept and an investigation of local needs. This group must also have an opportunity to visit successfully operating middle schools in other districts.

**Step Six:    Developing the Local Rationale and a Multiyear Plan**

The Steering Committee should develop a statement which elaborates on the decision to reorganize and the implications of this decision for the district. This statement might include an explanation of the characteristics of adolescent learners, general implications for school programs for this age group, descriptions of intended program modifications, a tentative time line for the reorganization, and some comments regarding staff development. The local rationale should be very clear about what program changes are contemplated, the time frame for those changes, and the staff development costs involved.

**Step Seven:    Designation of Staff**

Principals and teachers for the new facilities should be designated no later than this point. The success of the reorganization will depend on the willingness of teachers to participate—or to choose an alternative teaching post.

*Step Eight:*    Recontacting the Community

The absence of community involvement for a much longer time may create a climate in which suspicions of conspiracy develop. The community must not come to suspect that educators are foisting unwanted changes on them and their children.

*Step Nine:*    Staff Development Plans

The middle school movement is more than anything else a reorganization of people and the ways in which they work with each other. Without staff development there is no change. In addition, staff development must both precede and accompany the opening of new middle schools with workshops, seminars, and other activities planned with a maximum of teacher input. A school cannot depend on outside stimuli and visiting experts for continued growth.

*Step Ten:*    Plans for Formative and Summative Evaluation

This step begins by designing an evaluation process which emerges from the multiyear plan. Such plans will help to prevent the school board and other interested parties from requesting investigations which may violate the time frame approved earlier. A formative evaluation process provides enough feedback to certify that the school is in fact functioning as it should be. Summative evaluation should be used to decide, among other things, whether this form of educating youth should be continued.

# Topic 4 PHILOSOPHY AND MISSION STATEMENTS

## ▶ What are they?

Most schools have several different statements of philosophy or school objectives. Some were written because of local initiatives, some at administrative request, and some for accreditation. Frequently the faculty is not familiar with such statements, nor do they play a significant role in the decision-making process for the school.

In lighthouse middle schools, some of which have been operating for decades, these written philosophy and vision statements serve a far different purpose. They represent a major effort on the part of the faculty, administration, staff, and other shareholders to define and illustrate what they as a group believe to be true about students and schools. These documents serve as reference points for decision making. When a new idea, initiative, or innovation is proposed, the faculty can weigh the pros and cons of each proposal in light of the beliefs they have stated about teaching and learning for young adolescents. If the innovation reflects compatible and philosophically consistent reasoning, then the faculty can unite to make the effort successful. If the proposed change runs counter to the philosophy of the school, the mission statement becomes the basis for an alternative recommendation.

## ▶ How are they different?

In all too many schools and for a long time, teachers have been subject to the fads, bandwagons, and pet projects of decision makers outside the school itself. Often teachers coming to school in the fall found that they were expected to adopt a new method, organization, or technique. Sometimes these changes were based only on a single workshop someone had attended over the summer. While many significant changes in educational practices have sprung from grassroots movements, from workshops, and from teachers talking to teachers, the broad-scale changes required in making a transition to an exemplary middle school require large-scale agreement and collaboration.

A philosophy and a mission statement are not the same thing. A mission statement is usually very brief, succinct, and almost credo-like. A philosophy statement, on the other hand, is broader and more comprehensive. Philosophy statements usually have the following characteristics:

- They are very definitely site-based (decentralized).

- They represent the best thinking of all the shareholders in the school.

- They have been discussed sufficiently to ensure ownership and internalization by the shareholders.

- They represent the best thinking of the entire staff in terms of defining the developmental characteristics of these particular students and recognizing the implications of these characteristics for organization, curriculum, outcomes, instruction, and assessment.

# ► How do we get started?

In the last thirty years, the literature concerning middle level education has increased dramatically. Books, monographs, journal articles, multimedia sources, conference proceedings, and professional development handouts have contributed significantly to our knowledge base. Any faculty wanting to turn their school around can find a plethora of sources to help them make informed decisions about the nature of young adolescents and the best way to educate them. *This We Believe* (1992), the basic position paper of the National Middle School Association, is probably the best place to start to answer the question, What do you really believe about your students?

One of the most exciting aspects of the modern American middle school is that it continues to emerge. Someone asked Dr. William Alexander, Professor Emeritus of the University of Florida and an esteemed early promoter of the middle school movement, when he thought the middle school would finally arrive. His response was to express great fear and skepticism about any organization that "arrives." He believes that a healthy and vital organization must continue to emerge in order to remain healthy and vital. This sense of a constantly emerging middle school gives you considerable freedom for decentralized decision making. As a school-based professional participating in writing a valid philosophy statement you can

- Become informed about alternative ways of setting up a middle school

- Participate in serious and meaningful discussions

- Help to select the organizational patterns, curriculum, instruction, and assessment that are appropriate for your school

Your philosophy and mission statement will continue to grow and be revisited for a long time; but for now, you need a place to start. One way to begin:

1. Generate a list of philosophical and programmatic aspects of middle school education.

2. Ask all the shareholders in the school to prioritize the items on the list.

3. Reorder and revise the list to ensure that it becomes a set of "this we agree" statements.

At this point you would have the basic content for your philosophy statement.

Here is a sample initial list:

## WE BELIEVE IN

1. Use of diversified instructional materials and techniques

2. Increased flexibility in scheduling and student grouping

3. A wide range of exploratory opportunities, academic and otherwise

4. Cooperative planning, team teaching, and integrative curriculum efforts

5. Attention to the skills of continued learning, such as thinking and decision making

6. Increasing the student's ability to be independent, responsible, and self-disciplined

7. Attention to the personal development of students, such as instituting an advisor/advisee program

Let's assume that through a prioritizing process, your faculty decided that their number one priority from this list is number 7. Your philosophy statement would then begin with a statement about your school's desire to have an advisor/advisee program and the philosophical basis for that desire.

Rather than generating your own initial list, you might take a document such as Nancy Doda's *Indicators That the Middle School Concept Is at Work* (1992) as your starting point for discussion and consensus. Her list includes the following:

1. Interdisciplinary teaming efforts, including common expectations, structures, and learning opportunities devoted to common outcomes

2. Attention to personal development concerns: coaching, mentoring, daily assistance, support, and dialogue

3. Broad team and school student-recognition efforts

4. Diverse instructional opportunities with emphasis on hands-on, cooperative learning and integrative experiences

5. Exploratory learning experiences that emphasize interest, choice, and curricular enrichment

6. Heightened focus on health, hygiene, and physical activity

7. Collaborative models that include the nonteamed staff

8. Age-appropriate in-school socialization

9. Aggressive parent communication/inclusion

10. Flexible grouping, regrouping, and scheduling

Your school's actual philosophy statement might be two or three pages long with a motto or slogan or credo (your mission statement) growing out of the total statement. For example, your school may decide that your basic goal is for all students to participate in the total life of the school so that when they move on to the high school they are

### COMPETENT    CONFIDENT    CARING

When your faculty has had the opportunity to discuss thoroughly the key points of your philosophy statement, and the statement has found general acceptance, you are ready for the actual writing. Make your finished statement an important part of the faculty handbook. Make sure that you share it with parents. It will become the standard by which you can judge the effectiveness and desirability of the barrage of innovations, fads, and new ideas that schools constantly face.

## TIPS FOR TEACHERS AND TEAMS

Paul George spent some time with his son Evan in a Japanese junior high school. Evan enrolled as a student, and Paul was an observer studying the conditions of the equivalent of the American middle school. In their comprehensive account of their experiences, cowritten in *The Japanese Junior High School: A View From the Inside*, they proposed these three lessons.

1. We must teach our students a sense of reality and a new vision. We must teach our students to be ready and aware of our changing position in the world.

2. The skills of tomorrow—learning to work effectively in groups and developing consensus-building skills—must be a vital part of our instructional strategies.

3. More money is not the answer to a better educational program. The Japanese educate their students well with far less spent on building and equipment than in America. Commitment to quality education by everyone—parents, educators, the business community—is the key.

(George, 1989)

No matter what method you choose to write your mission or philosophy statement, it will probably share some common characteristics with other such documents. According to Robert Shockley (1992) these characteristics are

- A recognition of the uniqueness, importance, and formative nature of the young adolescent years
- A common commitment to build curricular and instructional programs and practices that are sensitive to the unique developmental needs of young adolescents
- A recognition of the transitional nature of the middle school as a bridge from the elementary to the secondary schools

## ► Where do we go for more information?

Lounsbury, J. 1989, November. As I see it—Strike while the iron is hot. *Middle School Journal.*
Gives some tips that individual teachers might use to strengthen the goals of the middle schools, such as increasing personal interaction, involving students more thoroughly in their studies, stressing critical thinking for all students, and sharing more of the curriculum and instruction strategies among the professional staff both on and off the team. Provides useful information for school staffs in the process of setting out the details of their mission and philosophy statements.

Middle Level Council. 1989. *Developing a mission statement for the middle level school.* Reston, VA: National Association of Secondary School Principals.
Argues that all effective organizations have a clear sense of their mission. Points out that from the largest corporation to the smallest clubs or special interest groups, a clear mission statement helps members decide on goals, set priorities, and monitor behavior. Provides examples and information on how to write such statements for middle schools.

# References

Doda, N. 1992. *Teacher to Teacher: Indicators that the middle school concept is at work.* Columbus, OH: National Middle School Association.

George, P. 1989. *The Japanese junior high school: A view from the inside.* Columbus, OH: National Middle School Association.

Middle Level Council. 1989. *Developing a mission statement for the middle level school.* Reston, VA: National Association of Secondary School Principals.

National Middle School Association. 1992. *This we believe.* Columbus, OH: National Middle School Association.

Shockley, R. 1992. Developing a sense of mission in middle schools. In *Transforming middle level education: Perspectives and possibilities,* ed. J. Irvin. Needham, MA: Allyn & Bacon.

# Topic 5  LEADERSHIP ROLES AND RESPONSIBILITIES

## ▶ What are they?

The advent of middle schools has created a new dialogue about school leadership policies. One long-advocated leadership trend would have principals move from being building managers to instructional leaders. Another trend would have the principal become an "executive steward." Still another would have all decisions about the school made by teachers in a site-based management model. Using program improvement councils as the primary site-based decision-making model is gaining strong support.

This rethinking of leadership roles raises some important questions. If all the faculty are building leaders, who is ultimately in charge of the whole school? Who are the actual building leaders? Who is ultimately responsible? However your organization answers these questions, an essential one remains: What do leaders do, and what are their most essential characteristics?

## ▶ How are they different?

At a time of renewed public interest in schools, parents and community members are frequently not familiar with many of the current concepts and practices. Therefore, the task of the middle school leader has broadened to include new duties and an even greater professional commitment. In a typical middle school organization, leaders have many roles and responsibilities. Usually they include the following:

- Instructional Leader
- Change Agent
- Provider of Services
- Communications Expert
- Listener
- Servant Leader
- Organizational and Social Architect
- Ethical Leader and Role Model

In many cases, middle school leaders are also responsible for

- Finalizing the master schedule
- Motivating teachers to grow professionally
- Providing direction and support for teams
- Helping to establish school goals and priorities
- Providing for relevant staff development
- Making final personnel decisions

# ▶ How do we get started?

If you are preparing to take on the challenge of being a building leader, the following suggestions will help you define your task. If you are already in a leadership role, you can use these suggestions to evaluate your current policies and set goals for the future.

1. Develop a heightened sense of mission, a clarity of vision, about the nature of your middle school, the teachers, and especially about young adolescents. Develop the ability to articulate these beliefs.

2. Base your direction on knowledge of and genuine respect for the characteristics and needs of older children and young adolescents.

3. Develop a deep understanding of the middle school concept, particularly its commitment to the personal, social, and emotional, as well as the intellectual, development of each student.

4. Display a willingness to assist others in implementing the team organization, advisory programs, integrated curriculum plans, alternative assessment strategies, and strategies for flexible scheduling and grouping.

5. Develop your skills in utilizing the building facilities and the daily schedule to support the faculty and staff as they develop and implement their collective vision for the school.

## CHARACTERISTICS OF MIDDLE SCHOOL LEADERS

Middle school administrators as well as other building leaders will be viewed most positively when they are

- COMMUNICATORS
- COLLABORATORS
- DECISION MAKERS
- RISK TAKERS
- RESOURCEFUL MANAGERS
- SELF-CONFIDENT LEADERS
- CHAMPIONS OF THE CAUSE

## ► Where do we go for more information?

George, P., and Alexander, W. 1993. *The exemplary middle school.* Orlando, FL: Holt, Rinehart, and Winston, Inc.
Takes a thorough look at building leaders in light of leadership and vision, maintaining the middle school, shared decision making, and the workings of a program improvement council (see the chapter on Middle School Leadership). Includes a section on the generative middle school of particular interest to those presently in fully functioning middle schools. Answers questions such as, If we already have teaming and advisory groups, where do we go from here?

George, P., Stevenson, C., Thomason, J., and Beane, J. 1992. *The middle school and beyond.* Alexandria, VA: Association for Supervision and Curriculum Development.
Contains vignettes and commentary by three building leaders as to what is needed by leaders and how leaders can be more effective and more successful (see the chapter on Middle School Leadership). Includes sections on vision, the high school versus the elementary experience, communication, school reorganization, shared decision making, collaboration, and several pages devoted to the goals, objectives, and roles of the program improvement council.

> "*Tentative expectations of administrators often stand in the way of developing effective middle level schools. The leadership job required at the middle level is often not to do, but to undo; not to add, but to subtract; not to organize, but to reduce organization.*"
>
> (Lounsbury, 1983)

## References

George, P., Stevenson, C., Thomason, J., and Beane, J. 1992. *The middle school and beyond.* Alexandria, VA: Association for Supervision and Curriculum Development.

Lounsbury, J. 1983, May. *Defining effective middle level schools: It's the principal of the thing.* Reston, VA: National Association of Secondary School Principals.

# Topic 6

## TEACHER ROLES AND RESPONSIBILITIES

### ▶ What are they?

If middle schools are really developmentally responsive and if students are the heart of the school, then teachers must surely be the soul. We can all remember the teachers who made us want to learn, those who seemed to truly care about us, and those who were demanding but fair. These relationships caused us to want to do our best. These teachers helped us though bad times and cheered our good times. They made a difference in how we performed in school and how we felt about the experience.

Effective middle school teachers, like middle school students, have some common characteristics. Some people claim that the best way to be a successful middle school teacher is to be much like the kids themselves. Effective middle school teachers take on some nontraditional roles and responsibilities along with the more traditional. They share a legacy of success and caring.

### ▶ How are they different?

Remember when you graduated from college? how young you were? how you were told to "keep your distance" from the kids? how many times you thought you might have stepped over some imaginary line by even talking candidly with your students? Business suits, a firm voice, no smiles until Christmas, and a tight ship were often the rule of thumb.

But also remember how difficult that was for many of you. You wanted to get to know your students as people. You cared about their fears and their triumphs. You wanted to help them have fewer bad times and more good things to remember about their teen years. Although you sensed that relationships were important, the suggested protocol was distance and control. Fortunately, things have changed. While there is little question that mutual respect, a sense of purposefulness, classroom control, and a professional demeanor are important as teachers work with young adolescents, one more thing may be just as important if not more so—the good relationship that can form between ten- to fourteen-year-olds and their teachers.

What do effective middle school teachers know about positive relationships with students? What characteristics do effective teachers share? What do successful teachers do?

## Characteristics of Effective Teachers

If you want to be successful with young adolescent learners, you will need to have

- A genuine desire to teach this age group

- A thorough understanding of students' distinctive developmental characteristics and needs

- An understanding and accepting attitude for the guidance role inherent in your job

- An accepting, positive, fairly uncritical attitude toward both students and colleagues

- Belief in a more democratic classroom and shared decision making

- The capacity to see things from others' points of view

- A respect for the value of independent, self-actualized individuals

## Teacher Roles and Responsibilities

As a middle school teacher, you will likely be asked to

- Be a member of a team

- Be responsible for a small advisory group

- Participate in decentralized decision making

- Establish long-term, personal, but still adult, relationships with students

- Establish communication channels with parents

- Balance teacher-directed activities with student interests

- Work in heterogeneous classrooms

- Develop lessons for cooperative learning and experiences

- Develop exploratory experiences for students

- Use diversified instructional approaches

EFFECTIVE MIDDLE SCHOOL TEACHERS ARE

- COMPETENT
- CONFIDENT
- CARING

# Special Education Teachers: the Value of Teaming

In a middle school situation, you as a special education teacher can perhaps for the first time become a valued member of a team of teachers dedicated to the best possible education for *all* students.

Historically, children with special needs were diagnosed and then placed in their own classrooms with their own teachers. The school's attitude seemed to be "out of sight, out of mind." Thus a stigma became attached to the student, the room, and the entire program. Today, these children are more likely to be part of a standard classroom. The purpose of regular placement is to remove the stigma as well as to capitalize on the true educational potential of the student. A regular classroom placement can also enhance the special needs students' social status among their peers. Why is teaming particularly beneficial for middle grade students with special needs?

- It provides a more flexible block schedule.

- It can improve self-concept for all students.

- It provides more opportunities to adapt experiences to include the special needs students.

- It can provide for a greatly expanded curriculum.

- It can improve instructional efficiency.

- It allows for more normal social interaction and therefore greater practice in developing social skills.

- It establishes partnerships between special education and regular education students.

- It broadens everyone's perspective on the talents and respective roles and responsibilities of the entire professional staff.

> "*Little separates the effective regular classroom teacher and the effective special education teacher. It is only a matter of degrees.*"
>
> (Public Law 94–142)

## ▶ How do we get started?

Following are some guidelines for developing positive relationships with young adolescents.

1. Be a supportive adult who meets the needs of your students as well as the needs of fellow team members.

2. Develop a strong personal self-concept.

3. Be available to students, sharing informal conversations with them.

4. Accept the role of guide and coach rather than mere lecturer.

5. Be a reliable, dependable role model.

## ► Where do we go for more information?

Doda, N. 1981. *Teacher to teacher*. Columbus, OH: National Middle School Association.
A collection of columns written for the *National Middle School Journal*. Still a remarkable work on the concerns and questions teachers have for themselves and their colleagues about being in the middle. Provides an insider's perspective on teachers, students, teams, advisories, and the gamut of middle school programs by a writer who has been a middle school language arts teacher and a team leader. Answers teachers' questions in an informative and readable style and in a minimum number of pages and words. If you want to know about teaching in the middle, read this book.

## References

Carnegie Council on Adolescent Development. 1989. *Turning points: Preparing American youth for the 21st century*. NY: Carnegie Corporation of New York.

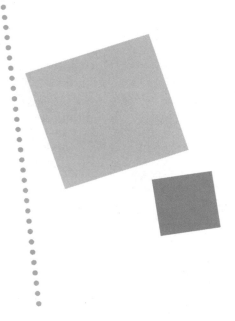

# 3 Middle School
# *Program Components*

The middle school is very different from other schools—both philosophically and organizationally. If you hope to create a fully functioning middle school, your school's staff must be aware of its students' developmental stages and be ready to make a conscious response to student needs. Besides this awareness, there are several program components vital to the middle school that the staff must value. These components include interdisciplinary teams of teachers working with shared groups of students, an advisory program, and an expanded exploratory and elective program. Also characteristic of middle schools are flexible time, space, and grouping arrangements, with most of the decisions in these areas made by the teams themselves.

This module helps you examine these characteristics and components of the effective middle school and suggests strategies through which each may be structured and implemented. You will also find resources that may be useful as you seek more information concerning team organization, decision-making processes, or new electives.

# MODULE 3

## *Contents*

# Topic 1

## GENERAL COMPONENTS AND CHARACTERISTICS

## ▶ What are they?

Not every middle-level school can be called a middle school just because it is organized around grades 6-7-8. Effective middle schools are the result of considerable professional planning; they are not merely an outgrowth of demographic facts or fiscal concerns.

The middle school concept is based on a commitment to the developmental needs of young adolescents. The middle school philosophy calls for active participation by all students and for a great deal of experiential learning. Much of the day-to-day decision making for any group of students is in the hands of those adults who work directly with them. Truly effective middle schools

- Strive to be developmentally responsive to the learner, both in philosophy and organization
- Provide learner-centered curricula and thought-provoking instruction
- Employ decentralized decision making on questions of scheduling, grouping, assessment, and discipline

## ▶ How are they different?

Since the 1940s, the prevailing organizational model for educating young adolescents has been the junior high school. All too often, these junior highs have simply been scaled-down models of the high school. The other widely used model has been K-8, with the upper grades set up differently from the primary grades. For the most part, however, K-8 schools were too elementary to meet the more sophisticated needs of the eleven- to fourteen-year-old. Teachers and administrators trapped in either form have had serious problems, even though they recognized that neither form was developmentally appropriate for the students they served.

## POINTS TO PONDER

In the old junior high and K-8 settings, what kinds of problems were created by each of these characteristics?

1. A curriculum with elementary school content

2. A curriculum with watered-down high school content

3. Teachers working in isolation with little support

4. Short-term and superficial relationships between students and teachers

What has resulted from their discontent is an evolution toward a more developmentally sound organization that enables teachers to control their environment and curriculum rather than simply respond to inappropriate conditions. For example,

- In the old models, control was centralized in the administration office. In middle schools, decentralized decision making has empowered teachers to exert a considerable influence on scheduling, grouping, curriculum, instruction, behavior management, assessment, and day-to-day concerns about their students.

- In the old models, teachers worked in isolation, viewing the learner through a single lens. In middle schools, teachers are members of a collaborative, interdisciplinary team that works with a common group of students. The result is a multifaceted view of students' capabilities, capacities, and needs.

# ▶ How do we get started?

While implementing the middle school concept is generally the responsibility of the central office, you as a teacher can start by reviewing the characteristics detailed in this section and by asking yourself or your team how your particular school measures up. When you find an area in which your school is doing particularly well, celebrate that accomplishment! Where you find areas in need of improvement, you have a place to institute further professional development and change.

## Middle School Characteristics

During these years of development and research, the following characteristics have gained general acceptance as typical of an effective middle school:

- The school is viewed as physically and psychologically safe.

- The atmosphere in the school is positive and supportive. Staff and students enjoy being there and move about the building in a congenial and purposeful manner.

- Each student is part of a team directed by a group of teachers. Each team is generally housed in one area of the building. Large buildings are divided into smaller houses, pods, teams, or families.

- Each student is a member of a small advisory group that includes an adult.

- Students are encouraged to participate in many varied experiences through an expanded exploratory program.

- Both scheduling and grouping are flexible and controlled most directly by the interdisciplinary team.

- Students regularly work and learn in cooperative groups that meet social, academic, and skill objectives.

- Parents are involved in most aspects of school life.

- All students have access to the same courses with little or no tracking or ability grouping.

- Discipline and behavior policies are determined by individual interdisciplinary teams in concert with the students; infractions are handled primarily by the team.

- The staff has received specific preparation for middle school teaching and shows strong commitment to this level.

- Students have opportunities to engage in community service.

- Special assistance is provided students with limited English ability or other limitations that hinder their educational experience.

- Teachers share in the decision-making process through a program improvement council or some similar structure.

# ▶ Where do we go for more information?

Epstein, J., and MacIver, D. 1990. *Education in the middle grades: National practices and trends*. Columbus, OH: National Middle School Association.

This publication is based on the authors' research studies of the emerging middle school concept across the country. It covers grade span, size of schools, homeroom and advisory teams, curriculum, instruction, report cards, teacher talents, and remedial instruction. Of particular interest is an authors' list of "signature practices" (p. 69). They include interdisciplinary teams, common planning time, flexible scheduling, students assigned to the same homeroom or advisory teacher for all years in the middle grades, cooperative learning, exploratory and minicourses, parent involvement in workshops, and parents as volunteers in the middle grades.

Lounsbury, J., ed. 1984. *Perspectives*. Columbus, OH: National Middle School Association.

This is excellent basic reading for those interested in beginning or refining their middle school. While the book presents no single model nor any "right" way of conceptualizing or implementing the middle school, there is widespread agreement on the basic principles of young adolescent education and the conditions which give rise to it.

Forte, I., and Schurr, S. 1993. *The definitive middle school guide: A handbook for success*. Nashville, TN: Incentive Publications, Inc. This book provides the perfect overview for middle school teachers, administrators, and others concerned with middle school success. The handbook is organized into independent modules for ease of use in workshops and in-service programs. Each module includes an overview, questions to be answered, a glossary, findings from the published literature, informational pages in a convenient top-ten format, and teacher activities keyed to Bloom's Taxonomy. Major topics include nuts and bolts of middle grades education, interdisciplinary teaming, advisory, cooperative learning, creative and critical thinking skills, assessment, and interdisciplinary instruction: a model for success.

## References

Alexander, W. M., and McEwin, C. K. 1989. *Earmarks of schools in the middle: A research report*. ERIC Document Reproduction Service. No. ED 312.

George, P., and Alexander, W. 1993. *The exemplary middle school*. Orlando, FL: Harcourt, Brace, Jovanovich.

# Organizational Arrangement

Effective organizational arrangement within your school is demonstrated by the following:

| | Always Evident | Usually Evident | Seldom Evident | Not Evident |
|---|---|---|---|---|
| 1. Interdisciplinary teaching teams at all grade levels | | | | |
| 2. Varied grouping and scheduling techniques used by teaching teams | | | | |
| 3. Staff commitment to the team approach | | | | |
| 4. Team spirit and unity of purpose among both students and teachers | | | | |
| 5. Common planning time provided for teachers to deal with team concerns of scheduling, grouping, and conferencing | | | | |
| 6. An administration based on decentralization of authority | | | | |

# Continuous Program for Students

Continuous progress for students is provided by the following:

| | Always Evident | Usually Evident | Seldom Evident | Not Evident |
|---|---|---|---|---|
| 1. A staff sensitive to unique age and learning characteristics of middle school students | | | | |
| 2. Instructional strategies providing individual attention to learners with recognition of diverse learning styles and levels of achievement | | | | |
| 3. Instructional experiences and exploratory activities that are short-term/high interest | | | | |
| 4. Cooperative team planning for continuous progress on a regular weekly basis | | | | |
| 5. An established program for basic skill improvement that is required of all students | | | | |
| 6. A special services staff available to all students for remediation and enrichment | | | | |

| | Always Evident | Usually Evident | Seldom Evident | Not Evident |
|---|---|---|---|---|
| 7. A curriculum management system that provides continuous monitoring of student skill mastery | | | | |
| 8. Written curriculum that contains special interest and enrichment activities for all students | | | | |
| 9. A staff and administration committed to sequential learning activities in the classroom | | | | |
| 10. An ongoing plan of continuous assessment and identification of student learning styles | | | | |
| 11. Communication between district schools for the purpose of recognizing individual student differences | | | | |
| 12. A balance between child-centered and teacher-centered learning activities based on students' needs | | | | |

# Middle School Hallmarks

## 1. Educators Knowledgeable About and Committed to Adolescents
Teachers share responsibility for the educational and personal development of each group of students.

## 2. A Balanced Curriculum Based on Adolescent Needs
A curriculum that includes academics, skills for continuous learning and personal development, participation (rather than spectatorship) encouraged in a wide variety of intramural activities, appropriate social activities that do not ape sophisticated high school programs

## 3. A Variety of Organizational Arrangements
Models that provide a gradual transition from the self-contained class of elementary school to the departmentalized structure of the secondary school: "houses" within schools; flexible scheduling within blocks of time; grouping strategies that maintain heterogeneous classes

## 4. Varied Instructional Strategies
Interdisciplinary approaches that help students integrate their studies (cooperative learning; strategic thinking) and a variety of materials

## 5. A Full Exploratory Program
Minicourses, exploratory courses, service clubs, special interest activities, and independent study projects that are available to all students

## 6. Comprehensive Advising and Counseling
Multiyear assignment of teacher-advisors to provide consistent individualized assistance to students

## 7. Evaluation Procedures Appropriate for Young Adolescents
Evaluation and self-evaluation that help adolescents discover and understand strengths, weaknesses, values, interests, and personality

## 8. Cooperative Planning
Interdisciplinary team planning in core subject areas and an understanding of what each contributes to the individual student's educational program is central to the middle school.

## 9. Positive School Climate
Both professional staff and students should show warmth, caring, and respect

(from Alexander and McEwin, 1989)

**Organization**

Flexible Scheduling and Grouping

Decentralized Decision Making

Collaborative Decision Making and Teaming

Vision/Mission/Strategic Planning

Articulation with Other Schooling Levels

Emphasis in Exploration

Teacher-Based Guidance System

**Curriculum**

Reading/Writing Across Subjects

Higher-Order Thinking Skills

Interdisciplinary/Integrative

Relating to Experience

Common Curricular Objectives

Equitable Content Coverage

Full Range of Electives

Exploratory Coursework

**Instruction**

Active Learning

Student Involvement

Paired/Collaborative Learning

Cooperative Learning

Educational Technology

Alternative Assessment

Heterogeneous Grouping

# Middle Level Education

## POINTS TO PONDER

Here is a list of questions about teaming that you may want to ask.

1. How are teams best organized?

2. What are the major benefits or advantages of teaming?

3. What are the characteristics of a successful team?

4. What are the roles of team leaders and team members?

5. How does a team build a sense of identity and community?

6. What goes on in a productive team meeting?

7. How do teams integrate curriculum and instruction?

8. How do teams handle decentralized discipline?

9. How can you avoid some team problems?

> "The factor needed to obtain the most benefits from interdisciplinary teaming is adequate, common planning time."
>
> (Epstein and MacIver, 1990, p. 461)

## ▶ What is it?

Interdisciplinary teacher teams are one of the most widely recognized features of a true middle school. Teaming is more than just a group of loosely organized teachers. It requires people working together on a day-to-day basis to see that the developmental needs of students—cognitive, emotional, physical, social, and character —are attended to. Teaming is a sort of professional bonding between adults with varied expertise and the group of students they teach.

As its highest priority, the middle school team develops and implements a set of team goals based on the needs of their students. These are goals which have been agreed upon after long, serious, and productive discussions. What do team members believe about young adolescents as persons and as learners? The goals they set are essential to the team's success, regardless of how diverse members' individual personalities, skills, and interests may be. To achieve these goals, team members have to support one another consistently, communicate openly, and collaborate willingly. That means there is no place for hidden agendas, unresolved conflicts in team relationships, or unfair workloads among team assignments. Teaming empowers each person in the group to share fairly in team responsibilities and in making team decisions.

It is critical that each team be given responsibility for a specific group of students that are housed in the same area of the building with the same block of uninterrupted time. Interdisciplinary teams function at their best when the individual classrooms are near each other. Proximity contributes to the necessary sense of community and "family."

## ▶ How is it different?

The most significant difference between being a member of a team and teaching alone is professional collegiality. Some of you may teach in a school where you see all of the teachers at the first faculty meeting and do not see all of them again until the holiday party in December. You may teach a whole day or even a whole week without seeing or talking to another teacher. Teaching can be and should be a shared job.

# ▶ How do we get started?

Teaming, as with most areas of middle school development, is never simple. But take heart! If it were simple, it probably would not be as developmentally responsive nor as effective. You probably still have questions about what teams do and what they are, how to begin to make some decisions, and how to avoid some problems. But the real issue is basic: How do you finally get these interdisciplinary teams up and running?

## How Are Teams Organized?

As in other areas of middle school organization, there really is no single, easy answer to this question. The answer depends on the size of the school, the philosophy of the faculty, the grade level, the configuration of the building, the state and local requirements for certification, and a host of other things. There are many decisions to be made while putting teams together—decisions that should be made collaboratively among school leaders and instructional staff.

Middle school teams generally range in size from two to five people. The number may vary from team to team. For example, a faculty might decide to have two-member teams for the sixth grade—more like elementary school organization—and four- or five-member teams at the eighth grade, more like a high school arrangement. Sometimes the decision is influenced by school or district requirements for gifted students or guidelines for mainstreaming learning-disabled or emotionally challenged students. The decision may be made simply on the basis of teachers' desires to work in a particular size team, or with a particular group of students or fellow teachers. The following chart suggests some advantages and disadvantages offered by teams of various sizes.

## CHARACTERISTICS OF SUCCESSFUL TEAMS

**The very best teams**

- Have a vision, set goals, make a plan, create a sense of family

- Prioritize their workload, roles, and responsibilities

- Do a few things really well

- Say "yes" more often than "no"

- Celebrate their accomplishments

- Develop ways of doing things

- Conduct *formal* team meetings

- Practice communication skills

- Balance weekly agendas

- Create and use a team calendar

- Keep records of team meetings as well as other important activities of the team

- Involve specialists and nonteam staff

- Utilize the steering or program improvement council

- Spend time on personal relationships

(Nancy Doda, 1991)

| | ADVANTAGES | DISADVANTAGES |
|---|---|---|
| **TWO-PERSON TEAM** | Fewer personality conflicts; students and teachers know each other sooner and better<br><br>Easier to find planning time and to integrate work in core subject areas<br><br>May ease transition from elementary school organization | Little team support or back-up if one teacher on the team is absent.<br><br>Students see only two different teaching styles and personalities. |
| **THREE-PERSON TEAM** | More support, more diversity, more backup<br><br>Each team member teaches one specific subject; all teach one subject in common. Result: more flexibility and subject integration<br><br>More opportunities to group and regroup students as needed | Difficulties in agreeing on the common subject to teach<br><br>"Two against one" problems in decision making |
| **FOUR- OR FIVE-PERSON TEAMS** | Increased diversity of teacher materials, delivery, personalities, and teaching styles<br><br>Team members have only one major subject to prepare; they may specialize in the subject each is most qualified to teach.<br><br>Ease in grouping and regrouping students for instruction; more flexibility and diversity in scheduling<br><br>Eases transition to high school organization | Difficulty in finding convenient planning times<br><br>Difficulties in integrating the disciplines<br><br>Greater number of possible personal and professional conflicts<br><br>Teachers continue to specialize, encouraging tendency toward departmentalization. |

Beyond size considerations, there are other variables you should think about when you organize teachers in teams. It is important, for example, that teachers on a given team are willing to work together and have had a choice in the matter. Besides being willing, team members should be different in their teaching and learning styles so that students are exposed to and matched with adults who may complement their talents and learning styles. Diversity of teacher interests, talents, skills, and even teaching experiences must be considered so that a versatile, but compatible, team is working together for the benefit of students. Learning style inventories, right- and left-brain exercises, and modality checklists can be used in forming teams. Once teams are active, you can also use these tools to help team members know their own strengths and weaknesses, as well as those of other team members.

Once a team has been organized and membership has been agreed on by everyone, there are some key decisions to be made within the team. These include the following:

■ Who will be team leader? What are this person's responsibilities?

■ How often will the team meet? For what purposes?

■ How will team meetings be managed and how will the team make decisions and handle conflicts or differences? What record of their meetings will be kept?

■ How will the team establish its yearly goals and objectives?

■ How will the team assess its effectiveness and plan for next year?

## Defining the Role of Team Leader

Now that you have some idea of how a team can be organized and what advantages can be gained from teaming, you need to take a look at the specifics of team roles and responsibilities. All core team members are equally responsible for their students' welfare and achievement. However, for teams to be most effective, there should also be someone in charge, and all team members need to agree on the role this team leader is to play. In most cases, such a role includes the following responsibilities:

■ PROVIDING LEADERSHIP in team activities: planning team meetings, implementing requests for grouping and scheduling, facilitating team efforts to develop guidelines for student discipline, planning for parent conferences, maintaining team records, delegating specific tasks to team members

■ OVERSEEING THE CURRICULUM in the core areas, working closely with others to see that the team is aware of state, local, and course objectives

## TIPS FOR TEAMS

- **Team development does not happen overnight.**

- **Team members can benefit from training in group dynamics.**

- **Don't expect every team member to show the same degree of enthusiasm for teaming.**

- **Expect some ups and downs as teams work together.**

- **Team members should be encouraged to maintain their own identity and teaching style so that they are complements—not clones!**

- **The benefits of teaming may not be immediately evident.**

- **Communication is the heart and soul of a team.**

- **Celebrations make the good times better and the trying times bearable. Try a social setting away from school.**

Judy Irvin (1992) suggests the following stages for middle school teams.

## FOR TEACHERS

**FORMING:** Insecure members depend on the leader for direction.

**STORMING:** Conflict in working toward consensus

**NORMING:** Group is finally working as a team.

**PERFORMING:** Increased student achievement and job satisfaction

**TRANSFORMING:** Change is enjoyed as teams constantly recreate themselves

## FOR BUILDING LEADERS

**MOBILIZATION:** Focusing on the assets and liabilities of the school and starting to implement the middle school concept

**IMPLEMENTATION:** Middle school concepts and programs introduced into the school, teams formed, advisory undertaken, exploratory program expanded

**INSTITUTIONALIZATION:** School community embodies the middle school concept fully and teams become a focal point of decision making and routine management

- REPRESENTING THE TEAM by serving on any program improvement council and in communicating the decisions of that council back to the team members

- ENCOURAGING PRACTICES that best meet the needs of young adolescents and that implement the middle school philosophy

# Building a Sense of Community

Once you have formed your team and chosen a team leader, how do you set about finding a team identity and creating a sense of community? If it is important for young adolescents to have a safe area in the building and a place where they belong; it is also important that students develop warm relationships with caring adults. A great deal of students' willingness to work and achieve is based on their relationship with their teachers.

Here are some ideas to help your team achieve these goals.

- Select a team name—one that teachers and students choose together and that gives the team a sense of identity.

- Design signs, logos, themes, colors, mottos, raps, or cheers to help set your team apart.

- Publish your team philosophy and goals. Let everyone know what you and your students have agreed upon as goals and expectations. The students will enjoy being "in the know" and actively participating.

- Hold a team orientation session that helps students feel they are welcomed participants.

- Schedule intramural events, field trips, and other events through your team.

- Assign projects that involve the whole team so that when they are completed everyone can celebrate and the rest of the school will know what the team has accomplished.

How do you manage all of this professional planning and these decisions that make a team successful? When, where, and how do you get together and get it done? Common planning time, well used, is essential to the success of the team.

# Using Planning Time Effectively

All teams will have issues to discuss and problems to solve. Too often, solutions are merely remedies that are not as well thought out as they might be and that do not always work in the long term. Think of times when you and your colleagues have talked a problem to death but never really arrived at any worthwhile solution. Try the techniques described below. They may help you arrive at more systematic and valid solutions for any of a number of issues that teams encounter. Each procedure can be used as an independent technique, but many teams find the techniques work best when combined or incorporated in a sequence.

## TECHNIQUES FOR QUALITY PLANNING TIME

### 1. ROUND-ROBIN BRAINSTORMING
Heightens originality and creative thinking; guarantees increased participation of all members rather than domination by a few

### 2. STRAW POLLS
Helps achieve consensus on issues that need maximum support and warrant further consideration

### 3. CAUSE-AND-EFFECT ANALYSIS
Provides a rational means of determining the true cause of a particular problem

### 4. DATA COLLECTION
Vital at certain stages of such issues as curriculum setting

### 5. DECISION ANALYSIS
Provides a systematic procedure for reviewing the decision-making process and determining the likely effect of the end result

### 6. GENERATING SOLUTIONS
When a specific list of recommendations is created, an implementation plan is likely to emerge.

### 7. PRESENTATION TO OTHERS
Keep the following points in mind for an effective presentation to others:
- Make positive statements.
- Use the personal viewpoint.
- Choose a moderator.
- Follow an agenda.
- Have a theme.
- Keep it short and simple.
- Use instructional/visual aids.
- Review all progress and accomplishments of the team on the issue, as well as your proposed course of action.

### 8. EVALUATION
Establish a set time (end of month, end of grading period) to review the team's planning process. Have individuals critique the way they personally functioned during the decision-making process, as well as the way the team addressed the issue as a whole.

# Integrating Curriculum

The team concept exists on varying levels of maturity and sophistication. Whatever its level of achievement, a team must have a common purpose to be as effective as possible. Often that common purpose is the integration of curriculum. While curriculum integration is discussed thoroughly in another module of this book, it warrants some attention here.

Curriculum integration, the process of moving from single discipline instruction to integrated curriculum, necessitates the following steps:

**STEP 1:** Discuss your students with other team members. As you get to know your students better, you will see that they perform differently for different teachers. Once you talk this over with the other teachers and begin to use some of their successful techniques, you are started on the road to curriculum integration as well.

**STEP 2:** Coordinate homework and testing. As you find out what your team members are assigning and requiring and how they are assessing students' work, you will begin to see common threads among the subjects. Sometimes it is thinking skills that everyone seems to be stressing; it may be relationships, causes and effects, topics, or themes. These common threads form the initial connections for curriculum integration.

**STEP 3:** Look at the specific goals your team members have. You may find that many of the goals are the same for all subjects and that emphasizing those common goals becomes the starting point for curriculum integration.

**STEP 4:** Work out a curriculum map for your team. You may be amazed at how simple changes in timing (teaching the short story in December rather than in September) will bring curriculum themes in line and move the process of curriculum integration along.

**STEP 5:** Make it your goal to have an integrated theme unit at least once each semester. Some units will be more complex than others, some you will have to develop, and some you can learn about from other teams. Just trying a relatively simple integrated unit will probably convince you and your team that there is something to this idea of integrating the curriculum. And the positive response of your students will confirm the value of the effort.

# Handling Behavior Management

Decentralized decision making is integral to the middle school philosophy. We know that the nearer the decision maker is to the students, the better the decisions are likely to be. Who is nearer to the students than their team teachers? Who is better able to set up team rules, expectations, rewards, and punishments than the adult team members *and* their students? So how do you start?

First, set common rules and common expectations. When young adolescents have to remember only one set of rules, rather than a separate set for each teacher, they are more likely not only to remember them but also to follow them.

Next, display the discipline plan that teachers and students have developed in each team room. Try to state the rules in positive terms such as "Come Prepared to Work."

Then work on behavior contracts and improvement plans for those students who require additional help in following the rules. The demerit system is ineffective—it almost guarantees the failure of certain students. A better system might be to start everyone off with a number of points, taking them away for misbehavior. In that way at least, every student has something to lose!

Set up valid ways in which to reward positive behavior. Middle school students are not going to be fooled by false praise, but they will generally respond to genuine praise when they do well. Just remember that most teacher praise must be done quietly and privately. A thirteen-year-old still finds it more important to be liked by friends than to be liked by you.

Schedule frequent recognitions and rewards. For example, it is far better to have a student of the week (thirty-six of them) than a student of the month (ten) or a student of the grading period (four or five perhaps). Remember, young adolescents do not have a long attention span and are not very likely to behave all that well for all that long.

Finally, it is important to get in contact with the parents and stay in contact with them. Present a united front across the team and keep parents informed of the good, the bad, and the improvements. Although there are a few parents who think their children never misbehave in school, all want their children to do well and will give you all the help you need, if approached properly.

Teaming takes effort and compromise—but the rewards are worth the work. Your team will have a good chance of success if you

- Work, think, talk, and act like a team of professionals

- Support the other members of your team

- Have a leader but share the responsibilities

- See that everyone is allowed to work from strength

- Deal with discipline in concert as a team

- Involve special staff and exploratory teachers

- Take control of the schedule but share time with others

## TIPS FOR TEACHERS AND TEAMS

- **Develop team identity and team spirit.**
- **Use team-building activities.**
- **Plan social interaction.**
- **Celebrate whenever you can.**

- Involve parents and present a united front
- Work to keep building leaders informed
- Set goals, assess your progress, fix what's broken

# ▶ Where do we go for more information?

Merenbloom, E. 1900. *The team process in the middle school: A handbook for teachers*. Columbus, OH: National Middle School Association.
In this book, Merenbloom provides a guide for classroom teachers who want to work in teams. He presents ideas, strategies, and a rationale for using teams to meet the unique learning needs of young adolescents. Most of the book describes the efforts of teachers working in real-life situations that the author found in his home area of Baltimore County, MD. Other teachers will readily see how the ideas and procedures he suggests can be applied in almost any middle school setting.

Erb, T., and Doda, N. 1989. *Team organization: Promise, practice, and possibilities*. Washington, D.C.: National Education Association.
This monograph gives a comprehensive overview of the interdisciplinary teaming process, beginning with the initial organization of the team. The authors go on to describe the factors necessary to implement the teaming concepts. Team meetings, team identity issues, and team decision-making strategies are discussed in great detail so that the reader gains a birds-eye view of all that is involved.

Forte, I., and Schurr, S. 1993. *The definitive middle school guide: A handbook for success*. Nashville, TN: Incentive Publications, Inc.
This guide provides a complete overview for middle school teachers, administrators, and others concerned with middle school success. Its utility is enhanced by its organization into independent modules, which are easy to use in workshops and in-service programs. Each module includes an overview, questions to be answered, a glossary, findings from the published literature, informational pages in a convenient top-ten format, and teacher activities keyed to Bloom's Taxonomy. Major topics include: nuts and bolts of middle grades education, interdisciplinary teaming, advisory, cooperative learning, creative and critical thinking skills, assessment, and interdisciplinary instruction.

# References

Doda, N. 1991. The very best teams. Unpublished handout: Teacher to Teacher, Inc., Burke, VA.

Epstein, J. L., and MacIver, D. J. 1990. The middle grades: Is grade span the most important issue? *Educational Horizons* 68(2): 88–94.

Irvin, J., ed. 1992. *Transforming middle level education: Perspectives and possibilities*. Needham, MA: Allyn & Bacon.

MacIver, D. J. 1990. Meeting the needs of young adolescents: Advisory groups, interdisciplinary teaching teams, and school transition programs. *Phi Delta Kappan* 71(6): 458–464.

# Team-Planning Process

### GOAL-SETTING MEETING

_____ Identify philosophy and goals

_____ Determine responsibilities within team

### INDIVIDUAL TEACHER PLANNING ACTIVITIES

_____ Select and organize appropriate content

_____ Identify and review available materials

_____ Determine appropriate methodologies

_____ Determine assessment plan

### DESIGN MEETING

_____ Present, critique, and modify plan

_____ Outline schedule

### TEACHER'S ACTIVITIES

_____ Preassess student

_____ Refine strategies and content

_____ Gather and prepare materials

### GROUPING AND SCHEDULING MEETING

_____ Present final plan to team

_____ Group students

_____ Finalize schedule, time, space, et cetera.

### TEACHER ACTIVITIES

_____ Teach unit, evaluate content/methods

_____ Refine with help of team members

# What Makes an Effective Team?

## AS A TEAM MEMBER, AM I ABLE TO COMMUNICATE?

1. Do I exchange ideas with my team members?

2. Do I "chat" with my team members?

3. Do I express my feelings and opinions during team meetings?

4. Am I aware of what unit each of my team members is presently teaching?

5. Do I share my problems with team members?

6. Am I sensitive to team members' needs?

7. Are other team members sensitive to my needs?

8. Am I afraid to disagree with other team members?

9. When did I last observe a teammate teach? Discipline students? Relate with students? Plan curriculum?

10. Do I complain about problems or try to solve them by going to the source?

11. What have I gained from working on this team?

## AS A TEAM MEMBER, AM I ABLE TO COOPERATE?

1. Do I follow through on team decisions?

2. Do I compromise and "give" or does everything have to be my way before I'm satisfied?

3. Do I assume my share of team responsibilities?

4. Do I cooperate with team members on covering classes, field trips, et cetera?

5. Do I help other team members who may be teaching subjects new to them?

6. Am I able to overlook personality differences I may have with team members?

7. Have I benefited by being on this team?

8. Do other team members view me as an asset?

## AS A TEAM MEMBER, AM I GOOD WITH TIME?

1. How long did it take me to be comfortable with my team members?

2. Am I on time for meetings and conferences?

3. Do I give advance notice of absence from team meetings?

4. Do I hand in things on time (to aides, counselors, team, et cetera)?

5. How much time during the day do I spend talking with team members?

## AS A TEAM MEMBER, AM I CONSISTENT?

1. Am I consistent in enforcing team decisions?

2. Do I consistently seek support from parents when a student has a problem?

## AS A TEAM MEMBER, AM I FLEXIBLE?

1. Do I expect other team members to use the same teaching style I do?

2. Am I tolerant of other teacher's and student's feelings?

3. Am I tolerant of other team member's ideas?

4. Do I enjoy working on a team?

5. Am I willing to adjust class times when necessary to aid another team member?

6. Do I feel the subject(s) I teach is the most important one?

7. Do I have reasonable expectations of my students?

*(Adapted from a handout by Dr. Nancy Doda, Teacher To Teacher, Inc. Burke, VA.)*

# Steps to Success with Teaming

**EVALUATION**

Yearly Growth Goals
Internal Evaluation
Formative Evaluation
Adjustments

**INSTRUCTION**

Skills
Progress Reports
Overlap Teaching
Units
Large Group Experiences

**MANAGEMENT**

Common Expectations
Discipline Plans
At-Risk Plans
Positive Recognition
Student Conferences

**IDENTITY**

Team Motto/Theme/Name
Team Activities
Intramurals
Goals
Decor

**ORGANIZATION**

Common Areas
Common Planning
Specialists Included
Personalities Balanced
Team Leaders
PIC (Steering Committee)
Block Schedule
Elementary/Secondary

*(Adapted from a handout by Dr. Nancy Doda,*
*Teacher To Teacher, Inc. Burke, VA.)*

# Topic 3  THE ADVISORY PROGRAM IN THE MIDDLE SCHOOL

## ▶ What is it?

**P**erhaps the most controversial program component in middle schools is the advisory program. Some call their particular program advisor/advisee; others refer to their program as teacher-based guidance. Still others call the component home-based guidance. Most schools with functioning advisory programs have chosen specific names— Prime Time, ACE, or STARs. One school refers to its advisory as QT—Quality Time. Ambiguity about the very name for the program attests to the conflicting feelings and ideas people hold about these decentralized guidance programs.

Some of the issues underlying this debatable nature of advisory programs include a reluctance by some teachers who are not trained guidance counselors to take on such a role. Some communities are wary of having what they view as a values-oriented curriculum within the school. For the most part, however, the advisory program is perhaps the most developmentally responsive program in a middle school and should therefore be able to weather these controversies.

If we think of the developmental nature of young adolescents in terms of their affective needs (emotional, social, and—in terms of how they feel about their developing bodies—physical), there is little question that student-teacher relationships, role models, and caring adults are essential to students' self-discovery. How to make these relationships possible may be a problem of simple logistics. Where can you find the time to be available for students who might just need a "friend in residence" for a few minutes during the day? Unless a specific time is set apart for an advisory program, the hectic daily schedules of most middle level schools make it unlikely that you will be available.

However, when schools are committed to respond to students' needs and teachers are willing to make the effort to provide a place and time in which long-term relationships between themselves and students can develop, the advisory program is a significant factor in making a middle level school a true middle school.

> " *. . . by age 15, substantial numbers of American youth are at risk of reaching adulthood unable to meet adequately the requirements of the work-place, the commitments of relationships in families and with friends, and the responsibilities of participation in a democratic society. These youth are among the estimated seven million young people—one in four adolescents—who are extremely vulnerable to multiple high-risk behaviors and school failure. Another seven million may be at moderate risk, but remain a cause for serious concern.* "
>
> (Carnegie Council, 1989, p. 8)

# ► How does it work?

You know that the teacher advisory is an affective program component scheduled into the regular school day as a time when teachers and their small groups of students can work at establishing long-term relationships as individuals. But how does it function? What are the goals of such a program? What do teachers, building leaders, guidance counselors, and students actually do during advisory? What are the characteristics of an effective advisory program? And how do you get started?

The advisory program is not just for the so-called at risk student—the potential dropout, the underachiever. Advisory programs are designed to accommodate the developmental needs of all young adolescents. Among the goals of the advisory are the following:

- Student self-awareness
- Student interpersonal competence
- Student self-respect
- Adult guidance and support
- Student self-discipline
- Teacher-student relationships
- Student moral development
- Student sense of community

## Characteristics of an Effective Advisory

Despite all variations, the following might be considered a standard list of characteristics of an effective advisory program:

- The group meets on a regularly scheduled basis.
- Time allotted is at least 20–25 minutes for a session.
- Multiage grouping is an appropriate option.
- Counselors help coordinate the program and support teacher-advisors.
- Students are randomly assigned.
- No teacher is assigned more than one advisory group.
- Virtually all certified personnel are assigned an advisory group.
- Homeroom duties may be included.
- Clearly defined procedures exist and are followed.
- Grades are not given.
- Good discipline is maintained.
- Handbooks and resource guides are readily available.

# Roles and Responsibilities

Every member of the school community has a role to play if an advisory program is to be a success. Here is a brief summary of the roles and responsibilities of each group.

**Administration:** The administration has a responsibility to generate a total school policy that supports the advisory program, to develop a management system for it, and to promote the program actively within the school and community. It also falls to the administration to provide appropriate in-service training for teacher-advisors. Finally, it is ultimately the administration's responsibility to allocate time and space for planning and implementing the advisory program.

**Counselors:** Perhaps the most significant role for school counselors is to serve as resource people for teacher-advisors. With their training and background, counselors are in a position to encourage and motivate teachers, who may at first feel out of their depth. Counselors can also serve as coordinators for team activities, as well as communications links between teams. Perhaps most important of all, counselors should faithfully respond to students referred to them by advisors.

**Teacher-Advisors:** As the backbone of the advisory program, teachers have the responsibility of providing a warm, caring environment and a time and place for advisees to freely share concerns. Perhaps their most significant role is to be good listeners and respond to advisees' needs. However, they also have the responsibility of referring advisees to appropriate resources. Advisors can assist advisees in monitoring their own academic progress—and personal and social development as well. Finally, there are responsibilities for record keeping, for communicating with parents and guardians of advisees, and (of course) for participating in staff meetings concerning the program.

**Students:** The all-important advisees should gradually assume their own responsibilities for developing open relationships with teachers, for helping to build a sense of trust, and for becoming involved in decision making and problem solving. They need to learn that they have a responsibility to raise questions and to develop a willingness to share problems. Students' basic responsibilities are for their own growth—being an individual as well as part of a group, learning to participate in discussion, and developing a sense of self.

## TIPS FOR TEAMS

**What creates a great advisory climate?**

- **An openness to exploring another person's point of view**

- **Listening with the purpose of understanding another person's point of view**

- **Empathy, which results only from careful listening**

- **A genuineness conveyed through warmth and interest**

- **The ownership of personal feelings**

- **Respect for differing points of view**

# ► How do we get started?

Once a school has established its rationale, philosophy, goals, and the competencies expected for those participating in the teacher-advisory program, there are several management questions that need to be addressed.

- Which grade level(s) should be included?

- Which teachers should serve as advisors? Should they be appointed by administration? Should they be accepted only if they volunteer?

- How should advisory groups be formed? Should students be allowed to select advisors? Should the administration make advisee/advisor assignments? Should that task fall to the teaching team?

Other questions will involve time and schedule. Should advisory groups meet daily? How long should each session be? How much planning time will be required? What materials and preplanned activities will be needed?

Believe it or not, it is good news that there are no magic answers to these questions. There are no givens. Middle schools are responsive and they are flexible. Your answers to these questions will depend on your philosophy statement, the demographic nature of your students, the competence and commitment of your faculty, and a host of other issues. Open discussion of these questions and as much input as possible will strengthen your teacher advisory program. In this case "answers may vary" is a healthy sign.

# ► Where do we go for more information?

Cole, C. 1992. *Nurturing a teacher advisory program.* Columbus, OH: National Middle School Association.
As a former middle school counselor, the author has worked extensively with teacher advisory programs. In this monograph, she deals with many pressing questions: Why have a teacher advisory program? What happens in such a program? Who is an advisor?; What kinds of activities work best? What are sources for advisory activities, and what pitfalls should you try to avoid when setting up a program? Her style is very "user friendly" and her examples are very helpful to beginning advisors.

> "For many youths 10 to 15 years old, early adolescence offers opportunities to choose a path toward a productive and fulfilling life . . . (yet) under current conditions . . . far too many . . . will not make the passage through early adolescence successfully. . . . Millions . . . will never reach their full potential."
>
> (Carnegie Council, 1989, p. 20)

Hoversten,C. et.al. 1991. *Treasure chest: A teacher advisory source book*. Columbus, OH: National Middle School Association.
This three-ring, custom-designed sourcebook for teachers contains 120 activities for a teacher advisory program along with valuable support materials. Activities are divided into sections: listening skills, nonverbal communication, goal setting, problem solving, self-awareness, and group skills. There are ready-to-reproduce handouts or worksheets with cartoons and student-centered illustrations. In addition to their use in a teacher advisory program, these materials and activities would be very beneficial for academic classes.

Forte, I., and Schurr, S. 1991. *Advisory: Middle grades advisee/advisor program*. Nashville, TN: Incentive Publications, Inc.
*Advisory* is a complete middle grades advisory program for three grade levels. The total curriculum incorporates four major themes: school culture and academic survival, communication, self-concept and relationships, and problem-solving and decision-making. Each theme contains a total of nine separate lesson plans that have a standard format and an optional set of advisory tasks for extension or follow-up activities.

Note: Additional resources on activities for teacher advisory are as varied as the number of schools which have advisory programs. Your local, regional, district, or state professional library may well have handbooks from other districts which will have suggestions for activities. The National Middle School Association in Columbus, Ohio, has materials available to members and nonmembers alike. Schools you might visit as you decide how to organize and implement your school-based program will almost always gladly share their resources and materials. Once you decide on your goals, topics, and schedules, finding appropriate activities should not be a difficult task at all.

# References

Carnegie Council on Adolescent Development. 1989. *Turning points: Preparing American youth for the 21st century*. New York: Carnegie Corporation of New York.

Cole, C. 1988. *Guidance in the middle level schools: Everyone's responsibility*. Columbus, OH: National Middle School Association.

Lewis, A. 1990. On valuing young people. *Phi Delta Kappan* 7(16): 420–421.

MacIver, D. 1990. Meeting the needs of young adolescents: Advisory groups, interdisciplinary teaching teams, and school transition programs. *Phi Delta Kappan* 7(16): 458–464.

Purkey, W., and Strahan, D. 1986. *Positive discipline: A pocketful of ideas*. Columbus, OH: National Middle School Association.

**SPECIAL THANKS:** Some materials used in this section were adapted from unpublished handout materials developed by Nancy Doda (Teacher to Teacher, Inc., Burke, VA) and Sharon Harris Lambert (Charlotte Mechlenburg Public Schools, Charlotte, NC).

# Steps in Setting up a Teacher Advisory Program

I.  RESEARCH/STUDY

    A. Read about advisory programs (see listed resources).

    B. Compare and contrast programs that are functioning effectively.

II. DETERMINE ADVISORS

    A. Teachers and administrators: how many will be needed?

    B. Staff : usually only certified staff function in advisory groups, but there are frequent exceptions.

        1) Custodial

        2) Cafeteria

        3) Health Services

III. PLAN (GROUP THINKING)

    A. Establish goals.

    B. Determine size of groups: somewhere between 12–20.

    C. Establish curriculum: topics, themes.

    D. Establish time for advisory periods: daily? weekly? morning, afternoon?

IV. TEACH

    A. Teach the advisors what is required of them—and how the role differs from that of teacher.

        1) Workshops

        2) Guest Speakers

        3) Observations

    B. Teach advisees how they are to participate.

        1) Model the process.

        2) Jointly establish guidelines.

    C. Plan activities (draw from common problems, needs, interests, or concerns).

V.  GROUP THE STUDENTS/ESTABLISH TEAMS

    A. Avoid ability grouping in advisory.

    B. Avoid tracking in advisory.

# What About Advisory Topics?

**ONE:** Advisory topics or themes are usually organized by weeks, months, quarters, semesters, or trimesters.

**TWO:** Some schools do not designate specific schedules for topics but allow teachers to devise their own schedule.

**THREE:** Some schools develop different topics at each grade level, while other schools use the same general topics for all three grades.

**FOUR:** Advisory periods may cover a variety of topics ranging from developing affective behavior skills, to predetermined topics, to the value of community projects. It is recommended, however, that while each grade level may have the same overall topics, activities for each grade level should vary. The needs and competencies of sixth graders quite likely are different from those of eighth graders.

## Sample Topics for an Advisory Curriculum

- Getting acquainted
- Organizing and study skills
- Celebrating yourself
- Peer relationships
- Family relationships
- Problem solving
- Decision making
- Career awareness
- Community Involvement
- Goal setting
- Self-esteem
- Drug awareness

- Leisure activities
- Health/fitness awareness
- Test-taking skills
- Sportsmanship
- Communication skills
- Conflict resolution
- Leadership skills
- Coping skills
- Life skills
- The future
- Emotions and feelings
- Cultural awareness

# Possible Advisory Activities

1. Periodic study sessions
2. Silent reading
3. Individual academic counseling
4. Special team projects
5. Special school projects
6. Current events
7. Guest speakers
8. Indoor and outdoor games
9. Intramural contests
10. Club or activity days

11. Holiday celebrations
12. Films or video tapes
13. Community projects
14. Storytime
15. Career exploration
16. School spirit week
17. Student council events
18. School pride events
19. Journal writing
20. Contests

---

### ADVISORY GROUP
### SAMPLE DAILY SCHEDULE

MONDAY — Group Discussion

TUESDAY — Study / Conference Day

WEDNESDAY — Group Activity

THURSDAY — Drop Everything and Read

FRIDAY — Group Activity/Discussion/ or Student Choice

---

# Cautions and Caveats for Advisory Groups

What is consistent with young adolescents is their inconsistency.

Young adolescents need strong adult role models.

Young adolescents are curious and need activity and interaction.

Young adolescents are egocentric — they believe the world revolves around them and their problems.

Advisory periods should not be free time.

Plan age-appropriate activities.

Be a positive influence; focus on affective development.

Let your advisees know they are special.

# Remember . . .

**ONE:** Have planned activities, but be ready to drop them when a real concern surfaces.

**TWO:** Be flexible.

**THREE:** Do not label or abandon students due to their record, interest, or attitude.

**FOUR:** Use variety to battle boredom and staleness.

**FIVE:** New and first-year teachers need inservice training.

**SIX:** Use guidance counselors as resources and for referrals especially for serious personal problems.

**SEVEN:** Strive to avoid advisor burnout.

**EIGHT:** Faculty must model positive relationships.

# Topic 4    EXPANDED EXPLORATORIES, ELECTIVES, AND INTRAMURALS

## ▶ What are they?

The varied experiences we cluster under the umbrella of exploration have one thing in common. All are designed to provide experiences that allow students to explore their constantly changing interests, identity, and aptitudes, and to broaden their horizons. Throughout the years, these courses have had various labels: unified arts, related arts, fine arts, applied arts, specials, and "explo." Whatever the label, the goal has always been to provide opportunities for student achievement in areas other than the traditional core subjects, giving every student a chance to succeed and even to excel.

The middle school years are a time when students need experiences that offer breadth rather than depth. We know that middle grade students are trying to find out as much as possible about themselves as persons. They are constantly testing their own abilities. They delight in projects that have relevance and some closure. They take pleasure in real work. Exploratory courses can help students have positive experiences by providing a safe, success-oriented environment, some choices of what to study, a variety of avenues for self-expression, and a chance for the applause of both peers and adults.

## ▶ How are they different?

When you were in junior high, did you take art, music, physical education, and "home ec" or industrial arts? Were those really electives or were they required electives? Did anyone ever offer you a special, short-term course based on a particular interest or need of your own? Were all teams competitive and only for the chosen? Were you the victim of the "unkindest cut"—not being selected for the team or the cheerleading squad, for example? Were your school newspapers and yearbooks compiled by a select group of students who won the journalism award so their sponsor could hang it on the wall? Did you explore or simply exist? That is the way it used to be.

> "*Changing social conditions require that we rethink the content and packaging of the exploratory strand of middle level schooling. Renewal of content needs to take into account newer definitions of gender and family roles and responsibilities, as well as the need to expose and enrich rather than to specialize and compete.*"
>
> (Messick and Reynolds, 1992, p. 130)

How have things changed? With a developmentally responsive middle school philosophy and adults who want to accommodate student needs, society may see significant changes in how students of the 1990s answer these questions when, as adults, they look back on their middle school experience.

For the purposes of this section, we will include all of the following as components of a full exploratory program for the middle school:

- The traditional required cycle of general electives such as art, music, et cetera

- Electives and exploratories in science and technologies

- Independent study

- Intramurals, athletic and otherwise

- Interest-centered minicourses such as special interest courses, hobbies, or other student-generated topics

- Cocurricular courses

- Clubs, organizations, and assemblies

Such a broad interpretation of the term *exploratory* is based on a belief that all such experiences should, first of all, be developmentally appropriate. Secondly, all should be open to anyone interested in joining—and joining should mean that everyone will get a chance to participate. The byword for exploratories should be "all come, no cut, all play!"

# Characteristics of an Effective Exploratory Program

Exploratory experiences should provide alternate ways of learning and encourage students to use their bodies and minds in creative ways. What are the characteristics of effective exploratories?

- Programs are noncompetitive.

- Teachers involved in the activities and courses understand the basic philosophy of the programs and are willing to abide by the guiding principles.

- All the exploratory experiences are regarded as safe time for students to try out new things in a nonthreatening environment.

- Experiences are interest-based, short in length, and usually graded by *pass/fail* or *outstanding, good, fair,* or *poor.*

Middle level schools working with a more traditional philosophy often grade exploratory courses with the letter grades used for core subjects. This reflects a basic opinion that all classes, subjects, and courses are offered for the same reasons and with the same expectation—content mastery. More progressive middle schools have

> "*The exploratory component of the curriculum is the one component that most directly and fully reflects the nature and needs of this age group.*"
>
> (Lounsbury, 1991, p. 64)

> "*For many, exploratory courses will be the last chance to sample the world of knowledge before they become committed to a particular program track at the high school.*"
>
> (Lounsbury, p. 63)

adopted less rigid or anecdotal reports of progress rather than letter grades. If the exploratory program is indeed a chance to pursue a wide range of interests, then it stands to reason that it is the experience rather than a set of facts which should be emphasized.

# ▶ How do we get started?

Many of the decisions about required electives will be administrative. There are state and local requirements and traditions about what has to be offered and to whom. Most schools have room for a truly *expanded* program of beneficial and enjoyable experiences and activities. There are a number of ways to get your program off the ground.

- Meet with interested teachers who are willing to participate.
- Survey current programs available in your school.
- Review your school's program goals to see what is needed.
- Capitalize on the experience of present exploratory teachers.
- Survey every faculty member for interests and strengths.
- Survey students about what they would like to see offered.
- Decide on topics and make format decisions (minicourses; clubs; in-school, after-school, community-based projects).
- Develop a trial schedule and roster of experiences.
- Appoint a steering committee.
- Present the trial plan to the entire faculty.

## Potential Electives and Experiences

Here is a list of exploratory areas you will want to consider.

- Art, music, physical education, home arts, industrial technology
- Foreign languages, foreign cultures, global studies
- Business education, apprenticeships, professional/career studies
- Student government, town (team or house) government
- Media studies, media production, critical viewing skills
- Clubs and special interest groups
- Special needs groups such as children of divorce or "newcomers"
- Transition experiences such as a move from eighth grade to high school
- All sports activities on the intramural roster, cheerleading, pep squad

## POINTS TO PONDER

What's in it for the kids?

An effective exploratory program

- Builds self-esteem
- Improves physical as well as cognitive skills
- Contributes to healthy relationships
- Enables all students to succeed
- Lets everyone have fun without pressure
- Gives students choices and the freedom to explore
- Emphasizes cooperative learning and social skills
- Boosts enthusiasm

# References

Bergman, S. 1992. Exploratory programs in the middle level school. In *Transforming middle level education: Perspectives and possibilities.* ed. J. Irvin. Needham, MA: Allyn & Bacon.

Lounsbury, J. 1991. *As I see it.* Columbus, OH: National Middle School Association.

Messick, R., and Reynolds, K. 1992. *Middle level curriculum in action.* White Plains, NY: Longman Press.

# Topic 5 FLEXIBLE BLOCK SCHEDULING

## ▶ What is it?

A truly flexible schedule is one that is responsive, effective, and efficient. It allows for individual needs and team requests. It can provide maximum time in class and on task. This is no easy task, as you well know. Shared teachers, buses, activities, lunch schedules, band schedules, and a myriad other factors influence decisions about schedule. Scheduling can become so complex that very often you just want to throw up your hands and leave the scheduling headache to the administration. However, schedules play a significant role in school and student achievement. You need to become skillful planners of time and space to implement team plans for curriculum, advisories, and exploratory programs. A guiding principle for your scheduling should be *to achieve a balance between daily stability and creative variety that is developmentally responsive to young adolescents*.

## ▶ How is it different?

Most elementary schools schedule large amounts of class time with one teacher in a self-contained classroom. High schools, by contrast, usually have a complex modular schedule with students moving every period to different subject area teachers—the schedule that is referred to as "cells and bells." That is, you put students into cells (classrooms), wait 45 minutes, ring a bell, and move them *en masse* to another cell. The ideal schedule for a middle school creates ways to use time that are neither too elementary nor too secondary. What an effective middle school needs is a schedule that combines some of the freedom of a self-contained elementary classroom with some provision for specialized teaching. To move toward that ideal, decision making about the schedule will need some degree of decentralization. It needs especially the input of the teams. Teams need the power to alter their share of the day if they are to achieve their goals.

*" The school schedule must be thought of as dynamic, alterable, and always subordinate to changing requirements of students and faculty. "*

(Superintendents' Middle Grade Task Force, 1987, p. 107)

# ▶ How do we get started?

Building a schedule is always a compromise. Everyone must give and take. Keep in mind that scheduling is the *budgeting of time*. Like the budgeting of money, the first thing you have to do is set priorities. And, like a budget, a schedule is the means—not the end.

After the priorities, there are some "nuts and bolts" questions to ask:

- What will be the average size of our teams?
- What are the pluses and minuses of the current schedule?
- What would the wish list of the teams look like regarding schedule?
- How many instructional minutes are desired/required per week?
- How many minutes of common planning time will be realistic?
- Do we have shared staff and when are they available?
- Are staff needed for lunch supervision or other duty assignments?
- What other constraints or givens must be considered?

## Developing a Team Schedule

You may want to review some of these questions in terms of how they affect your particular situation. Then begin to design two or three alternate schedules.

What grouping pattern would be best?
- heterogeneous
- homogeneous
- combination (which classes and how)

What teaming options would be best?
- self-contained
- two-, three-, four-person teams

What time periods do we need to consider for our schedule?
- rotating periods
- variations in the length of periods
- classes which meet four, five, six or more times a week
- recess
- other options

# ► Where do we go for more information?

Alexander, W., and George, P. 1993. *The exemplary middle school.* Orlando, FL: Harcourt, Brace, Jovanovich.
In this book, the authors talk about organizing time and space in the middle school (chapter 8). The many examples of building schedules from around the country point out the fact that there are probably as many schedules as there are schools.

Merenbloom, E. 1986. *The team process in the middle school: A handbook for teachers.* Columbus, OH: National Middle School Association.
Throughout this book, the author gives suggestions and examples as to how teams can design and implement a flexible, developmentally responsive schedule. Using flexible scheduling techniques, he gives many examples of building team schedules. His examples are good references for decentralized decision-making ideas.

## References

Alexander, W., and George, P. 1993. *The exemplary middle school.* Orlando, FL: Harcourt, Brace, Jovanovich.

Spear, R. C. Scheduling schools with middle grades. Unpublished handout from Powder Middle School, Southwick / Tolland Regional School District, Southwick, MA.

Superintendent's Middle Grade Task Force. 1987. *Caught in the middle: Educational reform for young adolescents in California public schools.* Sacramento, CA: California State Department of Education.

# Schedule A

**PROJECTED STAFFING NEEDS AT _____ MIDDLE SCHOOL
DURING THE 199__ – 9__ SCHOOL YEAR**

| | | |
|---|---|---|
| Advisory | 30 Min. | |
| Academic Block | 240 Min. + 9 | (5•48) |
| Exploratory Block | 96 Min. | (2•48) |
| Lunch | 25 Min. | |

Act. = Academic Plus Time (Team-Based)
Nancy M. Doda, Ph.D.
Educational Consulting
10363 Steamboat Lndg. Ln.
Burke, VA 22015

| 27 | 45 | 45 | 45 | 75 | 45 | 45 | 45 | |
|---|---|---|---|---|---|---|---|---|
| A D V | *L.A.* | *Math* | *Science* | L U N C H  *Lunch S.H. EUR* | Act. F.L.  *S.S.* | Health Health P.E. P.E. | Art Music H.Ec. Tech.  *Exploratory* | **6th** |
| A D V | | | | L U N C H | Health Health P.E. P.E. | Art Music H.Ec. Tech. or Typ. | Act. F.L. | **7th** |
| A D V | | | | L U N C H | Art Music Typ./H.Ec. Cmp./Tech. | Act. F.L. | Health Health P.E. P.E. | **8th** |
| A D V | Art Typ. Health/P.E. H.Ec./Tech. | Act. F.L. | Band Orch. Chor. Health/P.E. | L U N C H | | | | **8th** |
| A D V | Act. F.L. | Band Orch. Chor. Health/P.E. | Art H.Ec./Tech. Health P.E. or Typ. | L U N C H | | | | **7th** |
| A D V | Band Orch. Chor. Health/P.E. | Art H.Ec./Tech. Health P.E. | F.L. Act. | L U N C H | | | | **6th** |

# Schedule B

## MIDDLE SCHOOL
## FIRST TRIMESTER SCHEDULE

|  | W TEAM & T TEAM | D TEAM & M TEAM | C TEAM & B TEAM |
|---|---|---|---|
| 8:40 – 9:10 | Advisor/Advisee Time | Advisor/Advisee Time | Advisor/Advisee Time |
| 9:10 – 9:55<br>9:57 – 10:42 | Skills | Exploratory/<br>P.E. | Skills |
| 10:44 – 11:29<br>11:31 – 12:16 | Skills | Skills | Exploratory/<br>P.E. |
| 12:16 – 1:10 | Lunch | Lunch | Lunch |
| 1:12 – 1:57<br>2:00 – 2:45 | Exploratory/<br>P.E. | Skills | Skills |

**AFTER 1ST 12 WEEKS —**    W & T take D & M schedule
D & M take C & B schedule
C & B take W & T schedule

**2ND 12 WEEKS —**    Rotate ahead one block to complete cycle, etc.

# Schedule C

| TIME | UNIT I: 5/6 Y | UNIT II: 6/7 Y | UNIT III: 7/8Y |
|---|---|---|---|
| 8:00 – 8:55 | Teacher Planning Time | Teacher Planning Time | Teacher Planning Time |
| 8:55 – 9:25 | Advisor/Advisee | Advisor/Advisee | Advisor/Advisee |
| 9:30 – 11:00 | Reading/Language Arts | P.E./Expressive Art | Reading/Math |
| 11:00 – 11:30<br>11:30 – 12:00<br>12:00 – 12:30 | P.E./<br>Expressive Art | Social Science<br><br>Lunch | Social Science |
| 12:30 – 1:30 | Lunch | Math<br>Social Science | Spelling/<br>Language Arts<br>Lunch |
| 1:30 – 3:05 | Math | Reading/<br>Language Arts | P.E.<br>Expressive Art |
| 3:05 – 3:30 | Teacher Planning Time | Teacher Planning Time | Teacher Planning Time |

# Schedule D

| | | | | |
|---|---|---|---|---|
| **6th Grade** | 8:20 - 10:10<br><br>Exploratory<br>Physical<br>   Education<br>Careers<br>   Planning | 10:10 - 10:55<br><br>Basic<br>Curriculum | 11:00 - 11:45<br><br>LUNCH | 11:45 - 2:53<br><br>Basic Curriculum |
| **7th Grade** | 8:20 - 10:10<br><br>Basic<br>Curriculum | 10:15 - 11:55<br><br>Exploratory<br>Physical<br>   Education<br>Careers<br>   Planning | 12:00 - 12:45<br><br>LUNCH | 12:45 - 2:53<br><br>Basic Curriculum |
| **8th Grade** | 8:20 - 12:20<br><br>Basic Curriculum | | 12:30 - 1:10<br><br>LUNCH | 1:15 - 2:53<br><br>Exploratory<br>Physical<br>   Education<br>Careers<br>   Planning |

## ▶ What is it?

Flexible student grouping is often defined by what it is not. It is *not* tracking and it is *not* ability grouping. Tracking is an inflexible way of grouping students by ability, based often on standardized tests. While tracking is widely practiced and has been for many years, the practice is under considerable criticism, and there is growing skepticism about its effectiveness, based on continuing research. Likewise, ability grouping has become one of the most studied, most discussed, and most controversial topics in modern education.

The basic premise behind both tracking and ability grouping is a logical one. These methods aim at the goal of getting the most achievement out of the most students in the most efficient manner possible. If this is so logical, why are there so many problems? In what ways can middle schools work to group students flexibly so that the goal suggested above is not only met but far exceeded? How do we detrack and still teach and learn effectively?

## ▶ How is it different?

For middle schools and young adolescents, the question of tracking and grouping is particularly critical. If diversity is the hallmark of this age group, then supporting diversity within the school is an important way to be developmentally responsive. In the past, educators have tried many different ways of organizing and grouping students. The one-room schoolhouse used multiaged, heterogeneous grouping to the maximum. We have gone from this setting all the way to competitive, whole-group instruction. What are the alternatives? Flexible grouping of students is not an answer in itself, but it is a vehicle for helping you do what you know to be best for students and their learning.

> "The success of grouping depends on appropriate placement, flexible membership, appropriate instructional materials, teaching practices that reward students for progress, and other pedagogical and motivational factors."
>
> (Epstein & MacIver, 1990, p. 14)

## ▶ How do we get started?

If you are ready to begin detracking your middle school, you will need help and support from all on the staff who think as you do. Just re-arranging students into new groups is not the answer. It is what you do in those new groups that matters! Read, share, and exchange ideas. Replace the notion that there is only one way to group, assign, and assess with a multidimensional view that can create many ways for students to succeed. Find out what others are doing, ask questions, go see others in action, always be on the lookout for new ideas.

Robert Slavin, known for his works on cooperative learning (which can be a primary vehicle for detracking), suggests:

- As a starting point, group students for only one or two subjects, while leaving the remaining classes for the majority of the day grouped heterogeneously.

- Place students in groups based on demonstrated needs and not on standardized tests or simply on previous performance.

- Group students for instruction only when it will help them learn *new* material. For example, within-class ability grouping for learning a new math skill might be appropriate.

- If necessary, regroup into within-class ability groups to teach a *specific* skill. This method of grouping students at a similar level of talent and understanding on a temporary basis might be appropriate.

> "**B**right students are not held back when they are in mixed classrooms. And we can be quite certain that the deficiencies of lower students are not more easily remedied when they are grouped together. And, given the evidence, we are unable to support the general belief that students learn best when they are grouped together with others like themselves."
>
> (Oakes, 1985, p. 8)

- Within a group, vary the level and pace of instruction to meet different students' levels of readiness and understanding.

- Reassess strategies, assignments, expectations, and assessment frequently. Build in flexibility so that students can move from group to group as their progress or needs warrant. For example, individual pacing within and among groups in math would allow a student to move into a faster group when learning an easy process or concept, or move into another group if there is need for a slower pace.

As you consider various grouping alternatives, keep in mind what you know about your students' cognitive, emotional, social, and physical development. Since there is sometimes a decline in intrinsic motivation for young adolescents, they need additional involvement and tasks that appeal to their curiosity. Average and low-ability group assignments do not usually attend to this need. Young adolescents often become indifferent to their school work because their attention has shifted to other concerns—especially to their social development.

Middle grade students are often self-deprecating. However, they respond well when they succeed. If they do well at hard tasks, their sense of self-worth is rewarded and they are eager to try again.

# ► Where do we go for more information?

Oakes, J. 1985. *Keeping track: how schools structure inequality*. New Haven, CT: Yale University Press.
Oakes is both eloquent and persuasive about the need to rethink how we organize students in the name of equity and equality. She makes several excellent points about the way schools have locked themselves into structures that may benefit a few at the great expense of many others. She is forceful in her belief that tracking contributes to mediocre schooling.

*National Middle School Journal*. 1993, March.
This magazine contains several excellent articles on tracking and grouping specifically for the middle school grades. The articles would be very helpful for beginners who are looking for ways other schools have accomplished the task of detracking. One specific bonus in this issue is an extensive bibliography of resources which could help give background knowledge and lend support for any school or district that is ready to take on this complex and often hotly contested issue.

# References

Epstein, J., and MacIver, D. 1990. *Education in the middle grades: National practices and trends.* Columbus, OH: National Middle School Association.

George, P., and Alexander, W. 1993. *The exemplary middle school.* Orlando, Florida: Harcourt, Brace, Jovanovich.

Slavin, R. 1986. *Ability grouping and student achievement in elementary schools: A best evidence synthesis.* Tech. Rep. No. 1, Johns Hopkins University, Center for Research on Elementary and Middle Schools. Baltimore, MD.

Wheelock, A. 1992. *Crossing the tracks.* New York: The New Press (also available from National Middle School Association, Columbus, OH.)

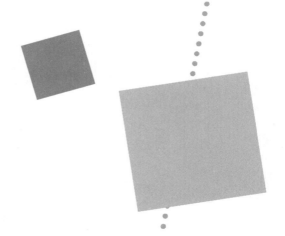

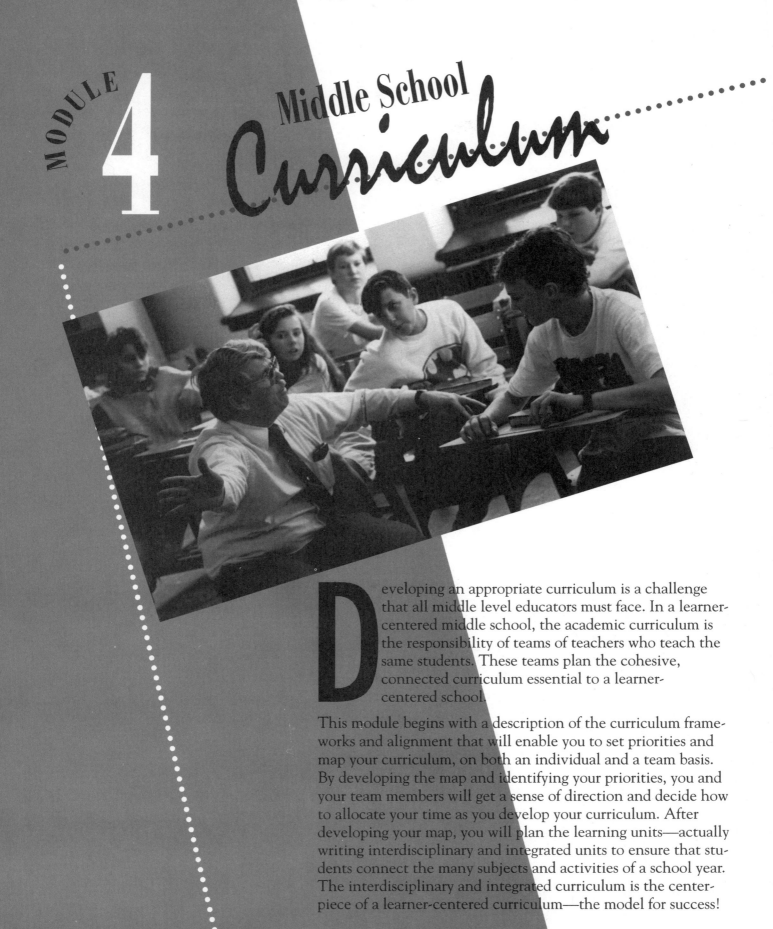

# MODULE 4

## Middle School *Curriculum*

**D**eveloping an appropriate curriculum is a challenge that all middle level educators must face. In a learner-centered middle school, the academic curriculum is the responsibility of teams of teachers who teach the same students. These teams plan the cohesive, connected curriculum essential to a learner-centered school.

This module begins with a description of the curriculum frameworks and alignment that will enable you to set priorities and map your curriculum, on both an individual and a team basis. By developing the map and identifying your priorities, you and your team members will get a sense of direction and decide how to allocate your time as you develop your curriculum. After developing your map, you will plan the learning units—actually writing interdisciplinary and integrated units to ensure that students connect the many subjects and activities of a school year. The interdisciplinary and integrated curriculum is the centerpiece of a learner-centered curriculum—the model for success!

# Contents

# Topic 1 CURRICULUM FRAMEWORKS

Since many states are replacing the traditional curriculum guides and checklists with curriculum frameworks, we have included a section in the Curriculum Module that explains what curriculum frameworks are and how best to use them. This section does not explain how to develop frameworks, since this tends to be done at the state level, but it does give you and your team a description of curriculum frameworks and how to use them.

## ► What are they?

Curriculum frameworks are documents that provide direction for schools and districts as they construct curricula to meet the needs of their students (Curry and Temple, 1992). Frameworks list and clarify desired learning outcomes for students—that is, what students should know and be able to do—and present key concepts, competencies, and performance criteria. Curriculum frameworks are not intended to be specific, highly prescriptive curriculum requirements. Instead, framework guidelines are more likely to

1. Use themes and concepts to link content rather than list isolated facts

2. Call for the use of thinking skills and problem solving/decision making rather than passive learning

3. Focus on instructional quality by including and connecting all aspects of instruction

4. Act as the core documents to support curriculum integration

### Traditional Curriculum Guides

In the past, state curriculum guides were used to encompass and communicate the arrangements schools made for students' learning and development in each subject area. These guides included the sequence, format, and content of courses, student activities, teaching approaches, and the ways in which classes were organized.

Curriculum guides created in the 1970s and 1980s usually consisted of goal statements, learning objectives, a minimum description of subject and course content, and a set of subject area skills in the form of a checklist or outline. They tended to reinforce the impression of the discipline as a laundry list of facts. The scope and sequence of the curriculum was usually in the form of a mandated, lockstep, sequential outline that focused on coverage. Such a curriculum often included so much material that it was difficult for teachers to teach in-depth knowledge or understanding. Students usually viewed curriculum as compartmentalized and focused on skills and irrelevant knowledge.

## The Curriculum Frameworks Concept

Newer, more progressive curriculum frameworks represent a significant departure from traditional curriculum guides. First, they incorporate the most recent information on how students learn. Second, they encourage integration of all components of the curriculum. Ideally, they provide an easily read map of ideas about instruction, an outline to be filled in and developed by teachers and learners. They not only let teachers focus on learners, but they encourage a learner-centered curriculum—a total learning environment.

Curriculum frameworks aim to align state goals with learner outcomes called for by recognized authorities, such as the National Council of Teachers of Mathematics (NCTM) and the National Academy of Sciences (NAS). They focus not only on what students ought to know, but also on what students should be able to do at various points in their school careers. They are not manuals to be looked into on Monday in order to determine the week's content. Instead, these frameworks present a range of options from which teachers choose, on the basis of what they think best for their students. As a result, while curriculum frameworks indicate important content and performance areas to be developed, they neither dictate how the presentation should be structured, nor specify a required scope and sequence that must be followed.

Curriculum frameworks foster a total learning environment in schools and classrooms. These frameworks assist teachers and administrators in designing exemplary, learner-centered programs and experiences at every grade level and enable learners to integrate all the parts of their education and experience into a whole.

# ► How do curriculum frameworks work?

Frameworks may include the following components:

- Goal statements
- Learning outcomes for students (also schools)
- Key concepts and competencies and areas of study
- Content and assessment performance standards
- Themes and concepts of the discipline
- Instructional strategies
- Technology strategies
- Interdisciplinary strategies
- Sample programs/curriculum units

Frameworks are organized around learning outcomes, competencies, and concepts in order to

- Encourage learners to focus on the essentials of performance rather than on getting through particular procedures
- Introduce rigor and reason into curriculum decisions and ensure that decisions are made in terms of broader learning goals for students
- Utilize students' prior knowledge effectively as part of the learning process.

# ► How do we get started?

Because curriculum frameworks start with learning outcomes and end with performance standards, they require educators involved in making curriculum decisions to answer the fundamental question, *What will students really know and be able to do as a result of engaging in particular learning activities?*

The following steps will help you and your team use curriculum frameworks as a tool to develop a learner-centered curriculum.

### Step 1: Set Curriculum Framework Priorities; Align Curriculum

Because your curriculum framework does not include a detailed list of "what to teach," your first step is to establish the curriculum priorities for your course.

The following activity has been developed to help teachers set curriculum priorities. Each member of the team should complete this activity.

1. Make a list of what you teach or pull such a list from your state curriculum guide.

2. Answer the following question, either individually or in subject-area groups: "What would I teach if I had only 90 days to teach this list, instead of 180?"

3. To help you answer this question, make a list of priorities and estimate the number of days you would allocate to each item on your list. Try not to use more than a total of 90 days. If you have concepts/skills left over after allocating your 90 days, decrease the number of days devoted to a topic or eliminate topics altogether.

4. If you are working in a group and teachers disagree on the number of days assigned to an item, compromise by assigning the difference to the remaining 90 days.

This process will highlight the most important content of the course, or the top 50 percent of skills, concepts, and facts. Most importantly, it will align all three parts of your curriculum—the written, the taught, and the tested curriculum. See the figure below for a diagram of curriculum alignment (English, 1988).

**R**emember that curriculum frameworks do not have lists of skills and knowledge to teach. With only broad statements of goals and outcomes, curriculum frameworks demand an aligned curriculum and require teachers to know and be guided by their priorities.

## THE WRITTEN CURRICULUM

Curriculum Quality Control (Alignment)

The Taught Curriculum

The Tested Curriculum

**Step 2:** Create a Curriculum Map

Use Copy Form 1 (Curriculum Map) to lay out your 90-day curriculum. This activity will give you and your team the opportunity to map each curriculum with priorities and organize your schedule of coverage. Once you have done this, you will have a map or guide of your course priorities for the academic year.

The chart below is an example from Heidi Jacobs (1991) of a sixth-grade team that set priorities and mapped its curriculum. The next step is for team members to rearrange and align their respective subjects to allow concurrent teaching of content areas.

## EXAMPLE OF CALENDAR CURRICULUM MAPPING

| | February | March | April | May | June |
|---|---|---|---|---|---|
| English/Language Arts | *Sarah, Plain and Tall* | | Wilson's Letters; Diaries of Immigrants | *Diary of Anne Frank* | |
| Social Studies | The Westward Movement | | The Industrial Revolution; World War I | World War II | |
| Mathematics | Fractions; Roman Numerals | | Metrics Compare Bases | Percents; Geometric Shapes; Scale; Area | |
| Science | Matter and Energy | | Electricity ←————Weather————→ | Magnetism | |
| Art | Color Western Landscapes | | Shape; Cubists Picasso; Gris | Photography: Documentary Purposes | |

A sixth grade team begins interdisciplinary planning by plotting the topics teachers teach month by month.

**Step 3:** Use the Prioritized, Aligned Curriculum

Once you have prioritized and mapped your curriculum, you and your team have many options for how you might use your maps. Some of the many possibilities follow:

- Build or develop your course around the priorities in order to ensure student learning and in-depth knowledge of these priorities.

- Use your curriculum map of priorities to provide a focus within your subject for possible thematic learning units.

- Compare your map with other team members' maps, looking for any topics or skills that are related to one another and could potentially be rescheduled for an interdisciplinary or integrated unit. You can make connections across curricula, not just with superficial activities, but with the most important content within subjects. (See Topic 2, Learning Units, for further discussion.)

- Use your map to ensure that your written, taught, and tested curriculum are aligned.

- If you and/or your team use mastery learning, use the prioritized curriculum to provide the content for both the enrichment and the corrective activities.

# ▶ Where do we go for more information?

California State Department of Education. 1988. *Curriculum frameworks*. Sacramento, CA: Department of Education.
A state frameworks document that includes curriculum frameworks in many disciplines, as well as suggestions on how teachers should use them.

Curry, B. and Temple, T. 1992. *Using curriculum frameworks for systemic reform*. Alexandria, VA: Association for Supervision and Curriculum Development.
A document reviewing existing state curriculum frameworks, it also includes a state-of-the-art curriculum frameworks literature review and recommendations for developing and using integrated, interconnected curriculum frameworks.

English, F. W. 1988. *Curriculum auditing*. Lancaster, PA: Technomic Publishing Co.
A text describing the evaluation activity of curriculum auditing. In addition to case studies, there is an extensive section to help districts, schools, and teachers align their curriculum.

New York State Department of Education. 1991. *A new compact for learning*. Albany, NY: NY State Education Department.
A document that describes a comprehensive strategy for improving public education. Based on the principle that all children can learn, it directs New York's reform efforts toward a learner-centered curriculum, assessment, instruction, and organizational focus.

# References

Curry, B. and Temple, T. 1992. *Using curriculum frameworks for systemic reform*. Alexandria, VA: Association for Supervision and Curriculum Development.

English, F. W. 1988. *Curriculum auditing*. Lancaster, PA: Technomic Publishing Co.

Jacobs, H. H. 1991. Planning for curriculum integration. *Educational Leadership* 49:27–28.

# Curriculum Map

**GRADE** . . . . . . . . . .

| MONTHS | DISCIPLINES | | | | |
|--------|---|---|---|---|---|
| SEPTEMBER | | | | | |
| OCTOBER | | | | | |
| NOVEMBER | | | | | |
| DECEMBER | | | | | |
| JANUARY | | | | | |
| FEBRUARY | | | | | |
| MARCH | | | | | |
| APRIL | | | | | |
| MAY | | | | | |
| JUNE | | | | | |

# Topic 2 · · · · · LEARNING UNITS

## ▶ What are they?

Learning units organize concepts and skills into meaningful structures for teaching and learning. They are *connecting tools* that facilitate student learning, communication, experience, and understanding. Learning units require large blocks of time, both to teach concepts and skills and to allow students to apply and extend what they have learned.

Traditional teaching structure has been based on the daily lesson. Even with flexible blocked schedules, teachers try to teach in 38- to 55-minute lesson periods. During the lesson period, teachers present content, have the students practice or use what they are learning, and routinely assess students' progress. In many cases, students have to provide their own learning structures and make their own connections to other subjects or to the outside world. Too often, a lesson is connected only to whatever lesson preceded or followed in a textbook. Students come to view the curriculum as meaningless, segmented, artificial, with little continuity, and related only to their lives at school.

Learning units provide a dramatic contrast to the daily lesson plan. Learning units not only extend learning time and provide connections with real life, they link prior knowledge to new knowledge. Such units allow the teacher to teach new skills and concepts and students to apply them by utilizing developmental characteristics. Learning units may teach and extend procedural and declarative knowledge (that is, knowing how to do something and knowing facts and concepts); create meaningful, authentic activities; develop student thinking and problem-solving skills; and link all these together for the student.

### Advantages of Learning Units

- Learning/Instruction
  Teachers can apply their knowledge of student learning styles. In contrast to the traditional lesson structure, the structure of a learning unit easily accommodates a diversity of student learning styles.

- Time

  Units extend teaching time to allow for the acquisition, generalization, and application of knowledge.

- Curriculum

  Units provide connections between subjects. The curriculum is more learner-centered.

- Assessment

  Units allow authentic assessment of student work. Teachers use more formative assessment concepts, which improve learning.

# ▶ How do they work?

Learning units are *thematic*. They tie many concepts and skills together around larger, central themes. These themes provide learners with connections and relationships which give meaning to the concepts and skills being taught, in contrast to the traditional series of lessons strung together with apparently unrelated content. The theme is the thread that holds concepts together to facilitate learning.

## Different Types of Units for Different Purposes

The focus of the unit will help you determine what type of unit to write. The types of units are defined with examples below. Teachers may plan any type of learning unit either within a single discipline or across two or more disciplines.

**Knowledge-Based Units** The main feature of a knowledge-based unit is the focus on declarative or procedural knowledge that is centered on skills or concepts. The readings, discussions, learning activities, and projects of a knowledge-based unit help students acquire the targeted knowledge. Usually the concepts and skills are emphasized more than the culminating activity or project, which simply reinforces the content of the unit. A knowledge-based unit may be within one discipline or interdisciplinary.

**Project-Based Units** The main focus of a project-based unit is the student project. While all learning units feature projects, in a project-based unit, the project itself is the "theme" of the learning unit. Almost all teacher and student activities in a unit are geared to the completion of the culminating project. Students' discussions, readings, research, and concepts/skills acquisition are directed toward the successful completion of the project.

## POSSIBLE THEMES FOR KNOWLEDGE-BASED UNITS

- The Civil War
- Ecology
- Poetry
- Statistics in Our World

## POSSIBLE PROJECTS FOR PROJECT-BASED UNITS

- Making a field guide and map of a local wildlife refuge
- Designing a community recycling plan
- Recording oral histories of local senior citizens
- Inventing work-saving devices

The following project categories are common:

- Problem/solution projects
- Design projects
- Construction projects
- School or community projects

**Literacy-Based Units** The purpose of a literacy-based unit is to integrate reading and writing skills into all content areas. Literacy-based units direct their strategies and activities toward the successful use of content reading, writing, and application. Therefore, literacy-based units' culminating tasks or projects usually revolve around written work. Students will read textbooks, periodicals, reports, and literature as they develop final projects or activities. They will also write daily journal entries, keep detailed notes, and use writing for gathering information, organizing their projects and daily activities, and as part of their final report or performance. The themes of literacy-based units appear very similar to the themes of other types of units, but the goal is the total integration of reading and writing, with the focus on the written product. Literacy-based units must be interdisciplinary.

**Inquiry-Based Units** Inquiry-based units concentrate on decision making and problem solving. By focusing their learning activities and culminating activity on inquiry and research, students develop the skills of finding and evaluating information. This, in turn, encourages proficiency in answering questions, taking positions, making decisions, and solving problems. The theme of an inquiry-based unit is almost always stated as a question, with intermediate activities leading up to a final product that "answers" the question. In many cases, students or student teams assume the roles of people who must solve a "real-life" problem. If you are trying to infuse thinking skills and processes into your curriculum, then inquiry-based units are particularly suited to your needs.

Even though we have defined each type of unit individually, teachers routinely combine aspects of various types of units. Many times this combination unit is a much richer learning experience for students.

**POSSIBLE THEMES FOR LITERACY-BASED UNITS**

- **Minerals and Geology: Publishing a local guidebook**

- **Exploring life's work: *60 Minutes* program and/or middle grades vocational guide**

- **Survival: A survival guide for our middle school**

- **Computer Technology: A how-to book for using computers in school assignments**

**POSSIBLE THEMES FOR INQUIRY-BASED UNITS**

- **How can we "buy the best"? Consumer magazine researchers report findings.**

- **Can diversity strengthen our community or country? Community leaders take a stand.**

- **What should be in a library of the twenty-first century? City planners develop policy, budget, and use.**

- **What will we do in Mexico? Travel agents plan a student trip.**

# Single Discipline, Interdisciplinary, Integrated

Teachers can design knowledge-based, project-based, or inquiry-based units either within a single subject or across two or more disciplines. By definition, literacy-based units must be across English/language arts and one or more other disciplines. However, once you decide to develop your unit(s) across disciplines, you must choose between an interdisciplinary or an integrated approach. Many teachers think that these two unit approaches are synonymous, but there are distinct differences. The following chart gives you a comparison of interdisciplinary and integrated units.

## COMPARISON OF INTERDISCIPLINARY AND INTEGRATED UNITS

| CHARACTERISTIC | INTERDISCIPLINARY | INTEGRATED |
|---|---|---|
| **NUMBER OF DISCIPLINES** | Teacher chooses two or more disciplines, usually tries to incorporate at least four to six | Teacher chooses two or more disciplines, based on relevance to theme and authentic activities |
| **FOCUS** | Discipline perspective linked through themes | Authentic life role and/or learner perspective linked through themes |
| **THEME BASIS** | Skills, knowledge, concepts of disciplines | Personal and social concerns of learners, authentic problems emerging from learners' daily lives |

## Ideas for Connecting the Curriculum

When the learning is authentic and connected, students learn more, retain that learning longer, and can apply and accomplish more with their knowledge. To help teachers plan this kind of connected curriculum, a planning wheel has been provided below. A planning wheel is a graphic tool to help teachers connect content and concepts within their subject and with other subject areas. (Palmer, 1991). Palmer's example on the following page will help you consider how a planning wheel might work for you.

# CURRICULAR CONNECTIONS PLANNING WHEEL

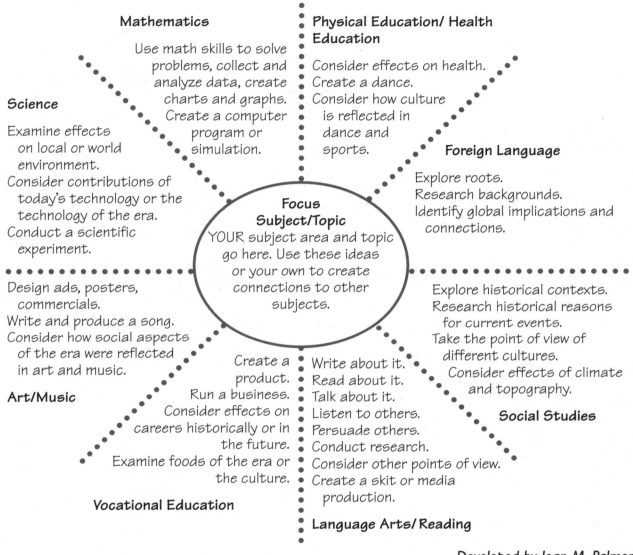

**Mathematics**

Use math skills to solve problems, collect and analyze data, create charts and graphs. Create a computer program or simulation.

**Science**

Examine effects on local or world environment.
Consider contributions of today's technology or the technology of the era.
Conduct a scientific experiment.

**Physical Education/ Health Education**

Consider effects on health.
Create a dance.
Consider how culture is reflected in dance and sports.

**Foreign Language**

Explore roots.
Research backgrounds.
Identify global implications and connections.

**Focus Subject/Topic**
YOUR subject area and topic go here. Use these ideas or your own to create connections to other subjects.

Design ads, posters, commercials.
Write and produce a song.
Consider how social aspects of the era were reflected in art and music.

**Art/Music**

Explore historical contexts.
Research historical reasons for current events.
Take the point of view of different cultures.
Consider effects of climate and topography.

**Social Studies**

Create a product.
Run a business.
Consider effects on careers historically or in the future.
Examine foods of the era or the culture.

**Vocational Education**

Write about it.
Read about it.
Talk about it.
Listen to others.
Persuade others.
Conduct research.
Consider other points of view.
Create a skit or media production.

**Language Arts/ Reading**

*Developed by Joan M. Palmer, Howard County Public School System, Maryland*

## Selecting Themes for Learning Units

The theme of a learning unit is the thread connecting all the content and activities of a unit. Many of us have developed units around themes by simply asking, "Will it be motivating for the students, and can I fit my activities and content into the topic?" However, research increasingly suggests that the interests and concerns of young adolescents can be directly related to broader issues in the outside world—an important consideration for the teacher in selecting themes. In the following chart, James Beane (1993) reveals how curriculum themes can be developed from the juncture of young adolescent concerns and social concerns. This is one way to ensure an authentic middle school curriculum that is connected to the real world. Such themes can easily incorporate a wide variety of outcomes and content.

## DEVELOPING CURRICULUM THEMES

| YOUNG ADOLESCENT CONCERNS | CURRICULUM THEMES | SOCIAL CONCERNS |
|---|---|---|
| Understanding personal changes | TRANSITIONS | Living in a changing world |
| Developing a personal identity | IDENTITIES | Cultural diversity |
| Finding a place in the group | INTERDEPENDENCE | Global interdependence |
| Personal fitness | WELLNESS | Environmental protection |
| Social status | SOCIAL STRUCTURES | Class systems |
| Dealing with adults | INDEPENDENCE | Human rights |
| Peer conflict and gangs | CONFLICT RESOLUTION | Global conflict |
| Commercial pressures | COMMERCIALISM | Effects of media |
| Questioning authority | JUSTICE | Laws and social customs |
| Personal friendships | CARING | Social welfare |
| Living in the school | INSTITUTIONS | Social institutions |

# Exemplary Units

The following description of exemplary units will allow you and your team to develop quality units, by adapting the ideas or concepts to your needs.

An exemplary unit usually has

1. A **concept of immediate curriculum goals within or across subjects,** an idea of what skills and concepts should be taught in the immediate future

2. A **theme** to link the curriculum and make it authentic. The theme ideally is presented as a concept or issue (*changes, choices, and conflict*) or as a question (*What if community service were required before graduating from high school?*) rather than as a topic (*the Civil War* or *poetry* or *transportation*).

3. A written list of the unit's **objectives** (within or across subjects)

4. A curriculum map that plans the **interdisciplinary connections** if the unit is interdisciplinary or integrated

5. A written list of **essential questions** that frame the choices of learning experiences. Teachers develop the list by using the content concepts/skills and the broad curriculum goals.

6. The unit has **outcomes** that link the broad outcomes to the unit's content, questions, and activities if a school has school or district outcomes.

7. Activities that include

   a. An **introductory activity**
   b. A variety of learning skills and **thinking skills activities** that extend, refine, and generalize the theme and content
   c. An authentic and meaningful **culminating activity** that helps the learner use and apply the declarative and procedural knowledge in the unit
   d. Opportunities for **student choice and involvement** in the decision making for activities

8. **Varied assessment techniques** to determine students' knowledge acquisition, level of skill development, and achievement. The alternative assessments have qualitative rubrics for learner and teacher use.

9. Opportunities for students to be **actively involved** in making decisions about objectives, activities, and assessment.

# A LEARNING-UNIT APPROACH

A middle school classroom that uses a literacy-based approach to integrate social studies, language arts, some aspects of science and math, art, and vocational studies might have the following sequence of learning units across a year:

1. **Becoming Myself: Looking at individual strengths, talents, and so on.**

2. **All Together: Studying communities and how individuals build them.**

3. **Adventures and Adventurers: The nature of those who dare.**

4. **Just Imagine: Exploring mysterious and bizarre events.**

5. **Tales from Here and There: Diverse cultures — common values**

6. **Survival: The challenge of survival**

## Characteristics of a Systematic, Unified Learning Unit Approach to Curriculum

For a curriculum centered on learning units to have maximum effect, there should be a systematic, unified approach throughout the year. The characteristics of this approach are

1. The logical sequence of units across the year in order to build on prior knowledge

2. Units that appeal to the varied interests and concerns of students

3. The use of a variety of sources including textbooks, media and technology, periodicals, literature, and real-life experts and experiences

4. Independent learning strategies

## ▶ How do we get started?

The following Teacher Team Planning Guide is provided to help you or your team plan learner-centered units. The guide takes the form of "decision questions" which you answer as you plan.

### Teacher Team Planning Guide

**Decision 1:** What will be the focus of the unit? Some options for selecting the focus were mentioned earlier, but a review is provided here for your convenience.

- If you wish to focus on acquiring and applying declarative and procedural knowledge, you might decide to plan a knowledge-based unit concentrating on concepts and skills.

- If you want to focus on student projects and authentic tasks, you might develop a project-based unit, with projects and activities chosen by you or the students.

- If you wish to integrate reading and writing into other subjects, then you may want to develop a literacy-based unit.

- If you are focusing on problem solving, decision making, and other thinking skills or processes, then you might develop an inquiry-based unit.

- You may want to combine two or more of these purposes into your unit. If so, remember that these combination units should definitely be interdisciplinary, integrated, and extend over a significant period of time (at least four to six weeks).

**Decision 2:** What is the central theme that will connect the concepts and skills in the unit? Is it content-related or issue-related? Can you frame the theme as a concept or question?

How can you bring this theme to life and encourage students to explore a wide range of materials, create something of their own, and share ideas with others?

**Decision 3:** What content knowledge, concepts, principles, procedures, and objectives form the basis of student learning?

**Decision 4:** If you are drawing your content objectives from more than one subject, have you developed a curriculum map of the content? If not, how have you connected the interdisciplinary content objectives?

**Decision 5:** Based on the content objectives, what are the essential questions (sometimes called *The Big Questions*) that learners must answer during the unit or during the completion of the culminating authentic activity?

**Decision 6:** If your district or school is outcomes-based, which of these outcomes or indicators will be included in this unit? Which outcomes fit with your content and essential questions?

**Decision 7:** What is your introductory or launch activity? Does it draw on students' prior knowledge? Does this activity "sell" the unit and get students motivated?

**Decision 8:** What are the intermediate instructional activities that generalize, extend, and refine the unit's content?

What are the thinking skills activities that allow students to use and retain the unit's content? Do these activities require students to know specific content and, most importantly, to apply that knowledge? The Content and Activities matrix, Copy Form 4 at the end of this section, will help you make decisions about activities.

**Decision 9:** What culminating activity will bring the unit to a meaningful conclusion? Is it a "real-life," or authentic, activity? Is there some kind of performance or product that results from the activity?

**Decision 10:** Are learning-to-learn skills, such as organizing skills, research skills, thinking frames, and study skills, built into the activities?

**Decision 11:** What kind of knowledge assessments will you design? How will you gauge students' progress?

Remember that formative assessment is to help learners *improve* and summative assessment is for learners to *prove* what they have learned. Be sure to include a number of formative assessments, which will provide cues, prompts, and learning support.

**Decision 12:** What alternative assessments will you design for your unit? Since the learning activities require students not only to know something but also to utilize that knowledge, how will you assess their work? Do your authentic assessments have qualitative rubrics that enable you to judge the quality of students' work? (See the Assessment Module.)

**Decision 13:** Is there a written overview that provides a general schedule of the unit? Do you have assignment sheets for the major activities of your unit? Does each assignment have quantity expectations and a quality rubric? Can each of your students answer the following questions about every assignment?

- What is my task?
- What should I do first? next?
- How should I allocate my time?
- What resources are available to me or my group?
- What role do others in my class/group play?
- What knowledge is important to the assignment?
- How will my work be evaluated?
- What will demand the most attention?
- How will I know where my performance or product is strongest and weakest?

**Decision 14:** What will be the schedule or unit time plan? Will it take the form of a matrix or calendar? Do all participating teachers and students have the time frame? Is it part of the written overview? You might use something like the Copy Form 5 Unit Sequence and Time Line provided at the end of this section to help you. As you create your time line, consider if it has an appropriate number of

- teacher-led, whole-class sessions
- student-directed learning sessions (either team or individual)
- teacher-guided student work sessions
- formative assessment times
- summative assessment times
- presentation times

# ► Where do we go for more information?

Association for Supervision and Curriculum Development. 1993. *Integrating the curriculum: Videos and facilitator's guide.* Alexandria, VA: Association for Supervision and Curriculum Development.
A videotape workshop with handouts, overheads, and readings that offers practical advice and guidance with classroom examples.

Beane, J. A. 1993. *A middle school curriculum: From rhetoric to reality* 2d. ed. Columbus, OH: National Middle School Association.
A description of an integrated curriculum that truly is learner centered and reflects the needs and concerns of young adolescents.

Fogarty, R. 1991. *The mindful school: How to integrate the curriculum.* Palatine, IL: Skylight Publishing Co.
Teachers will find this book useful, especially with its practical suggestions for integrating the curriculum. Several models for integrating are provided, along with examples and planning pages.

Jacobs, H. H. 1989. *Interdisciplinary curriculum: Design and implementation.* Alexandria, VA: Association for Supervision and Curriculum Development.
Makes curriculum more relevant to students by showing teachers six design options for an interdisciplinary curriculum. Included are two successful case studies of interdisciplinary programs.

Lounsbury, J. H., ed. 1992. *Connecting the curriculum through interdisciplinary instruction.* Columbus, OH: National Middle School Association.
A guide with activities and examples of interdisciplinary curriculum planning and instruction. Describes team planning and evaluating.

# *References*

Beane, J. A. 1993. *A middle school curriculum: From rhetoric to reality.* 2d. ed. Columbus, OH: National Middle School Association.

Palmer, J. M. 1991. Planning wheels turn curriculum around. *Educational Leadership* 49: 61–65.

# Learning Unit Planning Pages

These planning pages accompany the decision planning guide, in which each decision is explained in detail.

*DECISION 1:* Focus or primary trait of unit

_____

_____

_____

_____

*DECISION 2:* Central theme

_____

_____

_____

_____

*DECISION 3:* Content objectives or competencies

1. _____

2. _____

3. _____

4. _____

5. _____

6. _____

7. _____

8. _____

9. _____

10. _____

*DECISION 4:* Curriculum map if interdisciplinary/integrated
(See Copy Form 3, Curriculum Map.)

*DECISION 5:* Essential questions students must answer

1. _____
2. _____
3. _____
4. _____
5. _____
6. _____
7. _____
8. _____
9. _____
10. _____

*DECISION 6:* Unit outcomes

1. _____
2. _____
3. _____
4. _____
5. _____
6. _____
7. _____
8. _____
9. _____
10. _____

*DECISION 7:* Introductory or launch activity

_____

_____

_____

_____

_____

_____

DECISION 8: Extending, refining activities; thinking-skill activities, major instructional activities

_____

_____

_____

_____

_____

_____

_____

_____

_____

_____

DECISION 9: Culminating activity (meaningful use, authentic)

_____

_____

_____

_____

_____

_____

_____

_____

_____

_____

*DECISION 10:* Learning-to-learn skills in activities

_____

_____

_____

_____

_____

_____

_____

*DECISION 11:* Knowledge assessments (kind, sequence, formative, summative)
(See the Assessment Module.)

_____

_____

_____

_____

_____

_____

_____

_____

_____

*DECISION 12:* Performance and product assessment ideas with rubric

_____

_____

_____

_____

_____

DECISION 13: Written overview and assignment pages

_____

_____

_____

_____

_____

_____

_____

_____

_____

_____

_____

DECISION 14: Schedule and time plan ideas (See Unit Sequence and Time Line.)

_____

_____

_____

_____

_____

_____

_____

# Curriculum Map

|  |  |  |  |  |
|--|--|--|--|--|
|  |  |  |  |  |
|  |  |  |  |  |
|  |  |  |  |  |
|  |  |  |  |  |

**DISCIPLINES**

**WEEKS**

**Module 4** **141**

# Content and Activities Matrix

Down the left-hand column, fill in the skills, content objectives, or concepts that you want to emphasize in this unit. Then fill in the activities you have selected across the top of the chart. For each objective, have at least one activity.

**Activities**

**Skills/Objectives/Concepts**

# Unit Sequence and Time Line

| Monday | Tuesday | Wednesday | Thursday | Friday |
|--------|---------|-----------|----------|--------|
| | | | | |
| | | | | |
| | | | | |
| | | | | |
| | | | | |

# Activity Plan (A)

| | Monday | Tuesday | Wednesday | Thursday | Friday | | |
|---|---|---|---|---|---|---|---|
| Science | | | | | | | |
| Math | | | | | | | |
| Social Studies | | | | | | | |
| English | | | | | | | |
| Literature | | | | | | | |

# Activity Plan (B)

| Date of Activity | Activity/ What Will Be Assessed | Teacher Responsible for Activity | Materials and Equipment Needed | Resource People Needed | Other |
|---|---|---|---|---|---|
|  |  |  |  |  |  |
|  |  |  |  |  |  |
|  |  |  |  |  |  |
|  |  |  |  |  |  |
|  |  |  |  |  |  |

## Activity Plan (C)

| Evaluation | Subject Area | Activity | Check Point(s) | Activity |
|---|---|---|---|---|
|  |  |  |  | Monday |
|  |  |  |  | Tuesday |
|  |  |  |  | Wednesday |
|  |  |  |  | Thursday |
|  |  |  |  | Friday |

# Topic 3 THINKING SKILLS CURRICULUM

As we approach the twenty-first century, thoughtful educators are emphasizing the importance of thinking skills. In this Information Age, we must not only be literate and knowledgeable but also be competent in our thinking. However, thinking skills are not simply another program to be taught after the basics have been learned; nor are these skills just for the advanced students. In fact, educational research has shown us that real learning must involve thinking, and that thinking can be nurtured, practiced, and learned by everyone. The entire curriculum must be reconsidered so that thinking becomes integral to every lesson, activity, and educational purpose.

Research has shown that the most effective way of integrating thinking skills into the school curriculum is for districts, schools, or even a small team to establish a scope and sequence for thinking skills. Such a developmental exercise is extremely helpful when selecting activities, materials, lessons plans, and assessment strategies. In addition, this process makes teachers much more knowledgeable about thinking skills.

## ▶ What are they?

Defining thinking skills can be a complex activity. Advocates, scholars, and researchers have identified an enormous range of basic thinking skills, with estimates of the exact number of skills varying from 50 to more than 120. Similarly, while some experts have established a hierarchy of lower and higher order thinking skills, others reject such a distinction. Even the definition of the terms is surrounded by controversy. However, there is one point with which everyone seems to agree—we should infuse thinking skills into our instruction and curriculum plans.

## ADAPT, DON'T ADOPT

The purpose of this section is to help you infuse thinking skills into your curriculum. Therefore, many options are presented. These options give you flexibility as you plan a program for your objectives and activities. *Think of adapting, not adopting!*

Since there is little consensus among experts as to what constitutes thinking, this topic will present several definitions of critical thinking. Your task, both individually and as a team, is to consider these and other models you may have and then develop a framework for choosing and teaching essential thinking skills. A successful thinking, learner-centered curriculum depends on that task.

Glatthorn and Baron (1985) decided that comparing and contrasting good thinking and poor thinking would offer insight to teachers as they choose which thinking skills to include in their curriculum. The following figure provides their comparison.

## GOOD THINKING VS. POOR THINKING

| THE GOOD THINKER | THE POOR THINKER |
|---|---|
| ■ Welcomes problematic situations and is tolerant of ambiguity | ■ Searches for certainty and is intolerant of ambiguity |
| ■ Is sufficiently self-critical; looks for alternate possibilities and goals; seeks evidence on both sides | ■ Is not self-critical and is satisfied with first attempts |
| ■ Is reflective and deliberative; searches extensively when appropriate | ■ Is impulsive, gives up prematurely, and is overconfident of the correctness of initial ideas |
| ■ Believes in the value of rationality and that thinking can be effective | ■ Overvalues intuition; denigrates rationality; believes that thinking won't help |
| ■ Is deliberative in discovering goals | ■ Is impulsive in discovering goals |
| ■ Revises goals when necessary | ■ Does not revise goals |
| ■ Is open to multiple possibilities and considers alternatives | ■ Prefers to deal with limited possibilities; does not seek alternatives to an initial possibility |
| ■ Is deliberative in analyzing possibilities | ■ Is impulsive in choosing possibilities |
| ■ Uses evidence that challenges favored possibilities | ■ Ignores evidence that challenges favored possibilities |
| ■ Consciously searches for evidence against possibilities that are initially strong, or in favor of those that are weak | ■ Consciously searches only for evidence that favors strong possibilities |

## Thinking and You

The verb *think* has many shades of meaning. Consider the verb's meaning in each of these sentences.

- "Tomato soup always makes me think of my childhood."
  (remembering)

- "When the weather is very cold, I always try to think of the beach."
  (daydreaming or wishful thinking)

- "I think that this movie was her most famous."
  (believing)

- "He was trying to think through the process of building their house."
  (anticipate, figure out)

When teachers discuss thinking skills, they usually do not have these types of thinking in mind. They mean an intellectual activity that requires mental effort and serves a purpose. Numerous terms are used to qualify thinking. These include *critical, creative, inductive, deductive, higher, lower, convergent, divergent, lateral, vertical, left-brain, right-brain*, and so forth. There is a need to be specific about exactly what kinds of thinking you would like students to learn. You might begin this process by analyzing the kinds of thinking skills you are reinforcing now using Copy Form 9 at the end of this section.

## Defining Critical Thinking

**Lipman's Critical Thinking Definition** An example of a definition of critical thinking is supplied by Lipman (1988). He theorizes that critical thinking must employ criteria and standards, instead of reasoning alone, and compares ordinary thinking to critical thinking in the following manner:

## ORDINARY THINKING VS. CRITICAL THINKING

| ORDINARY THINKING | CRITICAL THINKING/REASONING |
|---|---|
| Guessing | Estimating |
| Preferring | Evaluating |
| Grouping | Classifying |
| Believing | Assuming |
| Inferring | Inferring logically |
| Associating concepts | Understanding principles |
| Supposing | Hypothesizing |
| Offering opinions without reasons | Offering opinions with reasons |
| Making judgments without criteria | Making judgments with criteria and standards |

The following chart by Lipman (1988) illustrates the differences between critical thinking and creative thinking.

## CRITICAL THINKING VS. CREATIVE THINKING

### THE NATURE OF CRITICAL THINKING

- Is purposeful and dominated by goals

- Is reasonable, reflective, and focuses on deciding what to believe and what to do

- Involves comparing and contrasting information with standards or criteria

### THE NATURE OF CREATIVE THINKING

- Involves taking risks

- Calls for continual recasting of ideas — creative thinkers are flexible in their approach to tasks

- Involves intense desire and preparation but uses flashes of insight from the subconscious

**Dimensions of Thinking** One of the most usable and complete frameworks for defining thinking was proposed by Marzano and others (1988). Their book, *Dimensions of Thinking: A Framework for Curriculum and Instruction*, provides a framework to help teachers, administrators, and curriculum specialists plan programs for incorporating the teaching of thinking throughout the regular curriculum. *Dimensions of Thinking* was the result of extensive work on the most current theory and research available. This is a good place to begin examining thinking skills curricula as you try to infuse thinking skills into your curriculum. The *Dimensions of Thinking* framework is summarized below:

*Metacognition:* refers to awareness and control of one's thinking, including inner speech, imagery, attitudes, and executive control, such as planning, monitoring, evaluating, and revising.

*Critical Thinking:* Reasonable, reflective thinking that is focused on deciding what to believe or do.

*Creative Thinking:* The ability to form new combinations of ideas to fulfill a need or to get original, appropriate results.

*Thinking Processes:* A complex sequence of thinking skills.

- Concept Formation
- Comprehending
- Decision Making
- Composing
- Principle Formation
- Problem Solving
- Research
- Oral Discourse

*Core Thinking Skills:* Thinking skills are relatively discrete operations that can be considered the "building blocks" of thinking. The following skills have a sound basis in research and theory, are important for students to be able to do, and can be taught and reinforced in school.

**Focusing skills** — directing one's attention to selected information
  1. Defining problems — clarifying problem situations
  2. Setting goals — establishing direction and purpose

**Information-gathering skills** — acquiring relevant data
  3. Observing — obtaining information through one or more sense.
  4. Questioning — seeking new information by formulating questions

**Remembering skills** — storing and retrieving information
  5. Encoding — storing information in long-term memory
  6. Recalling — Retrieving information from long-term memory

**Organizing skills** — arranging information so it can be used more effectively
  7. Comparing — noting similarities and differences between two or more entities
  8. Classifying — placing entities in groups by common attributes
  9. Ordering — sequencing entities according to a given criterion

**Analyzing skills** — clarifying existing information by identifying and distinguishing among components, attributes, and so on
  10. Identifying attributes and components — determining characteristics or parts of something
  11. Identifying relationships and patterns — recognizing ways elements are related

**Generating skills** — using prior knowledge to add new information
  12. Inferring — reasoning beyond available information to fill gaps
  13. Predicting — anticipating or forecasting future events
  14. Elaborating — using prior knowledge to add meaning to new information and to link it to existing structures
  15. Representing — adding new meaning by changing the form of information

**Integrating skills** — connecting and combining information
  16. Summarizing — abstracting information efficiently and succinctly
  17. Restructuring — changing existing knowledge structures to incorporate new information

**Evaluating skills** — assessing the reasonableness and quality of ideas
  18. Establishing criteria — setting the standards for making judgments
  19. Verifying — confirming the accuracy of claims
  20. Identifying errors — recognizing logical fallacies

**Beyer's Scope and Sequence** Barry Beyer, another noted expert on thinking skills, has developed a chart of the major cognitive operations and a model scope and sequence of thinking skills (1988). The major cognitive operations are as follows:

## MAJOR COGNITIVE OPERATIONS

### I. THINKING STRATEGIES

*Problem Solving*
1. Recognize a problem
2. Represent the problem
3. Devise/choose solution plan
4. Execute the plan
5. Evaluate the solution

*Decision Making*
1. Define the goal
2. Identify alternatives
3. Analyze alternatives
4. Rank alternatives
5. Judge highest-ranked alternatives
6. Choose "best" alternatives

*Conceptualizing*
1. Identify examples
2. Identify common attributes
3. Classify attributes
4. Interrelate categories of attributes
5. Identify additional examples/nonexamples
6. Modify concept attributes/structure

### II. CRITICAL THINKING SKILLS

1. Distinguishing between verifiable facts and value claims
2. Distinguishing relevant from irrelevant information, claims, or reasons
3. Determining the factual accuracy of a statement
4. Determining the credibility of a source
5. Identifying ambiguous claims or arguments
6. Identifying unstated assumptions
7. Detecting bias
8. Identifying logical fallacies
9. Recognizing logical inconsistencies in a line of reasoning
10. Determining the strength of an argument or claim

### III. MICRO-THINKING SKILLS

1. Recall
2. Translation
3. Interpretation
4. Extrapolation
5. Application
6. Analysis (compare, contrast, classify, seriate, etc.)
7. Synthesis
8. Evaluation

*Reasoning*
inductive
deductive
analogical

**A School District Example** The school district of East Islip, New York, used a core group of interested teachers and curriculum specialists to develop a scope and sequence for teachers to use in lesson and unit planning. Their continuum (illustrated below) shows which thinking skills should be introduced at a particular grade level and which should be taught continously from that point on.

## HIGHER ORDER THINKING SKILLS CONTINUUM

### Kindergarten
Classify ------------------------------------------------------------------►
Sequence ------------------------------------------------------------------►

### First Grade
Distinguish ------------------------------------------------------------------►
Conclude ------------------------------------------------------------------►

### Second Grade
Predict ------------------------------------------------------------------►
Categorize ------------------------------------------------------------------►
Detect ------------------------------------------------------------------►
Infer ------------------------------------------------------------------►

### Third Grade
Compare ------------------------------------------------------------------►
Compare/Contrast ------------------------------------------------------------------►

### Fourth Grade
Generalize ------------------------------------------------------------------►
Cause and Effect ------------------------------------------------------------------►
Organize ------------------------------------------------------------------►

### Fifth Grade
Summarize ------------------------------------------------------------------►
Create ------------------------------------------------------------------►
Discover ------------------------------------------------------------------►
Process Write ------------------------------------------------------------------►
Revise ------------------------------------------------------------------►
Edit ------------------------------------------------------------------►
Evaluate ------------------------------------------------------------------►

### Sixth Grade Through Twelfth Grade
Outline ------------------------------------------------------------------►
Originate ------------------------------------------------------------------►
Analyze Information ------------------------------------------------------------------►
Distinguish Fact from ------------------------------------------------------------------►
   Opinion
Distinguish Propaganda ------------------------------------------------------------------►
   from News

Although this type of plan provides little in the way of structure, it is very useful as a basic guide and allows teachers to develop their own strategies.

As middle school teachers, you need to be aware of students' prior experience with thinking skills. If there is no thinking skills curriculum in your district, you should begin to try to infuse thinking skills into learners' curriculum and instruction systematically, with checks on which skills have not been mastered by students up to this point.

**Bloom's Taxonomy** No compendium of thinking skills curricula would be complete without a discussion of Bloom's taxonomy. Many teachers, schools, and districts base their thinking programs on Bloom's taxonomy. It is so widespread that questions and activities structured around Bloom are included in most books and chapters about thinking skills. A complete listing of activities and lead questions based on Bloom's taxonomy can be found in Module 3: The Middle School Concept and Organization.

However, it is important for you to know that there is controversy about the effectiveness of a thinking skills program based on Bloom's taxonomy. Research has found that teachers rarely succeed in infusing instruction with higher order questioning based around Bloom's taxonomy. There is extensive evidence that Bloom's taxonomy does not guide a process of thought, even though it helps teachers set goals. Bloom's does not show how to assist or guide students individually. If you want to boost thinking skills, you must teach students strategies or frameworks that explicitly support effective thinking. Therefore, while there is nothing wrong with a program using Bloom's, the taxonomy activities should only be a part of a broader plan that includes other frames or strategies.

See the following references for more information on Bloom's taxonomy. (Beyer, 1987; Nickerson, 1985; Perkins, 1985; 1987; Swartz and Perkins, 1989)

## ▶ How do we get started?

There are three ways to start integrating thinking skills into your curriculum and instruction. You may choose one or more of the following strategies:

1. Use direct instruction of thinking

2. Infuse thinking skills into your curriculum

3. Employ strategies of instruction that foster thinking

In a direct instruction lesson, thinking skills or processes would be the reason for the lesson, as for example when students use a decision-making frame or organizer to help them make a decision about a scenario. A **direct instruction lesson** would have the following characteristics:

- A scenario
- An explicit thinking activity
- A clear understanding of the process on the part of students and teacher
- Evidence of students' metacognition, or their knowing what they are thinking and why
- Evidence of mastery and confidence
- *Process is the Goal.*

Actual infusion involves restructuring the strategies of regular curriculum to integrate specific thinking skills into lesson and unit design. Most experts recommend using this approach as much as possible. A **lesson that involves infusion** would have the following characteristics:

- An explicit thinking activity
- A clear understanding of the process on the part of students and teacher
- Relevant content
- Clear and planned transfer of the thinking skill
- Modeling by the teacher of good thinking throughout the lesson
- Evidence of learners' metacognition
- Evidence of mastery and confidence
- *Both Process and Content are the Goals.*

A third alternative for teaching thinking skills involves teaching methods that foster thinking while the content of the regular curriculum remains primary. A **lesson that uses methods to foster thinking** would have the following characteristics:

- Regular content-relevant activities
- Modeling by the teacher of good thinking
- *Content is the Goal.*

# Acquiring or Developing Thinking Skills Programs

Have you or your team considered the advantages and disadvantages of an acquired thinking skills program versus one developed by you or your school? You may prefer to acquire an independent thinking skills program instead of developing one. Here are some points for consideration.

## THINKING SKILLS PROGRAMS

| | ADVANTAGES | DISADVANTAGES |
|---|---|---|
| **PROGRAMS ACQUIRED FROM COMMERCIAL SOURCES** | 1. Wide choice. The market offers programs with different definitions of cognitive skills, objectives, and methodologies. <br> 2. Based on sound theory of cognition. Extensive research by experts is usually behind program. <br> 3. Lesson plans and instructional materials are on hand. <br> 4. In-service materials and procedures come with the program. <br> 5. Instruments for evaluation are available and identified. | 1. May be unrelated to local curriculum and content <br> 2. May be perceived as "another course" to be taught <br> 3. Implies that thinking can be taught in a prescribed number of lessons in a given number of semesters <br> 4. Programs may absolve the teacher from thinking — "because the materials do the job . . ." <br> 5. Specifications for in-service may be burdensome for district. |
| **LOCALLY DEVELOPED PROGRAMS** | 1. A participatory project. District teachers, curriculum workers, and administrators are involved in development. <br> 2. Final product acclaimed as "Ours!" by district teachers <br> 3. Final product geared to local curriculum and content <br> 4. High degree of acceptance and use by classroom teachers <br> 5. Program revised as local circumstances require. | 1. Process of development may be long — possibly years — and costly. <br> 2. Requires experts in cognitive knowledge for development <br> 3. Requires the creation of a theory of cognition and identification of thinking skills to be taught <br> 4. Developing evaluation instruments is a major undertaking. <br> 5. Production of in-service materials may constitute an obstacle. |

# Strategies for Fostering Thinking

If you decide to teach your content and foster student thinking rather than teach thinking skills directly, the following list of teaching behaviors may be helpful, as these are the behaviors that trigger student critical thinking. This list comes from Project IMPACT, directed by S. Lee Winocur, who has spent several years researching and validating his findings.

## STRATEGIES

| TEACHING BEHAVIOR | EXAMPLE |
|---|---|
| **MODELING/ DEMONSTRATING** | Teacher models or exhibits the thinking skills being taught. Encourages students to imitate the thinking skill after demonstration. |
| **CUING** | Teacher uses a vocabulary of phrases that prompt high-level thinking responses. Phrases become familiar as cues for reflection, analysis, or formulating hypotheses. |
| **HIGH-LEVEL QUESTIONING** | Teacher asks open-ended questions and encourages students to generate and explore alternative solutions. |
| **PROMOTING INTERACTION** | Teacher asks students to work in groups when engaged in problem-solving activities. Learning and thinking are social activities before they become cognitive activities. |
| **PROBING** | Teacher asks a planned series of questions leading students to produce a rule of generalization. |
| **SYMBOLIZING IDEAS** | Teacher presents graphics or visuals that help students to remember concepts. |
| **REFLECTING WITH WAIT TIME** | Teacher allows students enough time to formulate answers to high-level questions. |
| **TEACHING FOR TRANSFER** | Teacher helps students identify a variety of situations to which the skill being taught might be relevant. |

# A Plan for Introducing Thinking Skills

Thinking skills experts suggest adopting a systematic plan for infusing thinking skills into your curriculum. If you have been working without a plan, this approach to the instruction of thinking skills will be very uneven and haphazard. To ensure that your students are learning and applying thinking skills, your approach must be systematic and developmental.

A suggested plan would include the following steps. Compare this plan with your current approach and make the necessary adjustments.

1. **Needs Assessment:** Start with what you have currently.

   **a.** Review your curriculum's content objectives and your instructional strategies for the teaching of thinking.
   **b.** Review the objectives and strategies of the thinking skills programs or reasoning programs available to you. Reread the review in the first part of this section for suggestions.
   **c.** If you are using a thinking skills curriculum, select a few concepts or skills from it and identify how they are being taught now. Are you teaching thinking skills with direct instructional lessons, by infusion into your regular curriculum, or are you fostering thinking as you proceed?
   **d.** Identify how students currently practice thinking skills and how you assess their thinking.

2. **The Plan:** If you are concerned about the shortcomings of your current thinking skills curriculum, develop a plan for teaching thinking skills and acquire or develop a thinking skills curriculum. Develop a hierarchy of thinking skills and processes to guide lesson and unit planning. Take advantage of the many opportunities for infusing thinking skills into the regular curriculum. Try to make this infusion an integrated part of your approach.

3. **Staff Development:** If additional staff development is needed, determine how and when this will happen.

4. **Parents:** Organize a parent education and awareness plan.

5. **Lesson/Unit Planning:** Include a thinking extension or thinking activity in each lesson, either within your regular content or as an independent activity. You might consider the following questions as you plan:

   **a.** What are the components of the kind of thinking I want students to learn and practice?
   **b.** Is there content that can be used for this type of thinking?
   **c.** How can I organize my lesson or unit for this type of thinking?

6. **Assessment of Thinking:** Develop and/or adopt methods to assess students' growth in thinking.

# ► Where do we go for more information?

Forte, I., and Schurr, S. 1994. *Tools, treasures, and measures.*
Nashville, TN: Incentive.
The *tools* of the book's title are lively, effective student activities and assignments created specifically for middle grade students. The *treasures* are valuable lists, lesson plans, and information sheets for educators to use. The *measures* provide up-to-date assessment instruments, techniques, records, and reporting systems. All together, these tools, treasures, and measures form a significant collection of high-quality instructional materials and models. The book is divided into five modules, one of which is entirely devoted to encouraging and developing thinking skills across the curriculum. It includes prototypes of many different ways to individualize classroom delivery systems and to encourage the development and use of higher-level thinking skills.

## References

Barell, J. 1985. Self-reflection on your teaching: A checklist. In *Developing minds: A resource book for teaching thinking,* ed. A. Costa. Alexandria, VA: Association for Supervision and Curriculum Development.

Beyer, B. K. 1988. *Developing a thinking skills program.* Needham, MA: Allyn & Bacon.

Beyer, B. K. 1987. *Practical strategies for the teaching of thinking.* Needham, MA: Allyn & Bacon.

Glatthorn, A. and Baron, J. 1985. The good thinker. In *Developing minds: A resource book for teaching thinking,* ed. A. Costa, pp. 9–53. Alexandria, VA: Association for Supervision and Curriculum Development.

Lipman, M. 1988. Critical thinking — what can it be? *Educational Leadership* 46:1, 38–43.

Marzano, R. J. et al. 1988. *Dimensions of thinking: A framework for curriculum and instruction.* Alexandria, VA: Association for Supervision and Curriculum Development.

Nickerson, R. S., Perkins, D. N., and Smith, E. E. 1985. *The teaching of thinking.* Hillsdale, NJ: Lawrence Erlbaum Associates.

Perkins, D. N. 1987. An interview with David Perkins of Harvard University. In *Teaching thinking and reasoning skills,* ed. R. Pauker, p. 29. Arlington, VA: American Association of School Administrators.

Perkins, D. N. 1985. General cognitive skills: why not? In *Thinking and learning skills.* Volume 2: *research and open questions,* eds., S. Chipman, J. Segal, and R. Glaser. Hillsdale, NJ: Lawrence Erlbaum Associates.

Swartz, R. J. and Perkins, D. N. 1989. *Teaching thinking: Issues and approaches.* Pacific Grove, CA: Midwest Publications.

# Self-Reflection on Your Teaching: A Checklist

Using a scale of 1 to 5, rate your classroom and school according to the following items.

5 = Very Often     4 = Often     3 = Sometimes     2 = Seldom     1 = Hardly Ever

## CLASSROOM

1. When students pose unusual or divergent questions I ask, "What made you think of that?"   **5   4   3   2   1**

2. Whatever the text says is accepted as the right answer.   **5   4   3   2   1**

3. When a decision has to be made between involving the class in a discussion of an intriguing student idea (topic related) or moving on to "cover" content, I choose the latter.   **5   4   3   2   1**

4. I encourage students to seek alternative answers.   **5   4   3   2   1**

5. Students give reasons for making statements.   **5   4   3   2   1**

6. I use subject matter as a means for students to generate their own questions (or problems), which we then seriously consider.   **5   4   3   2   1**

7. When teaching, I sit or stand behind my desk.   **5   4   3   2   1**

8. Most questions posed during class can be answered with short or one-word answers.   **5   4   3   2   1**

9. Students spontaneously engage in critiquing each other's thinking.   **5   4   3   2   1**

10. Students relate subject matter to experiences in other subjects or in their lives.   **5   4   3   2   1**

11. I stress *what* to think, not *how*.　　　　　**5　4　3　2　1**

12. Students often set objectives for their own learning.　　　　　**5　4　3　2　1**

13. Students spend time working collaboratively to solve subject matter questions.　　　　　**5　4　3　2　1**

14. One focus in my classroom is trying to understand how and why people who are mentioned in texts created ideas, solutions, experiments, rules, principles, and so on.　　　　　**5　4　3　2　1**

15. Students actively listen to each other.　　　　　**5　4　3　2　1**

## SCHOOL

16. We talk about the nature of thinking.　　　　　**5　4　3　2　1**

17. My school stresses collaborative, instructional problem solving.　　　　　**5　4　3　2　1**

18. I learn from my colleagues by observing their teaching.　　　　　**5　4　3　2　1**

19. My supervisor, team, and I discuss how to challenge students to think in more complex fashions.　　　　　**5　4　3　2　1**

# Topic 4  WHOLE LANGUAGE IN THE MIDDLE SCHOOL

In many districts and schools, whole language philosophy has become the dominant mode of teaching language arts and reading in the elementary grades. As reading instruction has expanded into the middle grades, whole language has been extended also. The interest in and large-scale adoption of whole language in the late 1980s and early 1990s have many teachers asking the question, "Just what *is* whole language?" While whole language is not a curriculum, nor an instructional strategy, it is included in this handbook because it presents itself as the very model of learner-centeredness.

## ▶ What is it?

Advocates view whole language as a comprehensive philosophy or set of beliefs. The underlying premise of whole language is the belief that reading, writing, speaking, and listening skills are best learned when they are integrative and whole, not broken into separate, isolated skills.

"First and foremost: Whole language is *not* practice. It is a set of beliefs, a perspective. It must become practice but it is not the practice itself" (Altwerger, Edelsky, and Flores 1987).

Whole language instruction is based on what is known about language acquisition and the idea that the further one moves away from the natural process of learning, the more difficult learning is for students. Therefore, a whole language reading and writing curriculum is not overly structured or sequenced by a hierarchy of skills and experiences. The curriculum does not consist of a predetermined vocabulary and a set of isolated skills to be mastered, since that kind of learning is artificial, meaningless, and inappropriate.

In a whole language approach to reading and writing, students focus on meaning. The student is seen as constructing personal meaning based on cues found in the text and/or the social context in which reading or writing takes place. The key premise of whole language is that language learning must be based on natural acquisition — children acquire language through the natural use of language, not by practicing the separate parts mechanically and then putting them all together. Instruction that focuses on skills, particularly word identification skills, is seen as distracting the learner from meaning, which should be the essence of reading.

## WHOLE LANGUAGE BELIEFS

- **Reading and writing are a natural outgrowth of oral language development.**

- **Learners construct their own knowledge from within.**

- **Reading *is* comprehension, that is, creating meaning from text.**

- **Communication is the main focus of writing.**

- **Learning to read and write are social processes.**

- **Risk taking and making mistakes are critical to reading and writing well.**

# The Phonics Question

The role of phonics in language arts and reading instruction is a major point of contention in the whole language approach. Critics of whole language maintain that

1. Whole language slights or ignores completely letter-sound relationships

2. Reading is not as natural as speech (citing the huge numbers of illiterate people in the world)

3. Teachers cannot rely upon children to "discover" the writing/reading system, just by being exposed to books

Advocates claim whole language *does* teach phonics, but by focusing on meaning instead of sounds. Teachers help learners look closely at the patterns in the text, noting the link between letters and sounds.

In summary, whole language is a developmental, holistic, meaning-based approach to literacy, instruction, and learning. Students move through purposeful, contextualized experiences, rather than through a series of isolated skills. It is this link to context and meaning that has many middle school teachers adopting a whole language approach to guide their literacy program.

# The Whole Language Connection to Middle School Philosophy

There are many similarities between a whole language approach to literacy and the middle school philosophy, as the following chart reveals.

## CONNECTIONS

| STUDENT | PHILOSOPHY | TEACHER |
|---|---|---|
| Constructs knowledge | Holistic | Emphasizes strategies |
| | Process-oriented | |
| | Concepts | |
| Works cooperatively | Interactive | Structures learning environments |
| Participates | | Fosters community |
| Learns actively | Learner-centered | Facilitates |

# ► How do we get started?

This is the point at which much of the controversy begins. Some teachers and researchers adopt the "whole language theory" exclusively and resist any modification of the concept. Other teachers are more selective and strive for a compromise between traditional practice and an exclusive whole language approach.

Rather than looking for a prescription for practice, you might develop literacy-learning environments based on students' needs and experiences. Recently, certain strategies and practices have become almost synonymous with a whole language approach. Some of these strategies are for beginning readers or nonreaders. (See Where Do We Go for More Information? and References at the end of this section.)

For developing readers, such as the vast majority of readers found at the middle school level, there are three major guidelines to consider if using whole language. They are as follows:

**1.** Involve students in lots of reading.

**2.** Create an environment that accepts and encourages risk taking.

**3.** Maintain a focus on meaning (Goodman and Goodman, 1982).

Watson and Crowley (1988) list certain activities and procedures for the developing readers of a middle school. In their procedures, you

- Find out about students' interests, abilities, and needs and *use* that information in planning the curriculum
- Read to students or tell them stories every day
- Make sure that students have an opportunity to participate in authentic writing every day
- Make sure that students have an opportunity to read real literature every day
- Take advantage of the social nature of reading and writing in order to promote literacy. Have students work with and help one another often. Promote sharing of work.
- Initiate student discussions to consider the processes of reading and writing

As you can see, it would be very difficult for a middle school language arts teacher to accomplish all these activities without assistance. Using these strategies or elements across disciplines allows teachers to allocate the time necessary for students to learn and use these on a daily basis. Therefore, it is important to involve the entire interdisciplinary team in reading and writing across the curriculum. Such collaboration is necessary to implement a comprehensive literacy approach.

Many teachers in content areas find that building strategy lessons for students is helpful when using different kinds of texts. These strategy lessons are quick, meaningful, and lead to discussions of the reading process. The need to spend instructional time on these strategies and enabling skills should be more openly acknowledged by whole language advocates.

## Model Reading Strategies

An effective strategy for teachers to employ is modeling. Demonstrations of good reading appear to be crucial to successful whole language classrooms. In some classrooms, students experience very little successful modeling. The modeling phase is especially important for at-risk students whose communication skills need considerable upgrading. Some students are put in paired reading too soon; the model they hear is not of high enough quality. Also, some teachers move to silent sustained reading too quickly, before students are competent, independent readers of middle level materials. The following strategies provide you with some procedures that you can follow with students (O'Shea and O'Shea, 1994):

1. Activate Prior Knowledge

   – Tell students the purpose of the lesson.

   – Conduct a preview discussion to call up students' relevant experiential base.

   – If the passage is new, read the title and encourage prediction through questioning; conduct a K-W-L session.

   – If the passage is a continuation, ask questions to review several important points.

2. Model

   – Read aloud the first section of the passage.

   – Model self-questioning and summarizing.

   - Ask, "What is the main idea?"
     State, "The main idea is . . . "

   - Ask, "What are two key facts?"
     State, "Two key facts are . . ."

   - State, "This section is about . . ."

   – Define self-questioning and summarization; show examples.

   – Read the next section.

– Model self-questioning and summarizing.

  ■ Ask, "What is the main idea?"
    State, "The main idea is . . ."

  ■ Ask, "What are two key facts?"
    State, "Two key facts are . . ."

  ■ State, "This section is about . . ."

3. Relinquish

  – Read the next section.

  – Have a student imitate self-questioning and summarization.

  – Alternate teacher modeling and student imitation.

  – Provide corrective feedback about the quality of the self-questioning and summarizations; prompt students to self-question and summarize; or reteach self-questioning and summarization.

## Summary of Common Elements in a Middle School Whole Language Classroom

In middle school whole language classrooms, the following elements are usually evident:

■ Teachers presenting/modeling strategies for making sense of print
■ Teachers reading quality literature to students
■ Teachers and students sharing book experiences
■ Teachers using guided reading with summarizing
■ Students engaged in sustained silent reading
■ A language experience approach to writing and reading
■ Content and journal writing daily
■ Expository reading and writing strategies

Compare your classroom to the elements above to identify your next steps in creating a whole language environment for your students.

# ► Where do we go for more information?

Altwerger, B., Edelsky, C., and Flores, B. 1987. Whole language: What's new? *The Reading Teacher* 27: 144–154.
One of the most quoted and referenced articles on whole language. A substantive discussion of what whole language is and is not.

Goodman, K. S., Goodman, Y. M., and Hood, W. J. 1988. *The whole language evaluation book*. Portsmouth, NH: Heinemann Educational Books.
Provides teacher-developed evaluation techniques for whole language classrooms.

Lipton, L. 1992. Meaning is the method: Whole language in the thoughtful classroom. In *If minds matter*. Volume 2, eds. A. Costa, J. Bellanca, and R. Fogarty. Palatine, IL: Skylight Publishing.
Many strategies for starting and maintaining a whole language approach.

Newman, J. 1985. *Whole language: Theory into use*. Portsmouth, NH: Heinemann Educational Books.
This book is a fundamental resource for information on whole language tenets and practice.

# References

Altwerger, B., Edelsky, C., and Flores, B. 1987. Whole language: What's new? *The Reading Teacher* 27: 144–154.

Goodman, K. and Goodman, Y. 1982. A whole language comprehension-centered view of reading development. In *Basic skills: Issues and choices*. Volume 2, eds. L. Reed & S. Ward. St. Louis, MO: CEMREL.

Lipton, L. 1992. Meaning is the method: Whole language in the thoughtful classroom. In *If minds matter*. Volume 2, eds. A. Costa, J. Bellanca, and R. Fogarty. Palatine, IL: Skylight Publishing.

O'Shea, L. J. and O'Shea, D. J. 1994. What research in special education says to reading teachers. In *Teaching reading to at-risk learners*, eds. K. D. Wood, and B. Algozzine. Needham, MA: Allyn & Bacon.

Watson, D. and Crowley, P. 1988. How can we implement a whole language approach? In *Reading process and practice*, ed. C. Weaver. Portsmouth, NH: Heinemann Educational Books.

# Topic 5  OUTCOME-BASED CURRICULUM

**M**ost states will have mandated outcomes in their curriculum by the year 2000. Some states have based their entire restructuring process on outcomes, including rewriting all state curricula, while others are taking a more local, district by district approach. No matter which approach prevails, teachers must be able to see how outcomes affect their day-to-day planning and teaching. For that reason, a short module of outcomes-based education and curriculum is included. While most "exit" or graduation outcomes are developed at the district level, there are numerous examples of schools, and even individual teachers, developing curriculum around outcomes, even when outcomes do not exist at the district level.

## ▶ What is it?

An outcomes-based curriculum, quite simply, is a curriculum that specifies what students should know and be able to do after instruction and learning. An outcomes-based curriculum not only defines the desired content and knowledge, but also what students are able to do with that knowledge. It is that component that has been overlooked for so long in the curriculum. In the briefest possible explanation,

". . . an outcome is a culminating demonstration of learning. IT IS A DEMONSTRATION: what is it the kids will actually do . . . outcomes are not content, they're performances" (Spady 1993).

Exit outcomes are clearly defined and directly connect the knowledge, competencies, and orientations needed by adults in a complex, changing world. Students will successfully demonstrate these exit outcomes before they leave school. They are called exit outcomes because learners must demonstrate them before exiting the school system. They are based on beliefs and broad purposes of school as expressed by the parents, professional educators, and community.

In developing exemplary exit outcomes,

- Focus on the future

- Maintain a "life-role" focus

- Develop a concise list

- Consider the capacity of exit outcomes to drive the curriculum and affect all instructional staff

- Provide clarity of focus for everyone

- Express high expectations and standards

A list of typical **exit outcomes** with explanations follows:

### Self-Directed Learner

- Sets reasonable goals
- Monitors progress and clarifies, revises goals/plans
- Accesses a variety of information sources
- Strives for/maintains a positive self-image
- Uses appropriate technology
- Demonstrates independent learning

### Community Contributor

- Maintains physical and mental health
- Interacts with others in an ethical, caring manner
- Becomes involved in various groups (school, community)
- Initiates action in solving problems in the community

### Quality Producer and Performer

- Establishes plans
- Monitors progress and alters plans as necessary
- Meets requirements of task
- Applies best possible resources, technologies
- Creates original products of high quality
- Evaluates product

### Effective Communicator

- Conveys thoughts and feelings to others through a variety of methods
- Receives and reacts appropriately to expressed thoughts and feelings of others
- Reads appropriate level materials with understanding
- Writes effectively in a variety of formats

### Problem Solver and Decision Maker

- Develops and uses multiple frames of reference to identify, assess, integrate, and apply available information and resources in reasoning, decision making, and complex problem solving.

Obviously, there are many other possibilities for desirable exit outcomes.

Other, more specific outcomes are derived from the exit outcomes. These other outcomes are **program outcomes** (such as outcomes for K-12 math, K-12 art, K-12 English/language arts, etc.), **course outcomes** (such as outcomes for sixth-grade social studies, eighth-grade science), and **unit outcomes** (such as outcomes for learning units written in courses).

# ▶ How do we get started?

Most exit and program outcomes are determined by districts or state departments of education. Your actual planning or writing of outcomes comes in courses and units.

## The Design Down Model

The curriculum writing process that links or threads the exit outcomes to the actual classroom is known as the design down model, as the following illustrates:

### 1. Student Exit Outcomes

- Are drawn from district's mission statement
- Provide grounding for all curriculum

### 2. Program or Discipline Outcomes

- Focus on content-area knowledge/skills needed to meet choices and challenges of twenty-first century
- Select from current curriculum
- Address state guidelines comprehensively
- Spiral through all courses within a discipline

### 3. Course Outcomes

- Are generated from program outcomes
- Include specific content-area knowledge/skills

### 4. Unit Outcomes

- Are generated from course outcomes and prioritized curriculum
- Infuse higher-order thinking

Outcomes should be developed/designed from the general to the specific, in the sequence of the outcomes just listed. There should be a **thread** or **structure that links** every program, course, and unit outcome to one or more exit outcomes. There should be a tightly articulated curriculum framework that ensures clarity of focus on the exit outcomes.

The following is an example of how to "design down" from the exit outcomes, using eighth-grade language arts as a model.

| | |
|---|---|
| Exit Outcomes: | **COMPLEX THINKERS** — Access prior knowledge in new situations, make decisions consistent with set criteria, apply appropriate cognitive strategy where needed |
| Program Outcome: | **ENGLISH/LANGUAGE ARTS** — Produce clear judgments and analyses of a wide range of ideas, issues, and information, **by** analyzing and interpreting written and spoken language. The judgments and analyses should be based upon objective and personal criteria. |
| Course Outcome: | **EIGHTH-GRADE LANGUAGE ARTS** — Examine and compare plots **by** identifying key points and/or main ideas from two plots studied this year, examining and comparing the critical components of the plots, describing how the main character felt during phases of the plot, and assessing the significance of those feelings in relation to their own feelings when confronted with similar situations. |
| Unit Outcome: | *THE OUTSIDERS* — Conduct episode analyses of the book *The Outsiders*, **by** noting significant similarities and differences in how the main character in each episode felt (i.e., Ponyboy being attacked; Soda talking to the Socs, etc.) and **by** comparing the character's feelings to their own when confronted with similar situations. |

Notice the underlined words in each outcome link that outcome to the exit outcome of complex thinker. Also notice the use of the word **by** in each outcome indicates what the student should perform and/or demonstrate to prove what he or she has learned.

Another content-specific example from social studies is:

| | |
|---|---|
| **Exit Outcome:** | **EFFECTIVELY COMMUNICATE —** Demonstrate the ability to listen, read complex materials, and express oneself orally or in writing for various purposes and audiences. |
| **Program Outcome:** | **SOCIAL STUDIES —** Gather, _interpret_, evaluate, and _present_ data **by** formulating solutions, decisions, and/or conclusions and by _presenting_ information individually or in groups. |
| **Course Outcome:** | **AMERICAN HISTORY —** _Explain_ the cause and effect of a major development in U.S. history during the last 60 years **by** _writing_ a personal research paper and doing a group _presentation_ of the research in class. |
| **Unit Outcome:** | **WORLD WAR II —** Research and _explain_ the sociopolitical, military, geographic, and economic causes of World War II **by** _writing_ a cause-and-effect research paper and taking part in a jigsaw group _presentation_. |

## Writing Unit Outcomes

It is in the unit outcomes that an outcomes-based curriculum reaches the students. You should write unit outcomes as you write your learning units (see the Learning Units section in this module), and you should use performance and product assessment of your unit outcomes (see Module 6: Assessment). Copy Form 10 at the end of this section may help you in the actual writing of the unit outcomes.

# ► Where do we go for more information?

High Success Program on Outcome-Based Education. 536 Northridge Dr., Santa Cruz, CA 95066.
A leading organization for the Network for Outcome-Based Schools. Publishes newsletters and workshops for schools and teachers interested in outcome-based education.

Kentucky State Department of Education. 1991. *Learning goals and valued outcomes*. Lexington, KY: Department of Education.
A state document detailing Kentucky's plan and reasons for implementing outcomes in the Kentucky curriculum.

Marzano, R.J., Pickering, D., and McTighe, J. 1994. *Assessing student outcomes*. Alexandria, VA: Association for Supervision and Curriculum Development.
A compendium of outcomes and outcome rubrics for performance assessment outcomes.

New York State Department of Education. 1991. *A new compact for learning*. Albany, NY: NY State Education Department.
A state document detailing New York's plan for restructuring around outcomes and learning.

Redding, N. 1991. Assessing the big outcomes. *Educational Leadership* 49 (8):49–53.
One district's approach to outcomes and performance assessment of those outcomes.

Spady, W. 1993. On outcome-based education: A conversation with Bill Spady. *Educational Leadership* 50 (4):66–70.

Spady, W. G. 1988. Organizing for results: The basis of authentic restructuring and reform. *Educational Leadership* 46 (2):4–8.
Both articles describe Spady's concepts of OBE and the rationale of outcomes for schools.

## *References*

Spady, W. 1993. On outcome-based education: A conversation with Bill Spady. *Educational Leadership* 50 (4):66–70.

# Unit Outcome Development Organizer

Exit Outcome(s): _____

_____

_____

_____

| Knowledge/Skills/Concepts<br>(What) | BY | Application/Demonstration<br>(How/Where) |
|---|---|---|
| | • | |
| | • | |
| | • | |
| | • | |
| | • | |
| | • | |
| | • | |
| | • | |
| | • | |
| | • | |
| | • | |
| | • | |
| | • | |
| | • | |
| | • | |
| | • | |
| | • | |

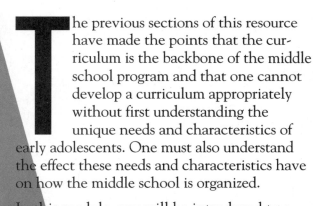

# MODULE 5 Middle School Instructional Strategies

The previous sections of this resource have made the points that the curriculum is the backbone of the middle school program and that one cannot develop a curriculum appropriately without first understanding the unique needs and characteristics of early adolescents. One must also understand the effect these needs and characteristics have on how the middle school is organized.

In this module, you will be introduced to a variety of instructional strategies ranging from those that are highly teacher directed to those that are highly flexible. It is important to keep in mind, however, that instruction in the middle school should involve hands-on activities, higher-order thinking skills, active learning techniques, self-directed experiences, cooperative enterprises, reflective exercises, personal choices, and authentic assessment options.

# MODULE 5 Contents

# Topic 1 ⋯ THE LECTURE METHOD

## ▶ What is it?

A lecture is an activity in which the teacher presents information and knowledge orally through a series of organized and structured explanations. Lectures can be both formal and informal. Formal lectures are predetermined talks generally given before a large group in such a way that student involvement or interaction is very limited or nonexistent. Informal lectures allow for some student participation in the form of questions and comments. Interactive or informal lectures (sometimes referred to as minilectures) increase student retention of information by 20 percent over formal lectures.

Minilectures are beneficial when the teacher wants to

- Establish a particular or different point of view or position

- Introduce or summarize major points of a new subject, unit, or activity

- Clarify difficult or conflicting pieces of information

- Develop connections among varied topics or theories

- Provide information when time is limited or when the information is not readily available by some other means

- Motivate learners and create interest in a given content area

- Adapt information to the unique needs, characteristics, and abilities of the students

- Regulate the pace and timing of the delivery of information

## ▶ How is it different?

In contrast to other instructional strategies used in the middle school, lectures generally involve limited student interaction and participation. Of course, even when you decide that a lecture is most efficient, encourage as much student involvement as possible.

### TIPS FOR TEAMS

Try giving a lecture as a team. Divide the lecture into sections and assign each section to a different team member. Students will benefit from the variety of lecture personalities.

66 The test of a good teacher: 'Do you regard "learning" as a noun or a verb?' If you see it as a noun, as a thing to be possessed and passed along, then you present your truths, neatly packaged to your students. But if you see 'learning' as a verb, the process is different. The good teacher has learning but tries to instill in students the desire to learn and demonstrates the ways one goes about learning. 99

(Schorske in McCleery, 1986, p. 106)

*The Lecture Method* **181**

Try to vary the types of lectures you use. Lectures for middle grade students should be limited to no more than twenty minutes, two or three times a week. Bonwell and Eison (1991) suggest several ways to vary lectures so that they are effective in the middle level classroom. Adaptations of these models are briefly described below.

**Feedback Lecture:** Provide students with a set of readings and an outline of the lecture notes prior to the lecture. Lecture for ten minutes, and then divide students into study groups for twenty minutes. During these study group sessions, assign student groups a question related to lecture material to consider. Reconvene the students for another ten-minute lecture, and address the assigned study question in your comments.

**Guided Lecture:** Provide students with a list of objectives for the lecture. Have them put down their pencils and listen carefully to the lecture for twenty minutes, attempting to remember the information given. At the end of the lecture, give students five minutes to write all the information they can recall individually. Next, involve students in small discussion groups to reconstruct the lecture by combining notes. Help students fill in missing information as they identify it.

**Responsive Lecture:** Devote one class period a week to answering open-ended, student-generated questions on any aspect of a given topic or unit of study. A few rules apply to streamline the question-and-answer process. All topics have to be presented as questions; students can submit questions as long as they specify why they think they are important; the class orders the questions in terms of general interest; and, the lecturer answers as many of the questions as time allows.

**Demonstration Lecture:** During the lecture, take time to stop and demonstrate a laboratory-type application to illustrate selected principles of the lecture content. Pose a series of "What will happen if we . . ." questions to encourage student interaction and to provide investigative opportunities as part of the lecture process.

**Pause Procedure Lecture:** Deliver a twenty-minute lecture, and have students take notes on the content. Every five or six minutes, pause during the lecture, and give students approximately two minutes to share their notes with a partner and to fill in any missing information or correct any mistakes.

**Think/Write/Discuss Lecture:** Prepare a set of three related questions to ask students throughout the lecture.

■ Give the first question—a motivational question that helps set the stage for the lecture—before the lecture, and have students write a two-minute response to it. For example, ask, "What are three things you know about mammals?" or "What would you like to know about the people of China?" or "What was your favorite childhood poem or nursery rhyme, and why?" If time allows, ask some students to share their responses orally with the whole group.

- During the middle of the lecture, pose another question to clarify the information given. Ask the students to write a short response to you, sharing some of their ideas aloud if possible. Questions that ask, "How would you define a rhombus?" or "What facts did you understand about tides?" or "Why do we use figurative language in poetry?" are good examples of these midpoint questions.

- At the end of the lecture, ask students to reflect on some type of feedback question, such as, "What was the most interesting idea you learned from the lecture?" or "What aspect of this topic would you like to know more about?" or "Why is poetry considered an art form?"

In short, the minilecture can be a good instructional tool if it is organized, short, to the point, and interactive.

Finally, you might want to improve your minilecture by incorporating these ideas from the research on effective instruction:

- Present the content in small steps or "chunks."

- Focus on a single idea at a time.

- Give many and varied examples to make a point.

- Provide alternative explanations for difficult points.

- Check for student understanding throughout the presentation.

# ▶ How do we get started?

In the planning and delivery of a lecture, consider several variables, including ways to establish rapport with the students and ways to hold the students' attention throughout the lecture. Also consider the length of the presentation; the scope and sequence of the content; the use of advanced organizers in presenting the material; the inclusion of examples, models, and audiovisual aids; methods for summarizing topics; and ways to solicit feedback about the effectiveness of the lecture.

## Steps for Planning the Lecture

Use the following steps to plan your minilecture:

**Step 1:** Decide what topics or content would best be delivered through the lecture method. Develop the purpose and objectives of the lecture.

## POINT TO PONDER

Have you observed the following during a lecture or formal presentation?

"Ten percent of the audience displayed signs of inattention within 15 minutes. After 18 minutes, one-third of the audience and 10 percent of the platform guests were fidgeting. At 35 minutes everyone was inattentive; at 45 minutes trance was more noticeable than fidgeting; and at 47 minutes some were asleep and at least 1 person was reading. About 24 hours later, the audience recalled only insignificant details that were generally incorrect." (Verner & Dickinson, 1967)

If this is the case with an intelligent audience, an adult learner, a knowledgeable speaker, and an interesting topic, what do you think the statistics would show about a middle school student in a lecture setting?

**Step 2:** Determine the length of the lecture—not more than twenty minutes for middle school students—as well as ways to modify it to accommodate a variety of learning styles and abilities.

**Step 3:** Prepare a detailed outline and/or a set of notes for the lecture. Plan to repeat key points and ask questions to check student understanding of the information presented. It is helpful to provide cues or symbols throughout the outline to remind yourself to pause, involve students, use supplementary materials, or ask questions. For example, you might use the letters *D* for discussion, *R* for reinforcement, *P* for pause, or *TQ* for teacher questions.

**Step 4:** Include humor, anecdotes, short stories, and many examples in your lecture to highlight important ideas and illustrate major concepts.

**Step 5:** Plan a special introduction or motivational gimmick at the beginning of the lecture to gain student attention and a comprehensive summary of the "big ideas" to close the lecture.

**Step 6:** Rehearse your lecture before giving it.

**Step 7:** Provide students with an outline or study guide of the lecture so they can fill in the gaps with their own notes and interpretations.

## Delivering the Lecture

The following tips may help you successfully deliver your minilecture:

- Don't talk too fast to "get it all in," and don't talk too slowly or you may "overkill" the message.

- Use changes in inflection, volume, and pitch to emphasize important points and generate enthusiasm for key ideas.

- Establish eye contact frequently with students, and move around the room to keep yourself and your students from losing interest or getting bored.

- Use vocabulary, examples, and audiovisual aids that are age-appropriate and that enrich the information given.

- Be alert to signs of restlessness, frustration, disinterest, or confusion. Vary the pace, change the voice level, ask a rhetorical question, dramatize a point, or throw in a provocative statement to get students back on task.

## Following Up the Lecture

Consider the following ideas for following up your minilecture:

- Hold the students responsible for the content of the lecture by using a short writing activity, a simple quiz, a small or large group discussion, or a related homework assignment.

- Establish a procedure for checking student notes and student knowledge of information presented.

# ▶ Where do we go for more information?

Bonwell, C. C., and Eison, J. A. 1991. *Active learning: Creating excitement in the classroom.* ASHE-ERIC Higher Education Report No. 1, The George Washington University, School of Education and Human Development, Washington, D.C.
Discusses active learning issues, including modifying lectures, developing questions and discussions, varied methods and strategies for incorporating active learning in teaching, and barriers to change in the classroom. Includes a full list of references.

## References

Bonwell, C. C., and Eison, J. A. 1991. *Active learning: Creating excitement in the classroom.* ASHE-ERIC Higher Education Report No. 1, The George Washington University, School of Education and Human Development, Washinton, D.C.

McCleery, W. 1986. *Conversations on the character.* Princeton, NJ: Princeton University Press.

Verner, C., and Dickinson, G. 1967. The lecture: An analysis and review of research. *Adult Education,* (Winter) 17: 85–100.

## POINT TO PONDER

How might you relate this quotation by Baltasar Gracian to the lecture method in your classroom: "Be content to act, and leave the talking to others"?

## ▶ What is it?

According to Clark and Starr (1991), a case study is a special problem-solving technique that gives students an opportunity to study an individual accounting of real events. Because these events represent a larger issue, students can draw conclusions about the issue as a whole. The best case studies describe events with realistic details, intriguing decision points, and provocative ideas that make the discussion group want to think and argue about them. The discussion group analyzes the details, tries to get into the minds of the characters, assesses the events that take place, and offers some recommendations for action.

Case studies can be a very popular instructional strategy for both students and teachers because they are written in a storylike format and feature a set of realistic anecdotes and situations.

## ▶ How does it work?

Effective case studies require some degree of story-writing and role-playing skills on the part of the teacher and the students. It is important that the teacher view the case study as a rather complex and sophisticated tool for problem solving that requires students to make choices and/or consider alternative solutions. Too often, case studies are limited to a mere accounting of a simple or single event that does not present the student with many opportunities to apply higher-order thinking skills. To be effective, case studies must have a variety of legitimate resolutions.

> "Learning is not a spectator sport. Students do not learn much just by sitting in class listening to teachers, memorizing prepackaged assignments, and spitting out answers. They must talk about what they are learning, write about it, relate it to past experiences, apply it to their daily lives. They must make what they learn part of themselves."
>
> (Chickering & Gamson, 1987, p. 3)

What is your response to this quotation in terms of the teaching and learning process?

# ► How do we get started?

**Step 1:** Collect several studies from textbooks, newspapers, teacher files, media productions, and data searches. Read through them and ask the following questions:

- How are characters portrayed and details presented?

- How do the case studies begin and end?

- How long are the case studies?

- How much background is given, and in what order do events occur?

- How are the sections of the case study divided or broken down?

- What and how many decision points are there?

**Step 2:** Choose a topic within your unit of study that might be taught effectively through the case study method. Write that topic in the form of a comprehensive story. Everyone appreciates a good story. Keep in mind, however, that although a case study has characters and events like a story, its special mission is to present students with a set of optional endings to stimulate discussion, not to provide a predetermined ending.

**Step 3:** Decide on names for the characters in your case study. Try to give them interesting names and personalities, perhaps using names that pun certain character traits. "Iva Problem" and "Hap Hazard" might be two characters in a case study involving disposal of toxic wastes or pollution of groundwater. Giving your characters names and traits helps bring them to life, which in turn makes case studies come alive to learners. Make the characters seem real. One way to do this is to involve the reader's five senses, rather than simply the intellect. Also, use realistic dialogue.

**Step 4:** Make certain the information you give is accurate, specific, and realistic to make your case study sound authentic. Avoid generalities in your descriptions; employ precise language. For example, using the toxic waste example, instead of calling something to measure the pH level of groundwater a tool, call it a calibrated omega pH meter. In addition, use the terminology, technical language, jargon, or personal expressions common to the situation in the case study. This is why research is so important to the writing process.

**Step 5:** Include important details at the beginning or end of paragraphs since students tend to skim the middle of each paragraph. Also, include all the facts students will need to discuss the issues of the case. Learners will follow the story better if you present events and information in chronological order. Avoid flashbacks and foreshadowing because they can be confusing to the students.

1. One cannot cover as much content in the time available.

2. Devising case studies takes a great deal of preparation.

3. Case studies can be difficult to manage in large classes.

4. Materials, space, and props needed to support case studies may not be available.

**Step 6:** Finally, be certain to make your case study both thorough and mysterious. Students must be given opportunities to make inferences, choose among alternatives, draw conclusions, and recommend some action. Nothing is more frustrating to students than the feeling that they have been set up to think a certain way or come up with a right answer. The secret to a good case study is leaving some loose ends to maintain a sense of interest, curiosity, mystery, and challenge.

# ► Where do we go for more information?

Engel, H. M. 1990. *Handbook of creative learning exercises*. 2d ed. Amherst, MA: HRD Press, Inc.
Describes the technical skills needed for designing effective learning exercises tailored to specific needs. Offers detailed explanations of how to develop case studies, role plays, and exercises ranging from the simple to the complex. Also contains an entire section of ready-to-use exercises.

Lowman, J. 1984. *Mastering the techniques of teaching*. San Francisco: Jossey-Bass.
Provides a systematic course of instruction in fundamental teaching skills: lecturing, leading discussions, motivating, and promoting independent learning. Discusses masterful teaching, classroom dynamics, developing interpersonal skills and teaching style, materials and presentations, integrating inside- and outside-of-class learning, and evaluating.

Silverman, R., Welty, W. M., and Lyon, S. 1992. *Case studies for teacher problem solving*. New York: McGraw-Hill.
True stories, adapted from the experiences of elementary and secondary teachers, that demonstrate how to apply theory to problem analysis and decision making. Covers classroom management, learning, effective teaching, diversity, evaluation, and contemporary teaching issues.

## *References*

Chickering, A. W., and Gamson, Z. F. 1987. Seven principles for good practice. *AAHE Bulletin*, (March) 39: 3–7.

Clark, L. H., and Starr, I. S. 1991. *Secondary and middle school teaching methods*. 6th ed. New York: Macmillan.

# Topic 3    GAMES AND SIMULATIONS

## ▶ What are they?

G ames and simulations are instructional activities operating under a given set of goals and rules, most often as a contest among adversaries. Games and simulations are most effective when their structure reflects a real-world process that enables the players to become working members of a system by analyzing information and making decisions.

In playing carefully designed games with clear instructional purposes, students can develop many valuable skills, including auditory, visual, motor, social, directional, and problem-solving skills. The use of games and simulations in the classroom can arouse students' curiosity, challenge their imagination, and stimulate their interest in the content.

## ▶ How are they different?

Too often the use of games and simulations has been reserved for a special occasion, an earned reward, or a break from the routine. With no real focus except for having fun and doing something different, these activities could be construed as wasting time. However, with planning and careful thought, games and simulations can be motivational and instructional—as well as entertaining.

According to Freiberg and Driscoll (1992), an effective game or simulation has four phases. They are (1) participant orientation, in which the game's principles are reviewed and the simulation processes are taught; (2) participant training, in which the students read background information and prepare themselves for the game's objectives; (3) participant simulation operations, in which students actually perform the activities through prescribed interactions with one another; and (4) participant debriefing, in which the teacher conducts a meaningful discussion and critique of the game's procedures, roles, and outcomes.

## ▶ TIPS FOR TEAMS

1. Consider assigning a student-made game as a product assessment for a unit of study.

2. Close an interdisciplinary unit with student-created simulations related directly to the objectives of the unit.

# ▶ How do we get started?

## Commercial Games

**Step 1:** Locate commonly used commercial games that lend themselves to classroom instruction and that may be played either as designed or with teacher adaptations. Games to consider include dominoes (addition and subtraction facts, visual and fine motor skills), bingo (sequence, auditory, visual, and kinesthetic skills), checkers (visual, spatial, and strategic skills), chess (higher-level thinking, visual and spatial skills), trivia games (visual, auditory, recall, and comprehension skills), and a wide variety of other board games.

**Step 2:** Determine how you might use a game in the classroom to meet and extend curricular objectives. Review the rules of play, select partners or teams, observe student interactions, and evaluate the results.

## Teacher-Adapted Games and Simulations

**Step 1:** Use a game format—such as bingo, charades, or ticktack-toe—with which you are comfortable, and adapt it to your subject.

**Step 2:** Determine the length of time you will spend on the game, the rules and procedures to be followed, and the desired outcomes.

## Teacher-Designed Games and Simulations

If you decide to create your own games or simulations, the following steps suggested by the professional game designer Dr. Clark C. Abt will be helpful (Heitzmann, 1987):

**Step 1:** Define the overall *objectives* (e.g., teaching, analysis, assessment, exploration).

**Step 2:** Determine the *scope* (duration, geographic area, issues).

**Step 3:** Identify key *actors* (simulated individual, groups, or organizations making the critical decisions).

**Step 4:** Determine the *actors' objectives* (power, wealth, influence, etc., in specific contexts).

**Step 5:** Determine the *actors' resources* (e.g. physical, social, economic, political, informational).

**Step 6:** Determine the *interaction sequence among the actors* (flow of resources and information to and from each actor).

**Step 7:** Determine the *rules* that govern how the actors decide what resources and information to transmit or receive or the actions to take.

**Step 8:** Identify *external constraints* on the actions of the actors (such as no violence being permitted in a competition among Quakers).

**Step 9:** Formulate the *scoring rules* and *win criteria* that reflect the degree to which the actors achieve their objectives.

**Step 10:** Choose the form of presentation (e.g., board game, computer simulation).

## Student-Designed Games and Simulations

Provide the following suggestions to students who choose to design their own board games as a class or team project.

**Step 1:** Pick a specific subject for your game from the topics studied in class. Choose a theme, such as "American Heroes," "Thesaurus Therapy," "Decimal Dodgery," or "Chemistry Creations," for your game. Think about a creative title for it.

**Step 2:** Create a rough draft of your game board. Consider using an interesting shape.

**Step 3:** Decide what kind of playing pieces you will have. Make or gather them.

**Step 4:** Make up twenty to forty questions and/or activity cards using reference books. Also add a number cube, spinner, or some chance cards based on your theme to make your game interesting, such as "lost the election—move back two spaces," or "failed the math test, lose a turn."

**Step 5:** Copy the rough draft on poster board to make your game board. Add illustrations, borders, or symbols to make your board attractive and fun.

**Step 6:** Make or find tokens for players. Use bottle caps, pebbles, wooden cubes, coins, and so on.

**Step 7:** Design a package (e.g., box, reclosable bag, large envelope) for your game equipment.

**Step 8:** Include an answer key, rules, and directions in the game container. Your rules should answer the following questions:

- How many players can participate?
- What is the object of the game?
- Who goes first? second? third?
- How do you move around the board?
- What do you do when you land on a section?
- Who checks the answers in the answer key?
- What happens if you answer a question correctly? incorrectly?
- When is the game over?

## ▶ Where do we go for more information?

Fischer, M. W. 1993. *American history simulations and world history simulations*. Huntington Beach, CA: Teacher Created Materials, Inc. Includes tools for teachers such as simulation information, suggestions for cooperative learning groups, more than twenty-five actual simulations for reproduction, and several efficient management tools.

Jones, K. 1987. *Simulations: A handbook for teachers and trainers*. New York: Nichols Publishing Co. Provides practical advice and guidance on all aspects of choosing, using, designing, running, and assessing simulations. Includes many examples and a complete list of references.

## References

Freiberg, H. J., and Driscoll, A. 1992. *Universal teaching strategies*. Needham, MA: Allyn & Bacon.

Heitzmann, W. R. 1987. *Educational games and simulations*. rev. ed. Washington, D.C.: National Education Association.

**POINT TO PONDER**

The cooperative-learning process works well with game and educational simulations in the middle level classroom. Cooperative teams play games and solve problems, building on each other's strengths and skills.

# Commercial Capers

**Directions:** After examining and discussing advertisements from a variety of media—including radio, television, theater screens, newspapers, and magazines—students working in groups of four to six form their own "Creative Commercials" companies. Each company selects an intended audience and chooses an advertising method that will be most effective with these prospective consumers. The groups design and present their commercials to the class and compete for a first prize, to be awarded by a panel of judges comprised of students, teachers, parents, and business leaders from the community. The first prize should be determined by the teacher and students together.

## Procedures for Students

1. Select a new product or service.

2. Name it.

3. Design its package.

4. Make a full-color drawing of the service or product and its package.

5. Decide on an advertising method, and then do one or more of the following tasks.

   a. Write a script.

   b. Design an advertisement.

   c. Create a catchy slogan or jingle.

   d. Produce a commercial.

   e. Perform a commercial.

## Debriefing Questions

- How did you go about organizing your company's people and resources to complete the task?

- How did you conduct your market research to make product decisions?

- How did you "gear up" for the competition from other commercial companies?

- What were the strengths and weaknesses of your business enterprise?

- What problems were most difficult for your group to deal with in completing this simulation?

- What would you do differently next time?

# Topic 4  ROLE PLAYING

## ▶ What is it?

Role playing is a popular instructional strategy with middle level students because it is interactive, involves physical movement, encourages improvisation, nurtures emotions or feelings, and can be designed to simulate real-life situations.

Role plays are usually short, somewhat spontaneous presentations that are structured and facilitated by the teacher. They should be based on an informal script that contains both sufficient background information and general character sketches. The teacher should provide the students in the audience with goals that have been established for the scenario so that they can be informed observers of pertinent developments and effective critics of the results.

Role plays can be used in any discipline to clarify attitudes, demonstrate concepts, deepen understanding of conflict situations, try out problem-solving skills, rehearse for lifelike situations, or practice leadership skills.

## ▶ What are the advantages?

Role plays, like case studies and simulations, provide students with situations that seem real and that allow students to develop and apply coping and higher-order thinking skills. Role plays are less structured and depend more on students' actions and interpretations than simulations and case studies.

Role plays offer many advantages to students because students are actively engaged in speaking, questioning, planning, thinking, and using data to solve problems. On the other hand, role plays can be time-consuming, they can be viewed as a frivolous activity rather than a learning experience if not well developed, and they can encourage students to resort to using stereotypes when they have insufficient time and guidance.

## TIPS FOR TEAMS

To introduce students to role playing, perform a role play of your own as a team. Enact a team-planning meeting, a parent conference, or a problem-solving session with the principal to show your students how it is done.

# ▶ How do we get started?

**Step 1:** To use role playing effectively, establish a climate that encourages trust, self-expression, and risk taking among students. Spend some time reading and discussing with the students stories of human emotions, conflicts, traumas, and personal relationships. Spend time nurturing the qualities of active listening among students so that they can respond to one another's feelings, ideas, and actions without judgment or censoring. Finally, spend some time with students encouraging spontaneity by placing them in several warm-up situations that require little, if any, prescribed behaviors. For example, have them act out their perception of the color red, the destruction of a tornado, or the antics of a clown.

**Step 2:** Choose the issue for your role play. Consider whether you want it to be light or serious, real or imaginary, past or present, light-hearted or conflict-oriented, and content-based or emotion-based.

**Step 3:** Brief the class on the goals and details of the role play. Be sure to keep the scenario simple and limited to no more than four characters. It is better to keep the number of players small and the plot short so that the role play can be repeated several times with different students and varied interpretations. In other words, describe the setting, characters, sequence of events, and issues to be addressed with enough detail to keep students on task but not so specifically that it inhibits their spontaneity.

It is also important to tell the audience members the purpose of the role play and what things they should be looking for as it unfolds. You might want to appoint certain observer roles so that some students focus on the verbal and nonverbal language of the actors while others focus on the enactments and outcomes of the portrayals.

**Step 4:** Select students for each of the roles, and give them time to think about their characters and the props they will need to set the stage for the drama.

**Step 5:** Have students enact their roles, following the predetermined script as planned. If students have trouble playing their parts well, don't hesitate to intervene and reorient them to the goals of the role play. Repeat and reenact the situation as long as new interpretations of the roles emerge or alternative actions are developed.

**Step 6:** After each enactment of the role play, allow ample time for debriefing and discussing what happened by asking the students to reflect on the diverse roles, actions, goals, and outcomes they experienced or observed. Be sure to help the students draw conclusions, form generalizations, and validate opinions at the end of the experience so that they can better see the connections between the concepts taught (as part of the script) and the methods used (as part of the role-play process).

## SOME POSSIBLE TOPICS FOR ROLE PLAYS

- A Teenager Involved in Shoplifting

- A News Reporter at a Political Rally

- A Scientist with an Important Discovery

- A Computer Genius Who Discovers a Virus

- A Meeting to Discuss Gun Control

- A Confrontation Between a Loyalist and a Patriot

- A Movement to Limit Violence on Television

- A Rally to Promote the Metric System

- A Discussion of Consumer Spending Habits

- A Meeting About a Proposal to Abolish Homework

# ROLE PLAYING CURRENT EVENTS FROM DIVERSE PERSPECTIVES

Older students can begin developing an appreciation for multiple perspectives by role playing current local or world events. One simple activity is to ask students to bring to class newspaper articles that address controversial or conflict-ridden issues. Assign students to groups, with each person briefly describing the article he or she brought. Each group then selects one article to pursue in greater depth and proceed through the following steps.

1. One student volunteers to read the article to the group.

2. The group identifies the conflict in the article and the diverse perspectives of the conflict.

3. Students determine potential roles represented by those involved in the conflict.

4. Each member of the group assumes a role.

5. The group role-plays the diverse perspectives.

6. The group discusses the role play, reflecting on the roles assumed, the validity of the perspectives expressed, and any insights gained.

7. The group next considers how the conflict might be resolved by using win/win approaches.

8. Each group shares its experiences with the whole class.

(Campbell, Campbell, & Dickinson, 1992, pp. 120-121)

## ► Where do we go for more information?

Engel, H. M. 1990. *Handbook of creative learning exercises*. 2d ed. Amherst, MA: HRD Press, Inc.
Describes the technical skills needed for designing effective learning exercises tailored to specific needs. Offers detailed explanations of how to develop case studies, role plays, and exercises ranging from the simple to the complex. Also contains an entire section of ready-to-use exercises.

## References

Campbell, B., Campbell, L., and Dickinson, D. 1992. *Teaching and learning through multiple intelligences*. Seattle, WA: New Horizons for Learning.

# Topic 5 COOPERATIVE LEARNING

## ▶ What is it?

**C**ooperative learning promotes teamwork among groups of students. Students, usually in heterogeneous groups, work together in a structured situation and follow specific rules, maintain assigned roles, and assist one another in the learning process to achieve a common goal.

There are five basic elements that must be in place for true cooperative learning to occur, according to Johnson, Johnson, and Holubec (1991).

**1. Positive Interdependence** provides a "sink or swim" situation in which students must cooperate to achieve mutual success. Group goals, joint rewards, divided resources, and role assignments are important aspects of this element.

**2. Face-to-Face Interaction** encourages eye contact and verbal and nonverbal responses. Students explain, discuss, solve problems, and complete assignments together.

**3. Individual Accountability** requires that students are accountable for individual tasks that will help the group meet its overall goal.

**4. Interpersonal Skills** are social skills that enhance positive interaction and communication among group members. Children learn intuitively at a young age to compete, but we must teach them to collaborate and use social skills in a cooperative group.

**5. Group Processing** is a discussion of how well the group has functioned. Key words for this element are *participation*, *feedback*, *reinforcement*, *expectations*, *clarification*, and *refinement*. This element allows for closure to occur when a cooperative assignment is completed.

Johnson, Johnson, and Holubec (1991) identified three types of cooperative learning groups: *formal groups* that relate directly to completing an assignment or task; *informal groups* that are temporary in nature and focus student attention on the material to be learned; and

> **"C**ollaboration is the key concept for success in the twenty-first century, whether in business, in government, or in international affairs. Teamwork has become the norm for getting positive results in the family structure, in the workplace, and in the globalization of the world. The Information Age demands that one be able to function in group settings of all sizes so that all involved can adapt to the phenomenon of rapid change and the complexity of technology.**"**
> (Forte & Schurr, 1992, p. 7)

**Do you agree or disagree with this quote? Why?**

base groups, which are long-term groups with a stable membership offering support, assistance, and encouragement to its members.

"What a daring idea: Have students face each other, rather than each other's backs. In the process of this revolution, we are all students, learning from and with each other."

(Kagan, 1992)

Do you agree or disagree with this quote? Why?

## How is it different?

Traditional group work includes some of the elements of cooperative learning and may be relatively successful in many instances. What is missing, however, is structure and group interdependence. Students in traditional groups sit together, talk about the assignment, and often allow the brightest or most motivated student in the group to take over and do the majority of the work; then all students put their names on it. There is no interdependence, no individual accountability, no social skill focus, and no group processing.

When the essential elements of cooperative learning are structured within the lesson, the teacher becomes the facilitator of the learning process, and students are empowered to fulfill their roles, complete their portion of the assigned task, and learn the material.

## How do we get started?

**Step 1:** Commit to trying cooperative learning, knowing that "practice makes perfect."

**Step 2:** Discuss the process with students.

**Step 3:** Provide several cooperative activities for students to experience. A few suggestions follow:

- Put together a jigsaw puzzle with no talking and with each student touching only the pieces in his or her stack.

- Complete a cooperative drawing. All team members have a piece of paper and colored pencils. Each begins a drawing of his or her choice for one minute. The teacher announces the end of the minute and students pass their papers to the left where the next person continues the drawing, and so on. This is also a nonverbal activity, although some students may giggle or moan.

- Create a cooperative collage. In groups of four, assign such roles as searcher, trimmer, paster, and sharer (the sharer could also search). The task is to find pictures and words that show or describe cooperation as the team understands it. Students paste these pictures and words onto construction paper or poster board.

These activities are not graded. Because they are nonthreatening and considered "practice," they help nurture group cohesiveness and acceptance of diversity.

**Step 4:** Practice random grouping of students and moving in and out of teams quietly and quickly. (Ideal group size ranges from two to five members.)

**Step 5:** At first, teach one or two social skills (e.g., active listening, sharing, encouraging participation). Have students practice these skills, and model them during the activities.

**Step 6:** Plan your lesson. Decide on the group task, and select the structure. Decide how you will assess student performance. Will students receive grades? Will groups that work well together earn a reward? Share your decisions with your students.

**Step 7:** Use a grouping strategy to place the students in cooperative teams. Some ideas for random grouping include using color strips, playing cards, birthdays, numbering off, and height. Other groupings may include rank-ordering achievement levels, marking period grades, test scores, or learning styles.

**Step 8:** Assign roles to each team member. Everyone must have a specific duty to perform. Some possible roles include:

- Leader to keep the team on task
- Recorder to write the answers for the team
- Timer to keep track of time
- Encourager to ensure that all team members provide input
- Reader to read directions or problems to the team
- Go-for who is the only team member who may leave his or her seat (to pick up and/or turn in materials, for instance)
- Quiet controller to reinforce the use of quiet voices
- Artist to illustrate and display projects
- Proofreader to check the final paper for sentence structure, capitalization, punctuation, format, etc.
- Checker to ensure each team member's understanding of the material
- Observer to keep notes on group processing and social skills

**Step 9:** Review the social skill that will be observed during the lesson. Ask students what they are looking and listening for. Remind them this is what you will be observing. A few of the many social skills important for middle level students include taking turns, encouraging participation, sharing information and materials, giving directions, using quiet voices, listening to a speaker, using time wisely, and criticizing ideas but not people.

Don't try too much too soon.

Practice! Practice!

Don't give up. Keep trying!

Keep your sense of humor.

Remember that we often learn more from our mistakes than from our successes.

In most instances, students should be grouped heterogeneously. It is important for groups to reflect diversity in achievement, ability, gender, socioeconomic status, interests, and ethnic backgrounds.

## POINT TO PONDER

According to researchers, more adult job losses are due to lack of interpersonal skills than to poor job performance.

**Step 10:** Establish and discuss classroom rules for cooperative learning. The rules should address the following ideas:

- Students are responsible for their own behavior in the group.
- Students are accountable for contributing to the assigned task.
- Students are expected to help any group member who wants, needs, or asks for help.
- Students will ask the teacher for help only when everyone in the group has the same need.
- Students may not "put down" another person in any way.

Post the class's rules on a wall or bulletin board for continued reference.

**Step 11:** Observe as students work cooperatively. Your role at this point is one of facilitator/troubleshooter. You are observing the social skill that has been discussed as the groups work collaboratively. If a student is off task or misbehaving, you might have to join the group to reinforce the rules or answer questions about the assignment.

**Step 12:** Involve the students in group and/or individual processing when the cooperative task is completed. Questions for students to answer might include the following:

- How well did I perform my role?
- How well did the other members of our team perform their roles?
- Was I successful with the social skill?
- Was my team successful practicing the social skill?
- What did I enjoy about the cooperative task today?
- What did I learn about the content covered?

**Step 13:** Evaluate the results of the learning that occurred during the cooperative activity. You might want to assign and grade a group product using predetermined criteria or give a traditional, individual paper-and-pencil test that covers the material to assess each individual's learning. Johnson, Johnson, and Holubec (1991) offer the following ideas on grading:

- Tally each individual's score plus bonus points based on all members' success in reaching the predetermined criteria.
- Add each individual's score to bonus points based on the lowest individual score in the group.
- Add each individual's score plus bonus points based on that person's improvement.
- Assign a group score to each group project.
- Randomly select a paper from one member of each group to score.
- Average the academic scores and a collaborative-skills performance score for each student.

# Sample Cooperative Learning Activity: Circle of Knowledge

This brainstorming activity is excellent for review and reinforcement of learned material or for creating interest in an upcoming unit of study. Group size is four to six. A recorder (who does *not* participate in the brainstorming because he or she is too busy writing responses) is assigned by the teacher. Other roles might be timer, encourager, and leader.

Give a question or prompt. Everyone takes one turn to respond in order, beginning with the person to the left of the recorder. Continue going around the group in the time allowed (usually two to five minutes) or until students have run out of ideas. When finished, allow the recorder to contribute an answer or two to the team list.

At this point, ask one of the class recorders to write on paper, chalkboard, or transparency the responses from each group or team as recorders share answers one at a time (with no repetition). This sharing may also be completed orally with no class recorder.

Team members now sign the recording sheet before turning it in to the teacher. Circle of Knowledge papers are not graded because all answers are accepted during brainstorming. You might make a positive comment on the recording sheet as feedback to the team.

# Sample Cooperative Learning Activity: Team Learning

Many teachers are comfortable with team learning because the recording sheet is similar to the worksheets students traditionally complete individually after direct instruction, discussion, and practice. Group size is four to six. Roles, such as recorder, reader, timer, proofreader, leader, go-for, and encourager, are assigned, and *all* team members participate in the assignment.

A team learning recording sheet has four to six activities or questions to be completed. The team must reach consensus, and all members must have input before the recorder writes the response. This paper is graded, usually as class work. Grading criteria needs to be shared before work begins. For instance, the teacher might require not only that content be correct but also that answers be written in complete sentences with correct spelling, capitalization, and punctuation.

When the work is complete, all team members sign the sheet, signifying that they have read it, have made necessary corrections, and will accept the grade they receive.

# Sample Cooperative Learning Activity: Roundtable

The purpose of Roundtable is to review material, to brainstorm, or to practice a skill. In Roundtable, a group of four or five students is given a problem to solve, a question to answer, or an activity to complete. Each student is asked to consider the problem and record his or her response in writing. The key here is that the group is given only one sheet of paper and one pencil; each person must record his or her response on the sheet as it is moved to the left around the group. No one is allowed to skip or pass a turn. Of critical importance is the question or problem. It should be one that requires discussion and higher-order thinking.

The students then agree on the best answer; answers should get better as the discussion ensues. A final stage might be for the groups within a class to share their answers with the rest of the class.

(Kagan, 1992).

# ► Where do we go for more information?

Rottier, J., and Ogan, B. J. 1991. *Cooperative learning in middle-level schools*. Washington, D.C.: National Education Association.
Synthesizes current research and basic information for educators who want to implement cooperative learning techniques. Includes recommendations for teaching social skills, sample lesson plans in many disciplines, and staff development suggestions.

Fogarty, R. 1990. *Designs for cooperative interactions*. Palatine, IL: Skylight Publishing, Inc.
Includes twelve different strategies that work with students of all ages and abilities in many disciplines. Includes descriptions of each interactive model, suggestions for its use, and anecdotes relating to its application.

Johnson, D. W., and Johnson, R. T. 1989. *Leading the cooperative school*. Edina, MN: Interaction Book Company.
Based on twenty-five years of theory, research, and practical experience, this book focuses on how school leaders can get extraordinary things done in their schools. Includes practical suggestions for changing the organizational structure of the school to a team-based cooperative structure.

# References

Forte, I., and Schurr, S. 1992. *The cooperative learning guide & planning pak for middle grades, thematic projects & activities.* Nashville, TN: Incentive Publications, Inc.

Johnson, D. W., Johnson, R. T., and Holubec, E. J. 1991. *Circles of learning: Cooperation in the classroom.* rev. ed. Edina, MN: Interaction Book Company.

Kagan, S. 1992. *Cooperative learning.* San Juan Capistrano, CA: Resources for Teachers, Inc.

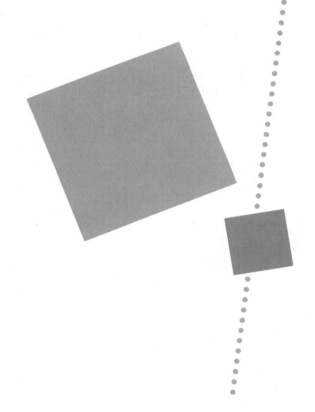

## ▶ What are they?

Learning stations are sometimes called "learning centers." According to Alexander and George (1993), a learning station is "an area for study and activity, in or near the classroom, that has been provided for the structured exploration of a particular subject, topic, skill, or interest. It is a place for using and storing materials that relate to a special interest or curriculum area."

Learning stations are powerful tools in culturally diverse classrooms because they can be used to address the academic and affective needs of students. Teachers use them to introduce or reinforce important concepts and skills and to help students become more self-directed and independent workers.

Effective learning stations have the following characteristics:

- They empower students because students are involved in their planning, implementation, and evaluation.
- They are self-directed and self-managed by students.
- They are designed to meet specific curriculum objectives.
- They offer a variety of instructional alternatives to meet diverse learning styles and ability levels.
- They are rich in resource materials.
- They allow for student choices and active involvement in decision making.
- They can require students to collaborate with others.
- They include at least one method for assessing student performance.

The purposes of learning stations are varied and can include one or more of the following options:

- **Interest stations** designed to capitalize on students' hobbies and personal interests
- **Exploratory stations** that allow students to learn more about contemporary issues, careers, or relevant hot topics
- **Skill development stations** that provide students with hands-on practice activities

- **Reinforcement and remediation stations** that provide for application of newly introduced or previously taught skills

- **Enrichment and extension stations** that offer students a variety of experiences to extend, enrich, and synthesize students' understanding of previously introduced material

A learning station offers a variety of options from which students might choose. The suggested activities below might be mixed and matched to the list of skills and resources in many ways.

| SKILLS | ACTIVITIES | RESOURCES |
|---|---|---|
| Vocabulary development | News stories | Audiotapes |
| Writing | Reports | Videotapes |
| Reading | Essays | Filmstrips |
| Listening | Diary entries | Records |
| Communicating | Journal entries | CDs |
| Problem solving | Letters | Laser discs |
| Researching | Poems | Computers |
| Classifying | Advertisements | CD-ROMs |
| Drawing conclusions | Editorials | Textbooks |
| Creating | Diagrams | Newspapers |
| Computing | Graphs | Magazines |
| Measuring | Pictures | Library books |
| Thinking | Scrapbooks | Pamphlets |
| Summarizing | Collages | Posters |
| Comparing/contrasting | Models | Pictures |
| Investigating | Displays | Maps |
| Preparing | Puzzles | Globes |
| Evaluating | Dioramas | Games |
| Demonstrating | Interviews | Puzzles |
| Record keeping | Games | Art supplies |
| Critiquing | Experiments | Flash cards |

# ▶ How are they different?

Learning stations are, by their physical setup, quite different from other areas, although they often include elements of other effective instructional strategies. The learning station format allows a teacher to mix and match elements of cooperative learning, games and simulations, creative and cognitive thinking skills, learning activity packets, interdisciplinary units, and technology.

- Extend learning stations beyond the classroom walls. Consider using the media center, an outside area, the hallway, the computer lab, another classroom, a multipurpose room, and the community.

- The library/media specialist can direct you to a variety of instructional media and print materials, including textbooks, library books, magazines, newspapers, vertical file pamphlets, pictures, clippings, CD-ROMs, computer programs, laser discs, videos, films, filmstrips, study prints, posters, professional books, and activity cards.

- Establishing an exploratory station can be a great way to seize the "teachable moment" of a presidential election, a space launch, or a front-page story that is not in the previously planned curriculum but should not be overlooked.

- Stations could be set up in one or more technologically linked classrooms to develop an interdisciplinary theme.

The use of learning stations can offer both the teacher and the students increased flexibility, variety, and choices. Learning stations follow specific guidelines: (1) objectives are clearly stated, (2) directions are simple and allow for self-direction, (3) activities are multi-leveled, (4) resources are varied and plentiful, and (5) record keeping and feedback systems are easily managed.

Learning stations can be organized around a theme or specific skill area, but activities can represent a wide range of abilities, learning styles, rates of learning, and student interests. Stations also allow for individualization and small-group instruction. Stations motivate students who might resist more traditional methods of instruction.

**In an interview, middle grade students and teachers responded to the question: "Do you like or dislike working at learning stations and why?" Their reasons for liking the stations included the following:**

### Students' answers

My grades have improved.

You can work at your own pace.

I can do more work because I do not have to wait for the rest of the class.

It is easier to get help when you need it.

The room is quieter. It is easier to concentrate.

Stations are more fun.

The room is more interesting.

I have more opportunities to express myself.

I can do extra stuff.

### Teachers' answers

The classroom is alive.

Students are more self-reliant.

Students are more focused on the task.

Grades are higher.

More gets accomplished; there's less time spent waiting.

The workload is less. There's more time to teach and to assess.

There's more time to work with individuals.

There's more student ownership in learning.

Students feel the classroom is a safer place. They are not as apt to be called on in front of the class.

Students feel freedom because of choice.

Students learn to research and ask questions.

# ► How do we get started?

The following steps suggested by Schurr (1989) represent a manageable outline for teachers to consider when setting up learning stations in the middle school classroom.

**Step 1:** Look around your classroom. What cubbyholes, counter-tops, cabinets, or shelves might you put to use? Cupboards or shelves placed flat against a wall might be turned perpendicular to the wall to create two divided learning station spaces and storage spaces for materials. House stations in cabinets with directions and activities on the insides of the cabinet doors. Use tabletops, desktops, counter-tops, and even the floor to make suitable work areas. Mount stations on bulletin boards, walls, easels, bookcases, file cabinets, boxes, aquariums, and doors. Hang them from a clothesline, a window shade, a screen, venetian blinds, a dead tree branch, or the ceiling. Use a shoe box, a basket, a manila folder, a bucket, a suitcase, or a shopping bag to hold the materials for a learning station.

**Step 2:** Decide how to set up your room. You might decide to set up your entire room with learning stations for a period of time, grouping the desks together near bulletin boards, cupboards, or book-shelves or adjacent to audiovisual or technology equipment. Or you might choose to leave your room arrangement as it is and use tables, counters, and floor space around the perimeter of your classroom. Another option would be to have portable stations that could easily be moved any place in the room.

**Step 3:** Determine the primary purpose and type of learning station to be developed. Is the purpose to introduce or teach a skill/concept, to reinforce or provide practice for a skill/concept, or to enrich or extend a skill/concept?

**Step 4:** Write a set of objectives that relate specifically to the skill/concept to be taught. What objectives of the regular classroom curriculum can be accomplished through the use of the station? How do the objectives relate to the abilities, interests, and instructional levels of the students?

**Step 5:** Choose the best possible location, setup, and design for the station. How much room will it take? What special equipment, furniture, or materials will it require?

**Step 6:** Obtain and organize the necessary furniture, materials, and equipment for the station. How will you arrange it in relation to other stations and/or classroom activities?

**Step 7:** Create a set of learning alternatives or strategies. What activity formats will you use? Are the strategies consistent with the objectives of the station? Are the strategies explained in such a way that the student knows what to do and how to do it? Do the strategies accommodate varying abilities, learning styles, and interests? Are the strategies written and displayed in such a way that they are easily accessible to students?

**Step 8:** Write a set of instructions for student use of the station. Who and when can students use the station? What can be done at the station, and what do students do with their finished products? How many students can be at the station at any given time?

**Step 9:** Determine a feasible management system. How many stations will operate at the same time? What organizational scheme can you devise for scheduling, handling, and evaluating students at the station? Does the system foster student self-discipline and self-management?

**Step 10:** Complete the physical setup of the station. How will you put all the pieces of the station together, including special directions, materials, equipment, resources, furniture, and displays?

**Step 11:** Orient all participating students, volunteers, parents, and support staff to the station. Do the students understand the objectives, procedures, and behavior standards for station activities? Is everyone informed about the expectations and guidelines for functioning in the station?

## Types of Learning Stations

According to Bee (1980), the various dimensions of learning stations may seem infinite, but they can be classified in one of two ways: maxi-stations and mini-stations. The choice of size will depend largely on the purpose of the station. The maxi-station is the larger of the two models and is normally semipermanent. A variety of learning activities are provided, covering several goals and objectives, and the maxi-station is designed so that several students can be active at one time. The mini-station is smaller and more portable. It is usually self-contained. Designed to be used by an individual student at his or her desk, this type of station can be incorporated into a maxi-station as one of its component parts.

Some examples of learning stations are described below.

- Bulletin boards covered with posters or pictures become interactive maxi-stations when students complete activities or investigation cards geared to what is on the bulletin board. A table or desks placed under the chalkboard would make a handy work space, as would the floor. This is a viable option for classrooms with limited space and furniture. Such a station could comfortably hold up to four students.

- Folding tabletop displays, such as those used for science fair projects, make great learning station formats. These display boards come in a variety of sizes for use with both maxi- and mini-stations. Covered with colorful contact paper, they create interest as they serve as a backdrop for various envelope pockets of activities and resources. Because they are so portable, these learning stations can easily be stored away for later use or shared with another teacher.

- A learning station in a file folder is compact and easy to store. Activity sheets or task cards can be attached to this mini-station, can rest on a chalkboard, or can stand on a bookshelf.

- Another easily stored mini-station is a "pocket packet." Designed around a central theme and stored in a 5" x 8" manila envelope, these task cards encourage student creativity and action. This format is portable for use at desks or as part of a maxi-station.

## Scheduling Students

Each type of learning station has its own scheduling options. For example, if the station is an interest station, not everyone should be required to work at it, and scheduling can be arranged to fit each student's availability. On the other hand, if the station is part of a major unit, all class members need to spend time there. Another factor that must be considered in the scheduling of learning stations is how many students the station can accommodate. As Bee (1980) points out, there are no cookbook recipes for scheduling classroom learning stations. Too many variables enter into the picture: time factors, the number of stations, the number of students each station can hold, and the difficulty and length of activities at each station. Start small and experiment. Some possible schedules include the following:

- All students are scheduled to attend each station on a specific rotation. The learning activities can be diverse, and students can have some choices, but the amount of time spent at a station is standard. The advantage of this schedule is that it is easily managed, with both teachers and students knowing where everyone belongs. The disadvantage is that time is not a variable, so that while some students will finish early, others will not have enough time. You can partially solve the time problem by varying the activities and providing numerous choices. Despite the problems, this schedule is often a comfortable one with which to begin. The rotation of such a schedule can be daily, every two or three days, or weekly.

- Another way to schedule learning stations is to have more stations than groups so that when a student has finished work at a given station he or she can go on to a station that is not being used. Using this format, the teacher might specify which activities all students are expected to complete by the end of a specific time period (one, two, three, or more weeks), and students could choose additional activities that they wish to explore. Not all students are expected to finish all stations in such a schedule. The flexibility of such a schedule, along with the opportunity to individualize student outcomes, makes this a very positive option, but it takes some experience to manage successfully.

- If the teacher is using the mini-station format, the schedule might be flexible and determined by when a student finishes some other assignment. On such days, the students may take their personal learning station and work under a tree in nice weather or find a comfortable spot somewhere in the room. Such mini-station formats also make nice partner activities. These formats are typically most appropriate for interest or enrichment stations.

- Another method for scheduling stations is to have students sign up for the stations based on their interests or learning needs.

## Record Keeping

It is also important to involve the students in record keeping and evaluation whenever possible. The purpose of the record keeping is more an accounting of who has used which station, what activities were accomplished, and which objectives and outcomes were met than the grading of each bit of completed work. Assessing students' progress as they move through the stations is more manageable than collecting everything at the end of all station work. This way students receive feedback as they go along, and they can make appropriate adjustments along the way.

Schurr (1994) describes several methods for keeping student records. Some are summarized below.

**Portfolios of Student Work:** Maintain a folder for each station or for each student. A checklist on the front of the folder reflects who has completed which stations or which tasks. Each folder stores samples of student work.

**Total Class Chart:** Keep or post at each station a chart showing the dates on which stations or tasks are completed.

**Observation Sheets:** Keep a simple observation checklist, which is divided into three columns. The first column lists students' names for each station. The second column lists dates of observations, and the third column contains notes on observed academic behavior of importance to the teacher.

**Student Performance Rating Scale:** Create an individual performance rating sheet for each student. The first column reflects the station performance standards such as: (1) makes good use of station time, (2) completes required assignments, (3) works well in groups or independently, (4) makes effective use of station materials, and (5) understands and follows directions. The second column provides a series of boxes with ratings such as excellent, good, fair, and needs improvement.

**Student Logs:** Students keep their own logs with daily entries reflecting the date, time, title of tasks completed, and personal comments on the quality of finished products.

**Individual File Boxes:** Use 3" x 5" or 5" x 8" file cards for each student to record student activity at learning stations. Label separate cards for each station or series of station tasks. Record student performance data such as the date, tasks completed, and grades.

**Library Pockets:** Post a series of library pockets in strategic spots to hold cards containing records of pupils and their activities.

**Daily Progress Reports:** Give each student a daily progress report to complete at the end of each learning station experience. Have the students include their name and date, the title of the station, the number of days the student is assigned to the station, the activities completed each day, the activities yet to be completed, and descriptions of personal reactions and comments or questions. (Schurr, 1994)

In summary, learning stations offer a manageable way for teachers to fulfill curricular demands and at the same time meet the social, physical, affective, and varied intellectual needs of their students.

## TIPS FOR TEACHERS

Don't color, cut, assemble, or paste learning station parts—let the students do it. They will get excited about completing the activities when the time comes. As an extra bonus, they will feel ownership and take better care of the materials in the stations.

Encourage other team teachers or colleagues to join in the creation of learning stations. By sharing, each person's workload is reduced and more ideas are generated.

A learning station rotation may look like this:

| Station # | Groups |
|-----------|--------|
| 1 | A B C D E F |
| 2 | B C D E F A |
| 3 | C D E F A B |
| 4 | D E F A B C |
| 5 | E F A B C D |
| 6 | F A B C D E |

# MORE TIPS FOR TEACHERS

Diane Ehlers, a teacher at Venice Middle School in Venice, Florida, varies the length of different stations to eliminate the burden of creating new stations all at one time. For example, in her sixth-grade language arts classroom the writing-workshop station is ongoing, while the skill introduction station changes each week.

If your students have access to computers and/or a video camera, you might want part of their station portfolio to be on disk or video-tape. You also could integrate all the technologies and have them keep a multimedia portfolio of their station work.

There are now computer programs that allow you to create your own bar codes (like on the packages at the supermarket). You can create an individual bar code for each student as well as bar codes describing observable behaviors such as "uses time wisely" or "works well with others." Using a light pen, the teacher can observe a student, read the student's bar code with the pen, and then read the behavior while facilitating the classroom. At the end of a class period, the observations can be down-loaded into the teacher's electronic grade book. There are even new handheld computers (for example, Macintosh Newton) that let you manage similar record keeping with just the touch of a stylus to the computer screen.

# LEARNING STATION CHECKLIST FOR TEACHERS

- Is the learning station attractive and inviting?
- Is it colorful and neatly arranged?
- Is it spacious and well defined?
- Are the printed words large and clear?
- Are the goals well displayed?
- Are the purposes and overviews of the activities evident?
- Are prerequisites clearly identified?
- Are the directions for completing the activities clear?
- Are there two to six objectives?
- Are the objectives specific and precise?
- Are there three to five activities for each objective?
- Are the activities varied for different ability levels and learning styles?

- Do the tasks represent a variety of instructional strategies such as reading, using audiovisual materials, using technology, writing, playing games, researching and writing reports, and working on cooperative group tasks.
- Are all the necessary resources available?
- Can the average student finish at least one activity in one class period?
- Are there enrichment activities that take students beyond the minimum requirements?
- Are activities challenging and fun?
- Are students receiving feedback on their progress while they work at the learning station?
- Are there any assessment choices?
- Does the assessment reflect the objectives of the learning station?

# ► Where do we go for more information?

Bee, C. P. 1980. *Secondary learning centers: An innovative approach to individualized instruction.* Santa Monica, CA: Goodyear.
Provides a step-by-step guide to implementing learning centers in the secondary classroom, including the types of learning centers, the components of learning centers, how to make learning centers, and how to schedule, keep records, and evaluate. The book has many examples of learning centers for all content areas.

Schurr, S. 1994. *Dynamite in the classroom: A how-to book for teachers.* Columbus, OH: National Middle School Association.
Focuses on instructional methods and activities that meet the needs of and are based on the characteristics of early adolescents. Provides an ample supply of tools and techniques.

Schwartz, S., and Pollishuke, M. 1991. *Creating the child-centered classroom.* Katonah, NY: Richard C. Owen.
The authors of this how-to book focus on the features of the child-centered classroom, whole language, and active learning. Their examples and recommended activities present the reader with a variety of practical, informative, and exciting ideas.

## References

Bee, C. P. 1980. *Secondary learning centers: An innovative approach to individualized instruction.* Santa Monica, CA: Goodyear.

George, P., and Lawrence, G. 1982. *Handbook for middle school teaching.* Glenview, IL: Scott, Foresman and Company.

Schurr, S. 1994. *Dynamite in the classroom: A how-to book for teachers.* Columbus, OH: National Middle School Association.

## Topic 7 · CREATIVE THINKING

# ▶ What is it?

Creative thinking is the act of imagining, visualizing, or conceptualizing something new and original. It requires an attitude, outlook, perspective, or view that breaks established rules or manipulates knowledge or experience in uncommon ways.

Today's world offers many challenges to the creative thinker, who is highly valued by top executives from the workplace and key leaders from educational institutions. The globalization of national economies, the competitive business environment, the pace of technological evolution, the movement to an information-based economy, and shifting demographics all require creative thinkers and problem solvers.

# ▶ How is it different?

Although creative and critical thinking skills overlap and complement one another, they have some distinct differences. Critical thinking is linear, convergent, and deductive, while creative thinking is spatial, divergent, and inductive. Critical thinking corresponds to left-brain thought patterns; creative thinking corresponds to right-brain thought patterns. Quality schooling in thinking skills must focus on both types.

# ▶ How do we get started?

There are several models to use in the teaching of creative thinking skills. Three of these structures are outlined here for you to review and experiment with in your classroom.

## COMMON TRAITS OF CREATIVE THINKERS

Open to new experiences

Willing to take risks

Playful with ideas

Flexible

Eager to experiment

Appreciative of humor

Curious

Self-confident

Often unconventional

Self-reliant

Highly tolerant of disorder and ambiguity

Motivated

Persistent

Courageous

Eager to explore complex issues or problems

# Williams's Taxonomy of Divergent Thinking and Feeling

**Step 1:** Become familiar with the eight levels of creative thinking described by Williams.

The Williams Model has been widely used in middle level classrooms to develop creativity in students. The first four behaviors are associated with the cognitive or intellectual domain, and the last four behaviors are associated with the affective or feeling domain. The eight levels of Williams's Taxonomy, four in each domain, are listed below along with selected behaviors.

## Cognitive Domain

**Fluency** enables the learner to generate a great many ideas, related answers, or choices in a given situation.

**Flexibility** lets the learner change everyday objects to fit a variety of categories by taking detours and varying size, shape, quantities, time limits, requirements, objectives, or dimensions in a given situation.

**Originality** causes the learner to seek new ideas by suggesting unusual twists to change content or come up with clever responses in a given situation.

**Elaboration** helps the learner to stretch by expanding, enlarging, enriching, or embellishing a list of possibilities that build on previous thoughts or ideas.

## Affective Domain

**Risk taking** enables the learner to deal with the unknown by taking chances, experimenting with new ideas, or trying new challenges in a given situation.

**Complexity** permits the learner to create structure in an unstructured setting or to bridge a logical order in a given situation.

**Curiosity** encourages the learner to follow a hunch, question alternatives, ponder outcomes, and wonder about options in a given situation.

**Imagination** allows the learner to visualize possibilities, build images in his or her mind, picture new objects, or reach beyond the limits of the practical.

# DISCUSSION TOPIC FOR TEAM MEMBERS

**DIRECTIONS:** Take a few minutes to complete individual responses to these questions. Discuss your responses at a team meeting to share personal perceptions of your own level of creativity.

- Are you more creative at home, work, or play? Give examples or reasons for your answer.

- What is the most creative activity or lesson you've done with students?

- Who is the most creative person you know? Why has he or she influenced you?

- How can you recognize creative students?

1. Is innovation highly valued by your team members?

2. Is innovation built into the overall mission of your team?

3. Is innovation implemented quickly into your lesson plans, activities, and events?

4. Do you hold team meetings to discuss creative opportunities as often as you do for discussing problems?

5. Are your assessment and evaluation systems on the team set up for judging qualitative as well as quantitative information on students and programs?

6. Do you celebrate innovation with ceremony on your team?

**Step 2:** Design a set of worksheets, task cards, or learning stations around Williams's Model similar to the one suggested here on superstars and superheroes.

**Fluency:** List as many of the world's important or famous superstars and superheroes as you can think of in three minutes.

**Flexibility:** Categorize your list of individuals in some way, adding others for variety and clarity when necessary to complete a comprehensive picture of the concept "superstar and superhero."

**Originality:** Invent a new superstar or superhero to fill a void or need that we have in our society. Describe the person's physical appearance, character traits, special talents or skills, accomplishments, and challenges.

**Elaboration:** Build on the idea that the word "hero" means different things to different people. It may also have several meanings for an individual.

**Risk taking:** What would you fear most about becoming a superstar or superhero in today's society? How would you overcome those fears?

**Complexity:** Suppose you were to establish a "Hall of Fame" for student heroes in your building. What criteria or guidelines would you use in the selection process, and whom would you choose as the first recipient?

**Curiosity:** If you could meet your favorite superstar or superhero in person, what would you want to ask of him or her?

**Imagination:** Visualize a world free of superstars and superheroes. What would it be like?

(Adapted from Williams, 1980)

## SCAMPER

SCAMPER is a mnemonic device, developed by Eberle, for different ways that students can expand and revitalize their thinking during brainstorming. Eberle's checklist is adapted from the work of Alex F. Osborn in his book *Applied Imagination*. The checklist is outlined on the next page and is followed by an example of how SCAMPER can be used in the classroom.

**Step 1:** Study the SCAMPER checklist on the following page to familiarize yourself with this device for improving an existing project or object.

## SCAMPER Checklist

**Substitute:** Have a thing or person act or serve in another's place.

**Combine:** Bring together or unite.

**Adapt:** Adjust to suit a condition or purpose.

**Modify:** Alter or change in form or quality.
  Magnify: Enlarge or make greater in quality or form.
  Minify: Make smaller, lighter, slower, less frequent.

**Put to other uses:** Use for purposes other than the one intended.

**Eliminate:** Remove, omit, or get rid of a quality, part, or whole.

**Rearrange:** Change order or adjust; create another layout or scheme.

Using SCAMPER as a systematic reminder of ways to generate new ideas or modify existing ones, a group of fifth graders generated the following list to design the "ultimate bathtub."

## Possible Objects for Scampering

**Kitchen tools:** can or bottle opener, spatula, whisk, egg beater, egg timer, oven thermometer, ladle, cheese slicer

**Hand tools:** screwdriver, wrench, hammer, pliers, tongs, measuring tape

**Household items:** toothbrush, comb, flashlight, umbrella, curling iron, Frisbee, stapler, cellophane tape dispenser, disposable razor, scissors, paper clip

---

**Substitute:** Instead of seats on the side, make the tub contoured to the body for maximum comfort.

**Combine:** Combine the rubberized soft material with a grooved surface on the bottom of the tub to prevent slipping and falling. Add a handrail to the sidewall.

**Adapt:** Create an entertainment center with TV, videocassette player, and special book holder and page turner for people who prefer to read in the bathtub. A robotic hand could turn the pages so they won't get wet.

**Modify:** Modify the sunlamp so that it is in the sides and bottom of the tub as well as overhead for an allover tan.

**Magnify:** Add movable partitions to the tub so it can be made larger.
**Minify:** Add partitions to make the tub smaller, depending upon the amount of time you have for your bath.

**Put to other uses:** Use the enlarged tub to practice aerobic exercises.

**Eliminate:** Eliminate spigots on the tub. Water could enter from jets in the sides of the tub.

**Rearrange:** Place a tub in the family room, where family members can relax together while they watch TV. Movable sidewalls will automatically enclose tub for privacy when desired.

(Carnow & Gibson, 1987)

**Step 2:** Divide the students into cooperative learning groups of three. Give each group a different object to study and improve. Kitchen tools, hand tools, or common household items work well for this exercise. Distribute copies of the reproducible page entitled "Using SCAMPER to Brainstorm Improvements" to guide their thinking.

**Step 3:** Design a series of "SCAMPER Innovation Awards" for groups who are successful with brainstorming patterns.

# Metaphorical Thinking

**Step 1:** Visualize the use of metaphors in literature, poetry, art, drama, advertising, and sales or marketing. They are forms of creative expression that force us to look at common things in uncommon ways. According to Thompson (1992), metaphors

- Enable you to go beyond the standard or ordinary definition of a concept, idea, or problem to see the bigger picture
- Focus your mind on interesting relationships of ideas, images, and symbols
- Make complex issues easier to understand
- Create tension (collisions of ideas) and fusion (an integration of ideas)
- Turn one idea into two or more

**Step 2:** Use Roger von Oech's (1983) metaphors about "The Meaning of Life" as springboards for creating metaphors for your own subject area.

## The Meaning of Life

Life is like a bagel. It's delicious when it's fresh and warm, but often it's just hard. The hole in the middle is its great mystery, and yet it wouldn't be a bagel without it.

Life is like eating grapefruit. First, you have to break through the skin; then it takes a couple of bites to get used to the taste; and, just as you begin to enjoy it, it squirts you in the eye.

Life is like a jigsaw puzzle—but you don't have the picture on the front of the box to tell you what it's supposed to look like. Sometimes, you're not even sure if you have all of the pieces.

Life is like riding an elevator. It has a lot of ups and downs, and someone is always pushing your buttons. Sometimes you get the shaft, but what really bothers you are the jerks.

Life is like a room full of open doors that close as you get older.

(Adapted from von Oech, 1983)

**What do you think life is like?**

Consider such starter statements as:

Middle school is . . .

Science is . . .

Solving mathematical equations is . . .

Reading a novel is . . .

Using a globe is . . .

Throwing a football is . . .

Cooking is . . .

Writing a report is . . .

Making friends is . . .

Taking a test is . . .

**Step 3:** Construct a metaphor bulletin board, compile a metaphor scrapbook, create a metaphor poster, or start a metaphor graffiti board for display or motivational purposes in your classroom. Encourage students to add their contributions throughout the school year.

# ▶ Where do we go for more information?

Bellanca, J., and Fogarty, R. 1986. *Catch them thinking: A handbook of classroom strategies*. Palatine, IL: Skylight Publishing, Inc.
Explains why teachers should teach thinking skills and shows how to make students more skillful thinkers. Contains easily adaptable strategies for novices; fifty strategies ready to "plug in" to classroom activities; complete lesson designs, adaptable to different subject areas; and interactive techniques to enhance lectures, activities, and textbook assignments.

## CREATIVE QUESTIONS TO PONDER

- Which is louder—joy or sorrow?

- Which has more flexibility—a circle or a square?

- Which has more intelligence—a question mark or an exclamation mark?

- Which is more playful— an electron or an atom?

- Which is more polluted— total agreement or agreement through compromise?

- Which is heavier to carry—a close friend or a worst enemy?

- Which has more bounce— a book or a tennis ball?

- Which is more fragile— someone's ego or someone's spirit?

Johnson, N. L. 1992. *Thinking is the key: Questioning makes the difference*. Beavercreek, OH: Pieces of Learning Division of Creative Learning Consultants, Inc.
Includes hundreds of divergent questions and activities to supplement the basic curriculum. Ideas and activities are designed to motivate reluctant learners as well as high achievers, especially focusing on global education, the environment, color, and visual and kinesthetic thinking. Includes an evaluation tool to assess the effectiveness of teacher questioning.

Michalko, M. 1991. *Thinkertoys: A handbook of business creativity for the '90s*. Berkeley, CA: Ten Speed Press.
Contains more than thirty meticulously outlined techniques to enhance creativity, written by a creativity consultant for businesses. Includes practical techniques that can be used by groups, including cutting-edge information on left-brain/right-brain thought and tips on how to overcome mental blocks to creativity.

von Oech, R. 1983. *A whack on the side of the head: How to unlock your mind for innovation*. New York: Warner Books.
A creatively packaged primer on how to be creative, written by a leading consultant on creativity in the business world, including tips on ten mental locks that prevent creativity and thirty-six tips on how to unlock them; why breaking the rules can be an avenue to innovation; how impractical ideas might be stepping stones to practical, creative ideas; where to hunt for ideas; how playing the fool may be an effective creative-thinking strategy; why play is the mother of invention; why the third right answer is usually more creative; how a little dose of ambiguity can stimulate your thinking; and why a "whack on the side of the head" can sometimes be the best thing to happen to you.

von Oech, R. 1988. *Creative whack pack*. Stamford, CT: U.S. Games Systems, Inc.
Provides a "creative thinking workshop in a box" of sixty-four strategies in the form of a deck of playing cards. Some highlight places to find new information. Some provide techniques to generate new ideas. Some lend decision-making advice. And some give you the "kick" you need to get your ideas into action.

# References

Carnow, G., and Gibson, C. 1987. *Prolific thinker's guide*. Palo Alto, CA: Dale Seymour Publications.

Thompson, C. 1992. *What a great idea: The key steps creative people take*. New York: Harper Collins Publishers-Harper Perennial.

von Oech, R. 1983. *A whack on the side of the head: How to unlock your mind for innovation*. New York: Warner Books.

von Oech, R. 1988. *Creative whack pack*. Stamford, CT: U.S. Games Systems, Inc.

Williams, F. 1980. *Creativity assessment packet*. East Aurora, NY: D.O.K. Publishers.

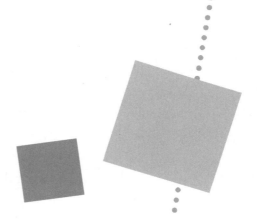

# Using SCAMPER to Brainstorm Improvements

## SCAMPER Checklist

**S**  **Substitute:**  Have a thing or person act or serve in another's place.

**C**  **Combine:**  Bring together or unite.

**A**  **Adapt:**  Adjust to suit a condition or purpose.

**M**  **Modify:**  Alter or change in form or quality.
**Magnify:**  Enlarge or make greater in quality or form.
**Minify:**  Make smaller, lighter, slower, less frequent.

**P**  **Put to other uses:**  Use for purposes other than the one intended.

**E**  **Eliminate:**  Remove, omit, or get rid of a quality, part, or whole.

**R**  **Rearrange:**  Change order or adjust; create another layout or scheme.

**Directions:**  Apply the SCAMPER model to brainstorm possible improvements to the object that the teacher has provided you and your small group for this project. Follow the guidelines given below. Write out your responses on a separate sheet of paper.

1. Briefly describe the object and its intended use.

2. Brainstorm some alternative uses for this object in its present form. Try to think of some unusual uses for it.

3. What could you do with the object that you can't do now if you . . .
   a. Made it 10 to 100 times larger?
   b. Made it 50 percent smaller?

4. What could you do with the object that you can't do now if you . . .
   a. Altered or eliminated one part of the object?
   b. Substituted something different for one part of the object?

5. What could you do with the object that you can't do now if you . . .
   a. Reversed any two or more parts of the object?
   b. Rearranged any two or more parts of the object?

6. What could you do with the object that you can't do now if you combined this object with another object or two?

7. Create a drawing, diagram, or description of an improved version of the original object using your best ideas from this exercise.

# Topic 8   CRITICAL THINKING

## ▶ What is it?

Critical thinking can be defined as a complex, reflective process that includes analysis of arguments, consideration of different points of view, understanding of relationships, and solving of problems.

One aspect of critical thinking, according to many experts, is metacognition, or the ability to think about one's thinking and to exhibit an introspective problem-solving ability as a conscious process. "Good problem solvers plan a course of action before they begin a task, monitor themselves while executing that plan, back up or adjust the plan consciously, and evaluate themselves upon completion" (Costa, 1985).

Another aspect of critical thinking to consider is the Socratic inquiry method, which probes the meaning, justification, or logical strength of a claim, position, or line of reasoning. "This . . . is based on the idea that all thinking has a logic or structure. . . . Its purpose is to expose the logic of someone's thought" (Paul et al., 1989).

## ▶ How is it different?

The didactic approach to learning can be fragmented and authoritarian. Teachers tend to lecture and drill; students tend to memorize, engage in repetitive practice, take notes, and repeat back the information learned. There is very little integration of subject matter, student interaction, or invited response. And, usually, there is little long-term retention of the material presented.

The critical thinking approach to instruction, however, produces quite different results. Students are actively involved in both the planning and implementing of integrated units. They are invited to share their opinions; justify their arguments; solve their problems; and apply, analyze, and synthesize the information that has been presented. This subsequently becomes more of a student-centered approach than a subject-centered approach to learning.

### TIPS FOR TEACHERS

**KEY POINTS OF SOCRATIC QUESTIONING**

- **Raises basic issues**

- **Probes beneath the surface of things**

- **Pursues problematic areas of thought**

- **Helps students discover the *structure* of their own thought**

- **Helps students develop sensitivity to clarity, accuracy, and relevance**

- **Helps students note claims, evidence, conclusions, questions-at-issue, assumptions, implications, consequences, concepts, interpretations, points of view**

> "*In this information era, schools must focus now on a fourth 'R'— how to reason.*"
> Lynne Young (1992, p. 109)

Another dimension of higher-order thinking is creative thinking, often defined as an intuitive, imaginative process that includes flexibility, fluency, originality, and elaboration. (Critical thinking relates more to logical and rational processes.) According to Young (1992), critical and creative thinking are complementary and considered comprehensive thinking skills. Both should be taught.

# ▶ How do we get started?

## Bloom's Taxonomy of Educational Objectives

One practical and manageable tool that you can immediately use in the classroom is Bloom's Taxonomy of Educational Objectives, a hierarchy of six levels of thinking skills and corresponding sets of student behaviors or action verbs. To use Bloom's taxonomy as a model for infusing thinking skills, use the following steps (Bloom, 1984).

**Step 1:** Make a conscious decision to emphasize higher-order thinking skills in your classroom, and include them in your daily lesson plans.

**Step 2:** Become familiar and comfortable with Bloom's taxonomy and the alternative delivery systems appropriate to each level.

**Step 3:** Introduce Bloom's taxonomy to your students. Explain its organization, purpose, and potential use in the classroom. Construct a Bloom poster for the bulletin board as a reference, reminder, and study aid for students.

**Step 4:** Create a series of worksheets, task cards, or learning stations on a common or well-known topic. The tasks should require students to complete one activity at each level of the taxonomy.

**Step 5:** Select a unit of study from the past that wasn't as successful as it could have been. Decide how you might use Bloom's taxonomy to restructure the assigned questions, tasks, minilectures, or quizzes.

**Step 6:** Use higher-order questioning strategies within every unit of study, and be sure to allow adequate wait-and-think time before calling on a specific student to answer.

**Step 7:** Be sure to allow students opportunities to evaluate the entire process of using higher-order thinking skills in your classroom through the use of learning logs, metacognitive journals, or personal diaries.

## BLOOM'S TAXONOMY OF EDUCATIONAL OBJECTIVES

1. *Knowledge:* Learning the information

2. *Comprehension:* Understanding the information

3. *Application:* Using the information

4. *Analysis:* Examining specific parts of the information

5. *Synthesis:* Doing something different with the information

6. *Evaluation:* Judging the information

(Bloom, 1984)

**DIRECTIONS:** Select one or more tasks from each level of Bloom's taxonomy below to create a unit on a topic of your choice.

## KNOWLEDGE

- Write 5–10 questions to answer about this topic.
- Identify at least ten key terms related to this topic. Define each.
- Record three to five specific sources/references to help you find information about this topic.
- Read the chapter(s) or assigned materials about this topic.

## COMPREHENSION

- Explain two key concepts about this topic in a one-page paper.
- Outline the information you have read and studied.
- Illustrate at least five important pieces of information about this topic.
- Suggest at least ten different ways you might share information about this topic.

## APPLICATION

- Develop a time line of important events that relate directly to this topic.
- Demonstrate your understanding of the topic by either presenting an oral report (two minutes) or creating a poster on the topic.
- Conduct an investigation or experiment on one important aspect or key idea related to your topic.
- Interview an expert on the topic. Construct at least ten interview questions in advance. Record the responses.

## ANALYSIS

- Classify the information you have learned about the topic in three different ways. Explain your classifications.
- Compare and contrast one aspect of the topic with another. How are they alike? How are they different?
- Diagram a flowchart to show the key ideas related to the topic.
- Examine your topic from three other points of view: a parent, a computer technician, and a media specialist.

## SYNTHESIS

- Generate a list of at least five predictions related to the topic.
- Compose a story or poem about the topic.
- Design a study guide on the topic for use by students younger than you.

## EVALUATION

- If you were to give an award to someone who has made a major contribution to the topic, who would you choose and why?
- Choose the ten most important facts you learned about the topic. Rank them from most interesting to least, giving reasons for your first and last choices.
- Consider one resource you used to find out more information about the topic, and give at least three recommendations for improving it.
- Decide which level of activities in this unit was most enjoyable and educational for you. Explain your answer.

## TIPS FOR TEACHERS

Copy the Chart of Bloom's Taxonomic Levels and Corresponding Verbs found at the end of this section. Put it in your lesson plan book for easy access.

Use the chart to

- **Prepare for classroom discussions**
- **Design lesson plans**
- **Create project assignments**
- **Plan learning stations**
- **Develop quizzes and tests**
- **Make homework assignments**

KNOWLEDGE

- Identify at least four characters from the novel.

COMPREHENSION

- Explain why Buck was stolen.

APPLICATION

- Compute the actual number of miles Buck traveled in the course of his journey.

ANALYSIS

- Determine the main events in the following plot outline:
  Introduction
  Rising Action
  Climax
  Falling Action
  Resolution

SYNTHESIS

- Design an original book cover for this novel. Include front and back cover and end sheets.
- Rewrite the final chapter.

EVALUATION

- Consider Buck's transformation from civilized pet to wolf that answers the "call of the wild." What characteristics were most important during this change? Why?

## SAMPLE STUDENT ACTIVITIES TO ACCOMPANY A UNIT ON THE PERIODIC TABLE

KNOWLEDGE

- List the elements of the periodic table.

COMPREHENSION

- Explain how the periodic table can be of great use to scientists, environmentalists, or archaeologists.

APPLICATION

- Demonstrate how you might use the periodic table in a science project, a science fair, or a science lab.

ANALYSIS

- Compare and contrast any two elements of the periodic table. Do this in graph or chart form.

SYNTHESIS

- Devise a simple lesson plan to teach a friend something about the periodic table. Your lesson plan should specify the objectives, time required, materials needed, procedures, and follow-up activities.

- Follow your lesson plan to educate your friend.

EVALUATION

- Judge the quality of your lesson plan by answering the following questions:

  - Were my objectives relevant and realistic in terms of intent and number?

  - Was I enthusiastic in my delivery?

  - Was I well prepared and well organized?

  - Did my friend understand what he or she was doing, and why he or she was doing it?

  - Were my directions clear and to the point?

  - Did I enjoy working with my friend during this lesson?

  - Would I do anything differently next time I used this lesson plan?

# de Bono's Colored Thinking Hats

Another critical thinking tool is the Six Thinking Hats model created by Edward de Bono, a pioneer in the field of thinking skills. "Thinking is the ultimate human resource . . . our most important skill" (de Bono, 1985). The concept of the six thinking hats is convenient and simple; it allows us to pay attention to one thing at a time by deliberately wearing a different color hat as we assume a thinking role.

Each of the six hats is a different color: white, red, black, yellow, green, and blue. Each represents a different attitude or viewpoint and becomes the "thinking hat" we put on to explore solutions and negotiate issues. Wearing the hat enables us to say things we might not say otherwise, to look at the issues from a different perspective, and to switch roles when necessary.

According to de Bono (1985), "the color of each hat is also related to its function."

**White** is neutral and objective. The white hat is concerned with objective facts and figures.

**Red** suggests anger (seeing red), rage, and emotions. The red hat gives the emotional view.

**Black** is gloomy and negative. The black hat covers the negative aspects—why it cannot be done.

**Yellow** is sunny and positive. The yellow hat is optimistic and covers hope and positive thinking.

**Blue** is cool, and it is also the color of the sky, which is above everything else. The blue hat is concerned with control and the organization of the thinking process. It is also concerned with the collaborative use and integration of the other hats.

**Green** is stretching and exploring new ideas. The green hat encourages creativity and risk taking.

When implementing the de Bono model, refer to the hats only by color and not their function. "Please take off the red hat for a moment and put on the white hat" is more acceptable than asking someone to stop being so emotional.

Using the colored hats as thinking tools will allow students to focus on their thinking in a variety of models, situations, and problem-solving settings.

To apply the six thinking hats in your classroom, follow these steps.

**Step 1:** Become familiar and comfortable with each of the hats and its function. Try using this model to address issues at your team-planning sessions for personal practice and application.

**Step 2:** Introduce the hat concept to your students. It would be wise to have six hats (each a different color or each one decorated with a different color). Explain and demonstrate the colored hat process by putting a problem or controversial topic, such as "School Dress Code" or "School Cafeteria Behavior," on the chalkboard. Then, actually put on each hat and demonstrate what the person who wears that hat might say about the situation under discussion.

**Step 3:** Conduct a cooperative learning activity similar to the one suggested here to give your students practice wearing de Bono's thinking hats in a hypothetical situation.

### Directions

- Divide your class into six small groups, and assign each group a different colored hat to wear. Assign roles and have group members spend a few minutes discussing the issues related to the fictitious problem: "What if no television broadcasting were available in your community for one month—no national channels, no cable, no rental videos, no video games, and no school/local broadcasts. What would happen and what would you do?"

- Give groups approximately five minutes to discuss the problem from the vantage point of their colored hat. Then, have each group briefly report on their discussion while the rest of the class determines whether or not that group followed the "type of thinking" associated with the assigned colored hat.

- Repeat this activity, switching colors each time so that each group has some experience with all six hats represented. Be sure to follow each small group session with a discussion about how each group fulfilled its role.

- When all groups have viewed the problem situation through all six hats, encourage students to write or talk about these questions with one another.

  – Which hat(s) do you think you wear most of the time? Why?

  – Which hat(s) is (are) most uncomfortable for you to wear? Why?

  – Why is it important to wear different colored hats during certain kinds of problem-solving situations?

**TIPS FOR TEACHERS**

Provide picture samples of different types of hats—straw hat, baseball hat, beanie, cowboy hat, beret, derby, top hat, helmet, etc. Have students select their favorite hat style. Reproduce six of each choice (on card stock) for students to cut out and color with all six colors.

Then as daily or weekly assignments are made, students pick the colored hat they want to wear as they focus on the specific thinking role they are to act out.

# ► Where do we go for more information?

Bellanca, J., and Fogarty, R. 1986. *Catch them thinking: A handbook of classroom strategies*. Palatine, IL: Skylight Publishing, Inc.
Includes strategies, lesson designs, and interactive techniques for teaching thinking.

Bloom, B. S., ed. 1984. *Taxonomy of educational objectives. Handbook 1: Cognitive domain*. New York: Longman.
This classic work fully explains all of the Bloom levels in the Cognitive Domain: Knowledge, Comprehension, Application, Analysis, Synthesis, and Evaluation. Bloom explains why he developed his taxonomy, what principles guided his thinking, and how the taxonomy can and should be used.

de Bono, E. 1985. *Six thinking hats*. Boston: Little, Brown and Company.
Divides thinking into six modes, which de Bono associates with six colored "thinking hats." Each hat represents a different style or mode of thinking. The colored hats make it easy and fun to teach students about their own thinking processes.

Paul, R. 1992. *Critical thinking: What every person needs to survive in a rapidly changing world*. Rohnert Park, CA: Center for Critical Thinking and Moral Critique.
Presents a program for better achieving our educational goals through critical thinking, including suggested classroom techniques and applications. This comprehensive guidebook also provides research, statistics, arguments, studies, teachers' views, a glossary, and recommended readings on the topic.

Schurr, S. 1994. *Dynamite in the classroom: A how-to book for teachers*. Columbus, OH: National Middle School Association.
Focuses on instructional methods and activities that meet the needs of and are based on the characteristics of early adolescents. This handbook provides an ample supply of thinking tools and techniques.

# References

Bloom, B. S., ed. 1984. *Taxonomy of educational objectives. Handbook 1: Cognitive domain.* New York: Longman.

Costa, A. L., ed. 1985. Teaching for, of, and about thinking. In *Developing minds: A resource book for teaching thinking.* Association for Supervision and Curriculum Development.

de Bono, E. 1985. *Six thinking hats.* Boston: Little, Brown and Company.

Paul, R. et al. 1989. *Critical thinking handbook: 6th–9th grades.* Rohnert Park, CA: Center for Critical Thinking and Moral Critique.

Schurr, S. 1994. *Dynamite in the classroom: A how-to book for teachers.* Columbus, OH: National Middle School Association.

Young, L. E. 1992. Critical thinking skills: Definitions, implications for implementation. *NASSP Bulletin*, December.

# Bloom's Taxonomic Levels and Corresponding Verbs

**KNOWLEDGE:** Knowledge is the remembering of previously learned material. This may involve the recall of a wide range of material, from specific facts to complete theories, but all that is required is the bringing to mind of the appropriate information. Knowledge represents the lowest level of learning outcomes in the cognitive domain.

## Related Action Verbs

| | | | | |
|---|---|---|---|---|
| Acquire | Follow | Locate | Quote | Reproduce |
| Choose |    directions | Match | Read | Select |
| Count | Group | Memorize | Recall | State |
| Define | Identify | Name | Recite | Tabulate |
| Distinguish | Indicate | Outline | Recognize | Trace |
| Draw | Know | Pick | Record | Underline |
| Fill in | Label | Point | Repeat | Write |
| Find | List | | | |

**COMPREHENSION:** Comprehension is the ability to grasp the meaning of material. This may be shown by translating material from one form to another (words to numbers), by interpreting material (explaining or summarizing), and by estimating future trends (predicting consequences or effects). These learning outcomes go one step beyond the simple remembering of material and represent the lowest level of understanding.

## Related Action Verbs

| | | | | |
|---|---|---|---|---|
| Account for | Differentiate | Generalize | Predict | Rewrite |
| Associate | Distinguish | Give examples | Prepare | Show |
| Change | Draw | Give in own | Put in order | Simplify |
| Classify | Estimate |    words | Read | Suggest |
| Compare | Expand | Group | Rearrange | Summarize |
| Conclude | Explain | Illustrate | Recognize | Trace (on map |
| Contrast | Express in | Infer | Reorder |    or chart) |
| Convert |    other terms | Interpolate | Reorganize | Transform |
| Define | Extend | Interpret | Represent | Translate |
| Demonstrate | Extrapolate | Measure | Restate | |
| Describe | Fill in | Outline | Retell | |
| Determine | Find | Paraphrase | Reword | |

**APPLICATION:** Application refers to the ability to use learned material in new and concrete situations. This may include the application of such things as rules, methods, concepts, principles, laws, and theories. Learning outcomes in this area requires a higher level of understanding than those under comprehension.

### Related Action Verbs

| | | | | |
|---|---|---|---|---|
| Apply | Differentiate | Generalize | Participate | Relate |
| Calculate | between | Graph | Perform (except | Restructure |
| Choose | Discover | Illustrate | in math or in | Select |
| Classify | Discuss | Interpret | public) | Show |
| Collect informa- | Distinguish | Interview | Plan | Solve |
| tion | between | Investigate | Practice | Track (in |
| Complete | Employ | Keep records | Predict | development, |
| Compute | Estimate | Locate | Prepare | history, |
| Construct | Examine | information | Present | process) |
| Convert (in | Expand | Make | Produce | Transfer |
| math) | Experiment | Manipulate | Prove (in math) | Translate |
| Demonstrate | Express in a | Model | Put into action | Use |
| Determine | discussion | Modify | Put together | Utilize |
| (calculate) | Find (implies | Operate | Put to use | |
| Develop | investigation) | Organize | Record | |

**ANALYSIS:** Analysis refers to the ability to break down material into its component parts so that its organizational structure may be understood. This may be relationships between parts and recognition of the organizational principles involved. Learning outcomes here represent a higher intellectual level than comprehension and application because they require an understanding of the content and the structural form of the material.

### Related Action Verbs

| | | | | |
|---|---|---|---|---|
| Analyze | Determine | Form general- | Outline | Sort |
| Break down | Diagram | izations | Point out | Subdivide |
| Categorize | Differentiate | Formulate | Put into | Survey |
| Classify | Discover | Group | categories | Take apart |
| Compare | Discriminate | Identify | Recognize | Transform |
| Contrast | Distinguish | Illustrate | Relate | Uncover |
| Criticize | Divide | Infer | Search | |
| Debate | Draw | Inspect | Select | |
| Deduce | conclusions | Make inferences | Separate | |
| Detect | Examine | Order | Simplify | |

**SYNTHESIS:** Synthesis refers to the ability to put parts together to form a new whole. This may involve the production of a unique communication (theme or speech), a plan of operations (research proposal), or a set of abstract relations (scheme for classifying information). Learning outcomes in this area stress creative behaviors, with major emphasis on the formulation of new patterns or structures.

## Related Action Verbs

| | | | | |
|---|---|---|---|---|
| Arrange | Derive | Integrate | Prescribe | Revise |
| Blend | Design | Invent | Present (an | Rewrite |
| Build | Devise | Make up | original | Specify |
| Categorize | Develop | Modify | report or | Summarize |
| Combine | Document | Organize | work) | Suppose |
| Compile | Explain | Originate | Produce | Synthesize |
| Compose | Form | Perform | Propose | Tell |
| Constitute | Formulate | (in public) | Rearrange | Transmit |
| Construct | Generalize | Plan | Reconstruct | Write |
| Create | Generate | Predict | Relate | |
| Deduce | Imagine | Prepare | Reorganize | |

**EVALUATION:** Evaluation is concerned with the ability to judge the value of material (statement, novel, poem, research report) for a given purpose. The judgments are to be based on definite criteria. These may be internal criteria (organization) or external criteria (relevance to the purpose), and the student may determine the criteria given them. Learning outcomes in this area are highest in the cognitive hierarchy because they contain elements of all of the other categories and conscious value judgments based on clearly defined criteria.

## Related Action Verbs

| | | | | |
|---|---|---|---|---|
| Appraise | Consider | Determine | Justify | Standardize |
| Argue | Contrast | Discriminate | Measure | Summarize |
| Assess | Criticize | Distinguish | Rank | Support |
| Award | Critique | Evaluate | Rate | Test |
| Choose | Decide | Grade | Recommend | Validate |
| Compare | Defend | Interpret | Relate | Verify |
| Conclude | Describe | Judge | Select | |

(Schurr, 1994)

# De Bono's Thinking Hats

Dr. Edward de Bono (1985) separates thinking into six distinct modes, identified with six colored "thinking hats." White-hat thinkers concentrate on facts, figures, and objective information. Red-hat thinkers deal with emotions and feelings. Black-hat thinkers emphasize logical negative thoughts. Yellow-hat thinkers look for positive, constructive thoughts. Green-hat thinkers search out the creative and new ideas, and blue-hat thinkers control the other hats and thinking steps. Summaries of the behaviors associated with each "color hat" are described below.

**Red-hat thinking** focuses on emotions, hunches, intuitions, feelings, and impressions. Wearing the red hat allows the thinker to say, "This is how I feel about the matter." The red hat allows a thinker to explore the feelings of others by asking for a "red-hat view." When a thinker is using the red hat, there should never be any attempt to justify the feelings or to provide a logical basis for them.

**Black-hat thinking** focuses on negative issues, logical consequences, truthful criticisms, and the role of devil's advocate. Black-hat thinking is specifically concerned with negative assessment. The black-hat thinker points out what is wrong. The black-hat thinker points out how something does not fit experience or knowledge. The black-hat thinker points out why something will not work. The black-hat thinker points out risks and dangers as well as faults in design.

**Yellow-hat thinking** focuses on positive and constructive features, optimistic outcomes, strengths, and bright possibilities. Yellow-hat thinking is concerned with positive assessment. Yellow-hat thinking probes and explores for value and benefit. Yellow-hat thinking then strives to find logical support for this value and benefit. Yellow-hat thinking is constructive and generative. Concrete proposals and suggestions come from yellow-hat thinking.

**Green-hat thinking** focuses on creative and new ideas, fertile thoughts, forward movement, and step-by-step innovations. The green hat is for creative thinking. The search for alternatives is a fundamental aspect of green-hat thinking. There is a need to go beyond the known, the obvious, and the satisfactory. The thinker seeks to move forward from an idea to reach a new idea.

**White-hat thinking** focuses on neutral facts, figures, information, and objectives. White-hat thinking is a discipline and a direction. The thinker strives to be more neutral and more objective in the presentation of information. The thinker does not offer interpretations or opinions. When wearing the white thinking hat, the thinker should imitate a computer.

**Blue-hat thinking** focuses on control, problem definition, questioning, and orchestrating. The blue hat is the "control" hat. The blue-hat thinker sets the focus, defines the problems and shapes the questions. Blue-hat thinking is responsible for summaries, overviews, and conclusions. The blue-hat thinker is like the conductor of the orchestra; the blue-hat thinker calls for the use of the other hats.

# Put on Your Thinking Hat

**Put on your red hat** to describe your feelings in the following situations:

- Your family just won the weekly state lottery.
- You found a wallet with $100 (and owner information) inside.
- Your best friend is going to a party, but you weren't invited.
- You tried out for the _____ and won or lost.

**Put on your white hat** as you share at least two facts about the following:

- your state
- parts of speech
- popular music
- newspapers

**Put on your green hat** to suggest a creative, alternative use for the following everyday items:

- a pencil with an eraser
- a textbook
- a toothbrush or dental floss
- a remote control device

**Wear your blue hat** to determine what you will do *next* in each of the following situations:

- You are halfway between your home and your destination when your bicycle has a flat tire.
- You have been given permission to have a birthday party.
- You have finished dinner; you have two major tests tomorrow.
- Your name is announced on the public address system, and you are supposed to report to the principal's office immediately.

**Use your black hat** to point out the difficulties in each of the following situations:

- The school year will be lengthened to a six-day week from mid-August through the end of July.
- No school lunch program will be offered.
- Movies and recordings will not be rated.

**Put on your yellow hat** to find some good points about each of the following situations:

- Your family won a one-year membership to the local YMCA.
- Instead of attending summer school, you will be working full-time for a lawn maintenance company.
- You must show your report card to the ticket seller at the theater before you can purchase your student-discounted ticket.
- You may watch television only one hour per day.

## ▶ What are they?

Investigation task cards describe hands-on activities for students to perform at each level of Bloom's taxonomy. Each set of cards focuses a student's attention on a common learning tool, such as a meterstick, microscope, dictionary, or globe, and then requires the student to investigate that object in some unusual ways.

Each set of investigation cards contains a minimum of eighteen activities—three at each level of Bloom's taxonomy. Students examine the designated tool by completing one or more of the activities for each level of the taxonomy. The teacher might suggest that students pick one card to do at each level or assign activities at any level. The student works independently with the cards and requires little outside help from the teacher or additional resources.

A simple self-assessment should accompany the investigation task cards so students can reflect on their work and analyze the results. Each card contains only one activity, simply stated, around a single taxonomic level. The student relies on his or her own background knowledge and ability to observe and discover interesting things about the object when working on the designated tasks.

Investigation task cards can be excellent instructional tools for learning stations, for homework tasks, for independent study, for cooperative learning groups, or for remediation or enrichment assignments. Investigation task cards could be designed around other learning hierarchies or models such as Williams's taxonomy or SCAMPER.

## ▶ How are they different?

Investigation task cards differ from most activity or task cards in that

- They are organized around a structure, such as Bloom's taxonomy, to promote creative and critical thinking skills
- They serve as a springboard to engage students in a series of discovery tasks rather than to teach a skill directly

### POSSIBLE TOPICS FOR INVESTIGATION TASK CARDS

*Science:* magnet, microscope, battery, rock collection, prism, gyroscope, insect specimen, shell, pulley, fossil, thermometer

*Social Studies:* globe, compass, newspaper, stamp collection, foreign money, cultural artifact, store directory, warranty, job application, menu

*Math:* meterstick, tangrams, compass, protractor, calculator, Cuisenaire rods, parquetry blocks, geometric models, templates

*Language Arts:* thesaurus, dictionary, poster, limerick, business letter, junk mail, card catalog

*Other:* piece of sculpture, audiocassette, Frisbee, jump rope, musical instrument, measuring tape, kitchen utensil, carpentry tool, sewing machine

- They require little teacher direction or access to other information resources
- They offer metacognitive opportunities for students

# ▶ How do we get started?

**Step 1:** Brainstorm a list of potential items, objects, tools, or topics that lend themselves to the investigation task card concept. Remember that investigations should encourage students to

- Work independently or with minimal teacher assistance
- Observe and explore a wide variety of concepts related to a given stimulus
- Discover information through the use of the five senses and such process skills as classifying, inferring, predicting, and experimenting
- Apply creative thinking across the disciplines

**Step 2:** Select one or more items, objects, tools, or topics from each of the basic skill areas for your investigation task cards.

**Step 3:** Collect information and resources associated with each object or topic, including textbooks, library books, encyclopedias, brochures, periodicals, and curriculum guides. Use these to identify major concepts, vocabulary, background information, or data related to the theme of the investigation task card.

**Step 4:** Write three questions, tasks, or activities for each of Bloom's taxonomic levels.

**Step 5:** Type or print each task on a different file card. Label each task with the appropriate taxonomic level.

**Step 6:** Make copies of the reproducible page entitled "Student Self-Assessment for Investigation Task Cards" for each student to use with the cards.

**Step 7:** Display selected objects and their accompanying investigation task cards for students to review and use. Cards may be illustrated and laminated for extra appeal and endurance.

(Adapted from Schurr, 1994)

# ▶ Where do we go for more information?

Schurr, S. 1994. *Dynamite in the classroom: A how-to book for teachers.* Columbus, OH: National Middle School Association.
Focuses on instructional methods and activities that meet the needs of and are based on the characteristics of early adolescents. The author provides an ample supply of tools and techniques in this popular handbook for teachers.

## References

Schurr, S. 1994. *Dynamite in the classroom: A how-to book for teachers.* Columbus, OH: National Middle School Association.

# Let's Investigate a Favorite Novel

**Knowledge-Level Tasks**

1. Identify the main characters of the novel.

2. Reproduce a map showing the setting of the novel.

3. List the key events that develop the plot of the novel.

**Comprehension-Level Tasks**

1. Describe your favorite character in detail.

2. Give examples of passages that summarize important elements to the setting.

3. Illustrate the climax in the story's plot.

**Application-Level Tasks**

1. Prepare a set of interview questions you might want to ask the antagonist or the protagonist.

2. Construct a diorama to depict some aspect of the setting.

3. Perform an important scene from the actions that take place.

**Analysis-Level Tasks**

1. Diagram the relationship of the characters to one another.

2. Make inferences about how things would be different if the novel took place in a different time period, geographic locale, or culture.

3. Compare and contrast any two scenes critical to the evolution of the plot.

**Synthesis-Level Tasks**

1. Create a series of name poems for the important people in the book.

2. Design an informative book jacket that indicates the time, place, and events of the book.

3. Compose a series of original greeting cards to celebrate key happenings or experiences in the book.

**Evaluation-Level Tasks**

1. Decide on criteria for judging the success of a novel, and use these to judge the quality of this one.

2. Assign a series of letter grades on an original report card you develop for the main character(s) in this story, and validate your choices.

3. Defend or negate the following statement: "This novel should be on the school's required reading list for students."

# Student Self-Assessment for Investigation Task Cards

**Title of investigation task cards:** _____

**Date work on investigation task cards began:** _____

**Date investigation task cards finished:** _____

**Directions:** When you complete each of the assigned investigation task cards, evaluate your results by circling the number that best describes your work. When you have completed the investigation task cards for a level, add up the total number of points circled and write the sum in the large triangle.

**Evaluation Key:**

**5** = Outstanding  **4** = Excellent  **3** = Good  **2** = Fair  **1** = Poor

### Knowledge Level

| | |
|---|---|
| Activity One | **1 2 3 4 5** |
| Activity Two | **1 2 3 4 5** |
| Activity Three | **1 2 3 4 5** |

Total points for knowledge-level activities:

### Application Level

| | |
|---|---|
| Activity One | **1 2 3 4 5** |
| Activity Two | **1 2 3 4 5** |
| Activity Three | **1 2 3 4 5** |

Total points for application-level activities:

### Comprehension Level

| | |
|---|---|
| Activity One | **1 2 3 4 5** |
| Activity Two | **1 2 3 4 5** |
| Activity Three | **1 2 3 4 5** |

Total points for comprehension-level activities:

### Analysis Level

| | |
|---|---|
| Activity One | **1 2 3 4 5** |
| Activity Two | **1 2 3 4 5** |
| Activity Three | **1 2 3 4 5** |

Total points for analysis-level activities:

## Synthesis Level

| | |
|---|---|
| Activity One | **1 2 3 4 5** |
| Activity Two | **1 2 3 4 5** |
| Activity Three | **1 2 3 4 5** |

**Total points for synthesis-level
activities:**

## Evaluation Level

| | |
|---|---|
| Activity One | **1 2 3 4 5** |
| Activity Two | **1 2 3 4 5** |
| Activity Three | **1 2 3 4 5** |

**Total points for evaluation-level
activities:**

## Performance Summary

**Directions:** Review your record-keeping sheet and complete each
of the self-evaluation statements that follow.

1. I received the most points in the level labeled _____.

2. I received the fewest points in the level labeled _____.

3. I enjoyed the activities least in the level labeled _____.

4. I enjoyed the activities most in the level labeled _____.

5. From this set of investigation task cards, I learned that _____.

6. I found this set of investigation task cards to be _____.

7. I think it would be interesting to do a set of investigation
   task cards on the following topics or objects: _____.

*(Schurr, 1994)*

# ▶ What are they?

Howard Gardner's Theory of Multiple Intelligences has made a significant contribution to the area of curriculum and instruction because it supports the idea that each middle level student has a unique set of needs and characteristics that must be addressed in the schooling process. In his book *Frames of Mind* (1983), Gardner states that there are at least seven different types or ways of knowing, perceiving, and understanding the world around us and that every student has all of these intelligences to some degree. Gardner also makes it clear, however, that one or two intelligences are often stronger and more fully developed in a person although everyone has the capacity for nurturing all seven. The challenge to middle school teachers is to turn on the intelligence potentials of all students and design lesson plans that teach and strengthen those multiple intelligences on a regular and consistent basis.

The following chart briefly defines all seven of the identified intelligences, suggests sample strategies for instruction, and cites specific career choices to illustrate each one.

| INTELLIGENCE | DESCRIPTION | STRATEGIES | CAREERS |
|---|---|---|---|
| VERBAL/LINGUISTIC INTELLIGENCE | Intelligence of words and production of language | Journal writing, making speeches, storytelling, reading | Novelists, comedians, journalists |
| LOGICAL/ MATHEMATICAL INTELLIGENCE | Intelligence of numbers, logic, and inductive reasoning | Developing outlines, creating codes, calculating, problem solving | Accountants, lawyers, computer programmers |
| VISUAL/SPATIAL INTELLIGENCE | Intelligence of pictures, mental images, and sight | Drawing, using guided imagery, making mind maps, making charts | Architects, mechanical engineers, map makers |
| BODY/KINESTHETIC INTELLIGENCE | Intelligence of physical self, control of one's body movements, and learning by doing | Role playing, dancing, playing games, using manipulatives | Athletes, inventors, mechanics |

| INTELLIGENCE | DESCRIPTION | STRATEGIES | CAREERS |
|---|---|---|---|
| MUSICAL/RHYTHMIC INTELLIGENCE | Intelligence of recognition and use of rhythmic or tonal patterns and sensitivity to sounds from the environment | Singing, performing, writing compositions, playing instruments, performing choral readings | Musicians, advertising designers, composers |
| INTERPERSONAL INTELLIGENCE | Intelligence of people skills, communication skills, and collaborative skills | Working with mentors and tutors, participating in interactive projects, using cooperative learning | Teachers, politicians, religious leaders |
| INTRAPERSONAL INTELLIGENCE | Intelligence of the inner self, intuition, and emotions | Using learning centers, participating in self-reflection tasks, using higher-order reasoning, taking personal inventories | Psychiatrists, counselors, entrepreneurs |

# ▶ How are they different?

Using the multiple intelligences to design instruction is a new way to teach basic skills and concepts because it provides a specific structure for the natural integration of subject areas and consistent development of thinking skills.

The multiple-intelligence theory, unlike many middle school textbooks and curriculum guides, gives you and members of your team considerable flexibility for creating challenging lesson plans that cater to varied learning and teaching styles and that adapt to different cultures and backgrounds by its total acceptance and promotion of multiplicity in the classroom.

Likewise, the multiple-intelligence approach to teaching and learning supports interdisciplinary teaming because it is centered around the premise that there are at least seven ways of knowing and seven ways of teaching—many of which should be represented by teachers on the team. Team teaching and team conferencing are both essential to the middle school program and to the multiple-intelligence approach to instruction.

## VERBAL/LINGUISTIC

Use storytelling.
Set up a debate.
Write a poem, myth, legend, short play, or news article.
Give a presentation.
Lead a class discussion.
Write journal entries.
Create a radio talk show program.
Write a newsletter, booklet, or dictionary.
Create an audiotape.
Conduct an interview.

## LOGICAL/ MATHEMATICAL

Create a time line.
Design and conduct an experiment.
Make a strategy game.
Make a calendar.
Interpret data.
Hypothesize.
Create story problems.
Categorize facts and information.
Use inductive or deductive reasoning.

## VISUAL/SPATIAL

Chart, map, cluster, or graph.
Create a slide show, video-tape, or photo album.
Design a poster, bulletin board, or mural.
Use a memory system.
Make a film or advertisements.
Invent a board or card game.
Illustrate, draw, paint, sketch, sculpt, or construct.
Use the overhead projector.

## BODY/KINESTHETIC

Rehearse and perform a play.
Role-play or simulate.
Create a movement or sequence of movements.
Choreograph a dance.
Invent a board or floor game.
Make task or puzzle cards.
Build or construct.
Devise a scavenger hunt.
Make a model.
Use hands-on materials.
Design a product.

## MUSICAL/RHYTHMIC

Sing a rap or song.
Indicate rhythmical patterns.
Give a presentation with appropriate musical accompaniment.
Explain the lyrics of a song.
Present a short class musical.
Use music to enhance skill building.
Create a musical game.
Collect and present songs.
Create a music collage.

## INTERPERSONAL

Conduct a class meeting.
Identify and assume a role.
Organize or participate in a group.
Use a conflict management strategy.
Accommodate learning differences.
Participate in a service project.
Participate in a mentorship, apprenticeship, or tutoring program.
Generate a variety of multiple perspectives on a topic.
Explain your perspective on an international issue.

## INTRAPERSONAL

Describe qualities you possess that will help you succeed.
Set a goal.
Describe how you feel.
Explain your personal philosophy.
Use self-directed learning.
Write a journal entry.
Explain the purpose in studying.
Explain your intuitive hunches.
Receive feedback from another person.
Self-assess your work.

(Adapted from Campbell, Campbell, & Dickinson, 1992)

# ► How do we get started?

**Step 1:** According to David Lazear (1991), there are at least three different types of lessons that are needed in the middle school classroom. Familiarize yourself with each of these in more detail and, with your team members find ways to infuse them into your planning and teaching process. Use the reproducible page entitled "Weekly Record of Multiple Intelligence Activities Used in Class" to record the specific tools, techniques, and tasks you have incorporated into your classroom lesson plans each week. Brief descriptions of the three types of lessons follow:

1. **Intelligence is a subject (teaching *for* multiple intelligences).** Teach each of the intelligences as a subject in its own right: music skills, language, art as a formal discipline, mathematical calculation and reasoning, skillful body movement (as in physical education, dance, and drama), and various social skills necessary for effective functioning in society. Teaching these "subjects" requires a grasp of the developmental stages of each intelligence and an understanding of the accumulated cultural wisdom on the subject, the formal knowledge base, and the practical methods, skills, and techniques of the intelligence.

2. **Intelligence is a means to acquire knowledge (teaching *with* multiple intelligences).** Teach students to use each of the intelligences as a means to gain knowledge: using body movement to learn vocabulary words, music to teach math concepts, art to bring to life different periods of history and different cultures, debate to explore various perspectives on current events, and comparative skills to analyze characters in a Shakespearean play.

3. **"Metaintelligence" is intelligence investigating itself (teaching *about* multiple intelligences).** Teach students about their own multiple intelligences—how to access them, how to strengthen them, and how to actively use them in learning and in everyday life.

**Step 2:** When teaching to the multiple intelligences, traditional subject matter lines fade, making it easier for a team of teachers to plan and implement interdisciplinary units. Discuss with your team members how you might create an interdisciplinary unit, using the multiple intelligences as the foundation for organizing the content and skills.

**Step 3:** Analyze the textbooks, supplementary materials, reference books, and software programs that you use on a regular basis. Ask yourself, "Which of the 'seven ways of knowing and teaching' do these materials foster most consistently and which do they neglect?" Then, add multiple intelligence activities to obtain a more balanced approach.

# ► Where do we go for more information?

Armstrong, T. 1993. *Seven kinds of smart: Identifying and developing your many intelligences*. New York: Plume-Penguin.
Provides an overview of the theory of multiple intelligences. Emphasizes ways to identify stronger and weaker intelligences in one's self and ways to practice and strengthen the weaker intelligences.

Campbell, B., Campbell, L., and Dickinson, D. 1992. *Teaching and learning through multiple intelligences*. Seattle, WA: New Horizons for Learning.
Surveys the theory of multiple intelligences and investigates the practical application of the theory to education. Suggests a variety of classroom activities and lesson plans for all ages and a variety of subjects. Includes tips on curriculum development, assessment strategies, and teaching skills.

Gardner, H. 1983. *Frames of mind*. New York: Harper Collins-Basic Books.
A leading psychologist argues that everyone possesses at least seven intelligences, most of which have been overlooked in our testing society, and that each person's blend of competencies produces a unique cognitive profile.

Lazear, D. 1991. *Seven ways of knowing: Teaching for multiple intelligences*. 2nd ed. Palatine, IL: Skylight Publishing, Inc.
Surveys the theory of multiple intelligences. Provides techniques for discovering and using the intelligences, including strategies for practicing them, strengthening them, and teaching them. Includes blackline masters and sample lesson plans.

Lazear, D. 1991. *Seven ways of teaching: The artistry of teaching with multiple intelligences*. Palatine, IL: Skylight Publishing, Inc.
Explores ways to teach the seven intelligences. Includes full lesson plans, activities, games, and diagrams for a variety of subjects in elementary through secondary grades. Also, includes lesson processing and graphic organizer blackline masters and a glossary.

# References

Armstrong, T. 1993. *Seven kinds of smart: Identifying and developing your many intelligences*. New York: Plume-Penguin.

Campbell, B., Campbell, L., and Dickinson, D. 1992. *Teaching and learning through multiple intelligences*. Seattle, WA: New Horizons for Learning.

Gardner, H. 1983. *Frames of mind*. New York: Harper Collins-Basic Books.

Lazear, D. 1991. *Seven ways of knowing: Teaching for multiple intelligences*. 2d ed. Palatine, IL: Skylight Publishing, Inc.

Lazear, D. 1991. *Seven ways of teaching: The artistry of teaching with multiple intelligences*. Palatine, IL: Skylight Publishing, Inc.

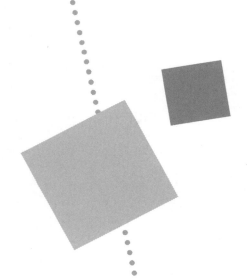

# Test Your Seven Kinds of Smarts

**Directions:** Check those statements that apply to you and each of your team members. What are the dominant intelligences of the teachers represented on your team?

## Verbal/Linguistic Intelligence

_____ Books are very important to me.

_____ I can hear words in my head before I read, speak, or write them down.

_____ I get more out of listening to the radio or a spoken-word cassette than I do from television or films.

_____ I show an aptitude for word games such as anagrams, Scrabble, or Password.

_____ I enjoy entertaining myself or others with tongue twisters, nonsense rhymes, or puns.

_____ Other people sometimes have to stop and ask me to explain the meaning of the words I use in my writing and speaking.

_____ English, social studies, and history were easier for me in school than math and science.

_____ When I drive down a highway, I pay more attention to the words written on billboards than to the scenery.

_____ My conversation includes frequent references to things that I've read or heard.

_____ I've written something recently that I am particularly proud of or that has earned me recognition from others.

Other Verbal/Linguistic Strengths:

## Logical/Mathematical Intelligence

_____ I can easily compute numbers in my head.

_____ Math and/or science were among my favorite subjects in school.

_____ I enjoy playing games or solving brainteasers that require logical thinking.

_____ I like to set up little "what if" experiments (for example, "What if I double the amount of water I give to my rosebush each week?").

_____ My mind searches for patterns, regularities, or logical sequences in things.

_____ I'm interested in new developments in science.

_____ I believe that almost everything has a rational explanation.

_____ I sometimes think in clear, abstract, wordless, imageless concepts.

_____ I like finding logical flaws in things that people say and do at home and work.

_____ I feel more comfortable when something has been measured, categorized, analyzed, or quantified in some way.

Other Logical/Mathematical Strengths:

## Visual/Spatial Intelligence

_____ I often see clear visual images when I close my eyes.

_____ I'm sensitive to color.

_____ I frequently use a camera or camcorder to record what I see around me.

_____ I enjoy doing jigsaw puzzles, mazes, and other visual puzzles.

_____ I have vivid dreams at night.

_____ I can generally find my way around unfamiliar territory.

_____ I like to draw or doodle.

_____ Geometry was easier for me than algebra in school.

_____ I can comfortably imagine how something might appear from a bird's-eye view.

_____ I prefer looking at reading material that is heavily illustrated.

Other Visual/Spatial Strengths:

## Body/Kinesthetic Intelligence

_____ I engage in at least one sport or physical activity on a regular basis.

_____ I find it difficult to sit still for long periods of time.

_____ I like working with my hands at concrete activities such as sewing, weaving, carving, carpentry, or model building.

_____ My best ideas often come to me when I'm out for a long walk or a jog or when I'm engaged in some other kind of physical activity.

_____ I like to spend my free time outdoors.

_____ I frequently use hand gestures or other forms of body language when conversing with someone.

_____ I need to touch things to learn more about them.

_____ I enjoy daredevil amusement rides or similar thrilling physical experiences.

_____ I would describe myself as well coordinated.

_____ I need to practice a new skill rather than just read about it or see a video that describes it.

Other Body/Kinesthetic Strengths:


## Musical/Rhythmic Intelligence

_____ I have a pleasant singing voice.

_____ I can tell when a musical note is off-key.

_____ I frequently listen to music on radio, record, cassettes, or compact discs.

_____ I play a musical instrument.

_____ My life would be poorer if there were no music in it.

_____ I sometimes catch myself walking down the street with a television jingle or other tune running through my mind.

_____ I can easily keep time to a piece of music with a simple percussion instrument.

_____ I know the tunes to many different songs or musical pieces.

_____ If I hear a musical selection once or twice, I am usually able to sing it back fairly accurately.

_____ I often make tapping sounds or sing little melodies while working, studying, or learning something new.

Other Musical/Rhythmic Strengths:

## Interpersonal Intelligence

_____ I'm the sort of person that people come to for advice and counsel at work or in my neighborhood.

_____ I prefer group sports like badminton, volleyball, or softball to solo sports such as swimming and jogging.

_____ When I have a problem, I'm more likely to seek out another person for help than attempt to work it out on my own.

_____ I favor social pastimes such as Monopoly or bridge over individual recreations such as video games and solitaire.

_____ I enjoy the challenge of teaching another person, or groups of people, what I know how to do.

_____ I consider myself a leader (or others have called me a leader).

_____ I feel comfortable in the midst of a crowd.

_____ I like to get involved in social activities connected with my work, church, or community.

_____ I would rather spend my evenings at a lively social gathering than stay at home alone.

Other Interpersonal Strengths:

## Intrapersonal Intelligence

_____ I regularly spend time alone meditating, reflecting, or thinking about important life questions.

_____ I have attended counseling sessions or personal growth seminars to learn more about myself.

_____ I have opinions that set me apart from the crowd.

_____ I have a special hobby or interest that I keep pretty much to myself.

_____ I have some important goals for my life that I think about on a regular basis.

_____ I have a realistic view of my strengths and weaknesses (borne out by feedback from other sources).

_____ I would prefer to spend a weekend alone in a cabin in the woods than at a fancy resort with lots of people around.

_____ I consider myself to be strong willed or independent minded.

_____ I keep a personal diary or journal to record the events of my inner life.

_____ I am self-employed or have at least thought seriously about starting my own business.

Other Intrapersonal Strengths:

(Adapted from Armstrong, 1993)

# Weekly Record of Multiple Intelligence Activities Used in Class

Have you taught the "seven ways of knowing" this week? Check by listing the specific strategies, techniques, and tools you have used in classroom lessons this week.

|  | Monday | Tuesday | Wednesday | Thursday | Friday |
|---|---|---|---|---|---|
| Verbal/ Linguistic |  |  |  |  |  |
| Logical/ Mathematical |  |  |  |  |  |
| Visual/ Spatial |  |  |  |  |  |
| Body/ Kinesthetic |  |  |  |  |  |
| Musical/ Rhythmic |  |  |  |  |  |
| Interpersonal |  |  |  |  |  |
| Intrapersonal |  |  |  |  |  |

(Lazear, 1991)

## Topic 11  INTERDISCIPLINARY INSTRUCTION

## ▶ What is it?

In an interdisciplinary approach to curriculum, teachers consciously relate different subject and skill areas of the school program. Students and teachers explore the relationships between and among the four core subjects, the fine arts, the practical arts, and physical education. Heidi Jacobs (1989) defines interdisciplinary instruction as "a knowledge view and curriculum approach that consciously applies methodology and language from more than one discipline to examine a central theme, issue, problem, topic, or experience."

Interdisciplinary instruction can take a variety of forms, ranging from better coordination among disciplines to a total blending of them. The simplest approach, parallel disciplines, leaves the individual disciplines intact but realigns course content so that related content is taught concurrently. In this fashion, the subjects are mutually reinforced. For example, when students read *Across Five Aprils* in English class, they also study the Civil War in history.

A more desirable approach is for teachers to create interdisciplinary units organized around a theme, problem, issue, or project. It should be noted, however, that interdisciplinary instruction does not necessarily mean that all disciplines must be involved in all units, or if they are involved, for the same length of time.

In summary, integration of subject matter can take place on a continuum from simple connections of course content to team teaching in a fully integrated model. For an overview, go to the end of this section and review "Ten Views for Integrating the Curricula: How Do You See It?" from Robin Fogarty's *How to Integrate the Curricula*.

## ▶ Why is it important?

Recent research on effective schools suggests that students learn and remember best when

- Subject matter is reinforced and integrated
- Activities require higher-order thinking

---

## TIPS FOR TEAMS

Respond to the following starter statements individually and then discuss your responses with your team:

- Interdisciplinary instruction means . . .

- One advantage of interdisciplinary instruction for teachers is . . .

- One advantage of interdisciplinary instruction for students is . . .

- A concern I have about interdisciplinary instruction is . . .

- To date, the closest we have come to interdisciplinary instruction is . . .

*"To students—curriculum is like working a jigsaw puzzle without the picture."*

What does this quotation by James Beane suggest to you about students' perceptions of a discipline-based curriculum?

- Students are actively involved in drawing connections among subjects, making decisions, and solving problems
- Choices are available and collaboration is encouraged
- Students see the whole context of what they are learning

Paramount to the success of interdisciplinary instruction is a team of teachers committed to making it work. Group dynamics play an important part. Working together collaboratively, developing a support system, and using effective interpersonal skills are very much a part of the interdisciplinary process for teachers. Going through the evolutionary stages of "forming, storming, and norming" takes time before a team can finally reach "performing." To develop integrated units within a team, four factors are necessary for success.

1. Team teachers must be willing to participate with enthusiasm and commitment.

2. The team must allot adequate time to plan and develop integrated units.

3. The team must have access to adequate materials to meet the needs of the unit.

4. The team must feel the support of the school administrator and district administration.

# ▶ How do we get started?

## Finding Parallels on Which to Build

In working toward subject matter integration, a natural starting place for many team members is the development of a planning matrix to organize the sequence of lessons across the disciplines. Finding parallels is often the first step in developing an interdisciplinary topic or theme. The steps for discovering parallels follow.

**Step 1:** Have each team member complete his or her section of a planning matrix using a tool such as the copy form entitled "Building an Interdisciplinary Planning Matrix" found at the end of this section.

**Step 2:** Record the completed information from all disciplines on a large sheet of paper or a chalkboard.

**Step 3:** As a team, look for the obvious and not so obvious curricular connections.

**Step 4:** Discuss where you can change the sequences to create or sharpen parallel themes.

**Step 5:** Plan how you might capitalize on the parallels you find.

## TIPS FOR TEAMS

Do some professional reading on the topic of integrating the curriculum. Select some current journal articles to read and discuss as a team.

Check with your district or regional professional development center to determine if it has videotapes about interdisciplinary instruction that you can borrow or a list of experienced speakers that you might invite to meet with your team on the topic.

If another team at your school or a neighboring school is successfully integrating the curriculum, try to arrange for release time when your team can visit. If it is impossible to go as a team, try covering for one another during visitation times.

- **Media specialists**
- **Physical education teachers**
- **Guidance counselors**
- **Guest speakers**
- **Films, filmstrips, videos, computer programs**
- **Off-site learning centers**
- **Reference books**
- **Commercial materials**
- **Members of the community**
- *Parents*

**When scheduling the unit, consider**

- **Putting activities and events on a calendar**
- **Reserving the media center, stage, gymnasium, or multipurpose room, if needed**
- **Contacting guest speakers and arranging for the equipment they may need**
- **Scheduling trips to off-campus learning sites. Be sure to arrange transportation, parent permissions, and a way to cover the costs**

**When spreading the word about the unit, consider**

- **Putting out teasers**
- **Decorating bulletin boards with lists of coming attractions**
- **Sending a letter home explaining the unit**
- **Advertising in the team or PTA newsletter**

**Step 6:** Look for an overriding theme, topic, problem, issue, or experience that might be developed into an interdisciplinary unit from these related concepts, skills, or strands.

## Developing the Connections

Once you have developed an organizational matrix, you need to generate a lot of ideas about the theme and how to use it in your classrooms. The next step in the process is brainstorming possible approaches. Not only should the team teachers take part, but students should participate as well. Allow some time for individual brainstorming first (some people need think time), then hold group brainstorming sessions. The interdisciplinary planning wheel recommended by Heidi Jacobs (1989) is useful in brainstorming. Follow these steps to develop an interdisciplinary planning wheel.

**Step 1:** Draw a circle, and in it write the central topic or theme.

**Step 2:** Draw spokes radiating out from the circle. Each spoke represents a standard school subject (e.g., math, science, social studies, language arts, physical education). Defining these standard subject areas encourages teachers and students to approach the theme from various perspectives.

**Step 3:** Begin the brainstorming. As with all brainstorming, accept all ideas without criticism, encourage creative and unique ideas, look for possible combinations of ideas, and then evaluate the ideas, eliminating those that are unusable.

**Step 4:** Next, to prevent the possibility of ending up with just a potpourri of activities, establish three or four guiding questions. The questions should transcend discipline lines and provide the structure to develop appropriate activities.

**Step 5:** Develop activities for implementation. These activities are the means for exploring the guiding questions. When planning student activities, use Bloom's taxonomy as a guide, include strategies for varied modalities, provide collaborative learning experiences, and implement varied delivery systems.

**Step 6:** Decide on special activities or events, such as having guest speakers, going on field trips, viewing films or videos, or presenting the unit findings in public, to open and close the unit.

**Step 7:** Finally, decide on ways to evaluate the unit. Administer a post test if desired. Survey students' attitudes about the unit. Analyze the experience from your perspective. Maintain a resource file. Decide which activities and events were most beneficial.

# ▶ Where do we go for more information?

Beane, J. 1993. *A middle school curriculum: From rhetoric to reality.* 2d ed. Columbus, OH: National Middle School Association.
Suggests that "curriculum themes should emerge from the natural overlaps between the personal concerns of early adolescents and the larger issues that face our world."

Fogarty, R. 1991. *How to integrate the curricula.* Palatine, IL: Skylight Publishing, Inc.
Focuses on integrated curriculum design. Describes ten models of curriculum integration.

Forte, I., and Schurr, S. 1993. *The definitive middle school guide: A handbook for success.* Nashville, TN: Incentive Publications, Inc.
Provides a comprehensive collection of resources designed for use in workshops and in-service training programs for middle-school educators, administrators, and others concerned with middle-school success. Also, includes a comprehensive index and bibliography.

Jacobs, H. H., *et al.* 1989. *Interdisciplinary curriculum: Design & implementation.* Alexandria, VA: Association for Supervision and Curriculum Development.
Describes a variety of integration options. Offers a step-by-step guide through the integration process. Also discusses the value of higher-order thinking and learning skills and provides a vehicle for integrating them into the curriculum.

Lounsbury, J. H. 1992. *Connecting the curriculum through interdisciplinary instruction.* Columbus, OH: National Middle School Association.
Articles that have appeared in the *Middle School Journal* along with many new thoughts and ideas are the backbone of this book. The author concentrates on four major themes in this practical, user-friendly, idea-packed volume: (1) what interdisciplinary instruction can do for you, (2) planning for interdisciplinary instruction, (3) interdisciplinary instruction in action, and (4) nurturing teaming and guiding growth.

Vars, G. F. 1987. *Interdisciplinary teaching in the middle grades.* Columbus, OH: National Middle School Association.
The focus of this monograph is on ways to organize for the implementation of integrated instruction. Readers will find clear explanations and ample examples to guide them. Planning, scheduling, and skill building are topics addressed.

# References

Beane, J. 1993. *A middle school curriculum: From rhetoric to reality*. Columbus, OH: National Middle School Association.

Fogarty, R. 1991. *How to integrate the curricula*. Palatine, IL: Skylight Publishing, Inc.

Forte, I., and Schurr, S. 1993. *The definitive middle school guide: A handbook for success*. Nashville, TN: Incentive Publications, Inc.

Jacobs, H. H., *et al.* 1989. *Interdisciplinary curriculum: Design and implementation*. Alexandria, VA: Association for Supervision and Curriculum Development.

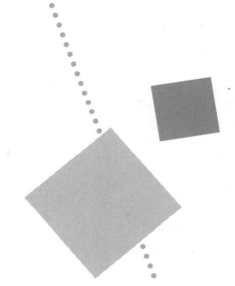

# Toward an Integrated Curriculum

## Ten Views for Integrating the Curriculum: How Do You See It?

### 1 FRAGMENTED

Periscope—one direction; one sighting; narrow focus on single discipline

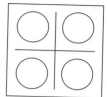

**Description**

The traditional model of separate and distinct disciplines, which fragments the subject areas

**Example**

Teacher applies this view in Math, Science, Social Studies, Language Arts OR Sciences, Humanities, Fine and Practical Arts.

### 2 CONNECTED

Opera glass—details of one discipline; focus on subtleties and interconnections

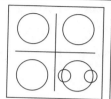

**Description**

Within each subject area, course content is connected topic to topic, concept to concept, one year's work to the next, and relates idea(s) explicitly.

**Example**

Teacher relates the concept of fractions to decimals, which in turn relates to money, grades, etc.

### 3 NESTED

3-D glasses—multiple dimensions to one scene, topic, or unit

**Description**

Within each subject area, the teacher targets multiple skills: a social skill, a thinking skill, and a content-specific skill.

**Example**

Teacher designs the unit on photosynthesis to simultaneously target consensus seeking (social skill), sequencing (thinking skill), and plant life cycle (science content).

### 4 SEQUENCED

Eyeglasses—varied internal content framed by broad, related concepts

**Description**

Topics or units of study are rearranged and sequenced to coincide with one another. Simlar ideas are taught in concert while remaining separate subjects.

**Example**

English teacher presents a historical novel depicting a particular period while the History teacher teaches that same historical period.

### 5 SHARED

Binoculars—two disciplines that share overlapping concepts and skills

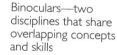

**Description**

Shared planning and teaching take place in two disciplines in which overlapping concepts or ideas emerge as organizing elements.

**Example**

Science and Math teachers use data collection, charting, and graphing as shared concepts that can be team-taught.

### 6 WEBBED

Telescope—broad view of an entire constellation as one theme, webbed to the various elements

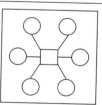

**Description**

A fertile theme is webbed to curriculum contents and disciplines; subjects use the theme to sift out appropriate concepts, topics, and ideas.

**Example**

Teacher presents a simple topical theme, such as the circus, and webs it to the subject areas. A conceptual theme, such as conflict, can be webbed for more depth in the theme approach.

*(continues on page 260)*

## 7 THREADED

Magnifying glass—big ideas that magnify all content through a metacurricular approach

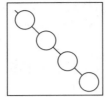

### Description

The metacurricular approach threads thinking skills, social skills, multiple intelligences, technology, and study skills through the various disciplines.

### Example

Teaching staff targets prediction in Reading, Math, and Science lab experiments while Social Studies teacher targets forecasting current events and thus threads the skill (prediction) across disciplines.

## 8 INTEGRATED

Kaleidoscope—new patterns and designs that use the basic elements of each discipline

### Description

This interdisciplinary approach matches subjects for overlaps in topics and concepts with some team teaching in an authentic integrated model.

### Example

In Math, Science, Social Studies, Fine Arts, Language Arts, and Practical Arts, teachers look for patterning models and approach content through these patterns.

## 9 IMMERSED

Microscope—intensely personal view that allows microscopic explanation as all content is filtered through lens of interest and expertise.

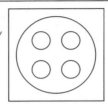

### Description

The disciplines become part of the learner's lens of expertise; the learner filters all content through this lens and becomes immersed in his or her own experience.

### Example

Student or doctoral candidate has an area of expert interest and sees all learning through that lens.

## 10 NETWORKED

Prism—a view that creates multiple dimensions and directions of focus

### Description

Learner filters all learning through the expert's eye and makes internal connections that lead to external networks of experts in related fields.

### Example

Architect, while adapting the CAD/CAM technology for design, networks with technical programmers and expands her knowledge base, just as she had traditionally done with interior designers.

# Building an Interdisciplinary Planning Matrix

**Directions:** With your team, list all the major concepts, units, skills, or topics each of you will cover this year. Look for overlaps or changes that could be worked into interdisciplinary units.

| | Sept. | Oct. | Nov. | Dec. | Jan. | Feb. | Mar. | Apr. | May |
|---|---|---|---|---|---|---|---|---|---|
| Science | | | | | | | | | |
| Mathematics | | | | | | | | | |
| Social Studies | | | | | | | | | |
| Language Arts | | | | | | | | | |
| Exploration | | | | | | | | | |
| Physical Education | | | | | | | | | |

(Forte & Schurr)

# Topic 12  CONTRACTS AND LEARNING ACTIVITY PACKETS

## ▶ What are they?

A learning contract is a prearranged agreement between the teacher and a student in which the student commits to doing specific learning tasks and completing certain academic requirements within a given time frame, usually to earn a grade. Contracts take many forms ranging from simple plans describing what the student must do to more complex plans that specify not only what work is to be done but also criteria for earning a specific grade.

Learning activity packets are self-contained and self-directed instructional packages prepared by the teacher for students to complete independently or with a minimum amount of supervision. These packets most often contain background information on a topic for the student to read; directions for a variety of academic exercises, activities, and problems for the student to complete; a list of references; and a series of materials for the student to review and self-correct to assess his or her daily progress.

Contracts and learning activity packets are excellent tools for varying instruction and individualizing assignments. This topic contains partial examples of student contracts and activity packets.

## ▶ How are they different?

Both contracts and learning activity packets place heavy emphasis on shared decision making between teacher and student, on alternative instructional strategies for students, and on optional delivery systems for teachers. As with other instructional methods, the successful use of contracts and learning activity packets depends on explicit directions for students, consistent checkpoints for teachers, and regular conferences to encourage shared decision making.

---

**TIPS FOR TEAMS**

Consider the theme or topic for your next interdisciplinary effort. Decide if it would be appropriate to use a contract or a learning activity packet.

---

# ▶ How do we get started?

The following are some general guidelines for preparing a contract or a learning activity packet appropriate for middle grade students:

**Step 1:** Determine the topic or specific area of study to be covered by the contract or the activity packet. Write the curricular objectives to be addressed.

**Step 2:** Plan and prepare the required and optional tasks, exercises, and assignments for the contract or activity packet.

**Step 3:** Decide on the requirements for satisfactory completion of the contract or activity packet. Include point values, descriptors, or benchmarks for success where appropriate.

**Step 4:** Create a test or a set of guidelines to assess student performance.

**Step 5:** Gather the resources, references, and instructional materials students will need to complete the contract or activity packet.

**Step 6:** Orient students to the goals, time lines, directions, and assessment procedures of the contract or activity packet.

**Step 7:** Set up a varied structure for monitoring student progress. Consider using journal entries, student conferences, self-reports, and informal observations.

## SUGGESTIONS FOR CONSTRUCTION AND USE OF ACTIVITY PACKETS

Try using a different color of paper for each part of the packet. For example, the activities might be printed on green, the objectives on blue, etc. Color coding makes locating parts much easier for you and your students. Also, it increases the attractiveness of the package.

Keep consumable materials separate or have students use their own paper for writing activities. This adds to the life of the packet.

When writing a packet for a heterogeneous class, use vocabulary appropriate for the low-average student. A large number of students must be able to read and understand the packet for it to be a useful tool.

Orient students to the use of learning activity packets before they start working on them. They need an adjustment period. Plan to work closely with them during the first packet.

Give yourself some adjustment time before you make any judgments on the value of using packets in your classroom. Don't give up too soon. Any effective device needs fine tuning before it fits well in your unique situation.

Learning activity packets, like any other teaching tool, are best used in combination with other tools. A teacher or team of teachers can effectively use a combination of learning centers, packets, and a teacher-directed activity such as demonstration, minilecture, or discussion.

(George and Lawrence)

# ▶ Where do we go for more information?

Clark, L. H., and Starr, I. S. 1991. *Secondary and middle school teaching methods*. 6th ed. New York: Macmillan Publishing Company. Designed as a methods textbook, this resource serves as a reference work for teachers. It includes detailed information about learning, motivating, managing, planning, guiding the learning process, and evaluation.

## *References*

George, P,. and Lawrence, G. 1982. *Handbook for middle school teaching*. Glenview, IL: Scott, Foresman and Company.

Schurr, S. 1992. *The ABC's of evaluation: 26 alternative ways to assess student progress*. Columbus, Ohio: National Middle School Association.

**Directions:** This week for your reading points, you must complete this contract. You may choose any of the activities you wish, but you must accumulate 25 points by Thursday. If you are absent on Thursday when the new contracts are filled out, it is your responsibility to complete a new contract when you return to school.

**Name** _____

**Date** _____

_____ 1. I will write a daily entry in my reading response log. Each entry will consist of one paragraph (at least five sentences) summarizing what I read that day and one paragraph explaining why I liked or did not like what I read that day. (5 points for each entry)

_____ 2. I will draw a picture illustrating a specific scene or event from my book and share it with a friend in class. (5 points)

_____ 3. I will write a letter to one of the characters in my book, telling him or her how I feel about how he or she is handling the situation in the book. The letter must be at least two paragraphs long. (10 points)

_____ 4. I will write an advertisement for my book, trying to "sell" the book to another student who will read it. (5 points)

_____ 5. I will write a letter to the author, telling him or her what I thought of the book and why. The letter must be at least two paragraphs long. (10 points)

_____ 6. I will begin reading a book by an author I've never read before. (5 points)

_____ 7. I will describe one of the main characters in my book, explaining his or her looks, personality, relationships with others, likes and dislikes, etc. This description must be at least eight sentences long. (10 points)

_____ 8. I will find three new words in my book, write each word, give the dictionary definition that fits the way the word was used, and use it in a sentence of my own. (5 points)

This will give me a total of _____ points.

**Student's Signature** _____

**Teacher's Signature** _____

# WRITE RIGHT!

This learning packet covers writing skills as they relate to your classes. Some of the materials will serve as review; other activities will introduce new concepts and provide practice. When you have completed the learning packet, you will be able to communicate in writing in many different ways, and you will be able to apply these new skills in your classes as well as in your everyday life.

## Objectives

1. Write summaries of information using a variety of formats.

2. Practice note taking in diverse situations that involve reading, writing, and listening skills.

3. Use outlining skills for studying, writing, speaking, and teaching.

4. Write paragraphs with supporting details and chronological descriptions of events. You will also write compare-and-contrast paragraphs and cause-and-effect paragraphs.

5. Write an informal report by selecting a topic, gathering information, and writing an outline. Develop an introductory paragraph, write the body of the paper based on the outline, and end with a concluding summary.

## Student Information

The package contains five major objectives. You will be asked to complete a certain number of activities for each objective.

You will need to keep a spiral notebook or folder and supply your own writing materials. All sample materials, filmstrips, books, articles, and magazines suggested for use are available in the classroom or media center. You also will need your textbooks.

When you finish each objective, show the teacher your notebook and all required work. Then move on to the next objective. Work on the objectives in the order they are presented. Good luck and good writing!

**OBJECTIVE #1:** Do either activity 1.1 or 1.2 and at least four more of the activities suggested. Keep your work in your notebook. Be sure to label all your work.

1.1 Read the section on writing summaries in your grammar/composition textbook. Complete the practice exercises provided.

1.2 View a filmstrip from your media center about summarizing. List the key points.

1.3 Write a summary of the chapter or unit you currently are studying in class.

1.4 Summarize an article of your choice from a current magazine. Be sure to include a brief statement of the main idea, details that support the main idea, important names, dates, numbers, and places.

1.5 Summarize one episode of your favorite television program. Pretend that your audience knows nothing about the program and has never seen it.

1.6 Choose your favorite movie. Write a summary that could be published in your school newspaper or presented on videotape.

1.7 Create a step-by-step illustrated study guide on how to summarize for younger students.

1.8 Design a poster for your classroom explaining how to summarize correctly.

1.9 Summarize one recent class period in which a new concept was introduced and practiced.

**OBJECTIVE #2:** Activity 2.1 is required. Select at least four more activities to complete. Continue working in your notebook.

2.1 Read the section on note taking in your grammar/composition textbook. Complete the practice assignments provided.

2.2 Identify as many situations as you can in which note taking would be helpful or necessary. Can you think of ten?

2.3 Note taking varies in different situations. List the guidelines for taking notes for oral presentations as well as those for reading selections. How are these guidelines similar? How are they different?

2.4 Select a filmstrip of your choice to view, and take notes.

2.5 Take notes on a chapter in your textbook.

2.6 Read a magazine article of your choice. Take notes. Use your notes to write a summary.

2.7 Take notes on a classroom lecture.

2.8 Plan an illustrated bulletin board display on note taking for your classroom.

2.9 Summarize the main points related to taking notes.

**OBJECTIVE #3:** Do either activity 3.1 or 3.2 and at least four more of the activities.

3.1 View a filmstrip on outlining from your media center. Take notes.

3.2 Read the section on outlining in your grammar/composition textbook. Take notes on the material presented.

3.3 Determine the difference between topic and sentence outlining. When would you use each type? Which is your favorite and why?

3.4 Write a topic outline for a current chapter in your textbook.

3.5 Write and explain the basic rules for outlining.

3.6 Choose a topic for a short report. Construct a sentence outline for your topic.

3.7 Select a topic for a three-to five-minute speech. Arrange a topic outline.

3.8 Create a lesson with visual aids to teach outlining to a class of younger students.

3.9 Explain the importance of summarizing, note taking, and outlining to academic success.

**OBJECTIVE #4:** Activities 4.1, 4.3, and 4.6 are required. Choose at least three more activities to complete.

4.1 Use the glossary and index in your grammar/composition textbook to help you define the following: *paragraph, topic sentence, main idea, supporting detail, chronological, compare and contrast,* and *cause and effect.*

4.2 Choose a favorite color, food, or sport to use as the topic of a paragraph. Decide on your topic sentence and at least four details that support the topic. Use ink and write your paragraph with proper margins and indentations.

4.3 Develop a chronological-order paragraph. This might focus on how to do or make something or a description of a sequence of events. Some key words that show order include *then, soon, next, first, after, now, later,* and *finally.*

4.4 Using proper paragraph form, compare and contrast television and radio, summer and winter, dogs and cats, baseball and football, or two items of your own choosing.

4.5 When you explain *why* something happens, you explain a cause. When you explain *what* happens as a result of something, you explain its effect. Develop a paragraph of cause and effect using a topic of your choice.

4.6 Some topics are too broad or general to be written about in just one paragraph. A few examples might include animals, nature, war, food, and movies. It is important to know how to narrow a topic. Explain how you might narrow a broad topic for a writing assignment.

4.7 Select a picture from a magazine or a textbook to use as the topic for a paragraph. Determine the kind of paragraph that will best develop your ideas about the picture.

4.8 Design an outline shape depicting a holiday, an animal, or a sport. Write a paragraph about the topic within the shape. Decorate it if you wish.

**OBJECTIVE #5:** When you complete all the following activities in the order presented, you will produce a two-to three-page informal report.

5.1 Brainstorm a list of possible topics for an informal report for your class. Try to think of at least twenty.

5.2 Select the one topic that interests you most and narrow it down to fit the report requirements.

5.3 Explore your topic by reading, viewing media, and gathering available sources.

5.4 Develop a correct topic or sentence outline for your report. Decide on a title.

5.5 Take notes from various sources. Be sure to select material that relates to your outline.

5.6 Write an introductory (opening) paragraph that includes a topic sentence.

5.7 Use your outline to develop your paper. Each main section of the outline will be the basis for at least one paragraph. Be sure to follow the order of your outline.

5.8 Write a conclusion to your paper and limit it to a one-paragraph summary.

5.9 Design an original cover for your report.

# Topic 13 · GRAPHIC ORGANIZERS FOR THINKING

## ▶ What are they?

Graphic organizers are tools students can use to establish patterns for their thinking, writing, and reporting. These organizers help middle level students develop intellectual discipline and the ability to think in the abstract and reason logically.

Although there is consensus among educators that the infusion of creative and critical thinking skills is essential to middle level schooling, little curriculum is available to them on "learning how to learn." Teaching graphic organizers is one way to help students develop inquiring minds and experience the joys of successful decision making and problem solving.

The most common graphic organizers, discussed in this section, include the following:

- Prediction Trees
- KWL Charts
- Data-Gathering Grids
- Venn Diagrams
- Fish Bone Diagrams
- Web Diagrams
- Flowcharts
- Stepladder Diagrams
- 5Ws and How Charts
- Compare and Contrast Diagrams

# ► Why are they important?

Graphic organizers provide students with a structure for recording ideas, information, predictions, or options on a given topic or theme. These diagrams, grids, and charts are study aids that allow middle level students to practice their creative and critical thinking skills in such a way that they can record important thoughts in a consistent and manageable way. No longer do they have to rely on their own underdeveloped methods for recording, retaining, and relating information in a given content area. Also, because these graphic organizers are generic, they help in the transfer of skills and data across grade levels and subject areas.

# ► How do we get started?

Review each of the following strategies for teaching graphic organizers. Determine which organizers are most appropriate for your subject, and begin using them on a regular and consistent basis. To begin, introduce the designated diagram, grid, or chart to the students. Explain the purpose, vocabulary, and process of the organizer while demonstrating its use in a minilecture, demonstration, or directed teaching activity. Assign students a follow-up task that involves applying the organizing principle to something they are asked to do in class. Encourage students to discuss the benefits of each organizer and to compare and contrast their recorded results with those of other students in the class.

## Prediction Trees

Prediction Trees, developed by James Bellanca (1992), help students develop predicting skills that can be useful when reading literature or using lab materials that encourage the anticipation of outcomes or results. Students complete this treelike organizer by brainstorming a list of predictions and reasons for each prediction in response to a given question or stimulus from the teacher. Students should be given time to discuss and agree upon relevant details and elaborations of their predictions and probable outcomes. Refer to the Prediction Tree on the following page for the story *The Giving Tree* for an example of this organizer.

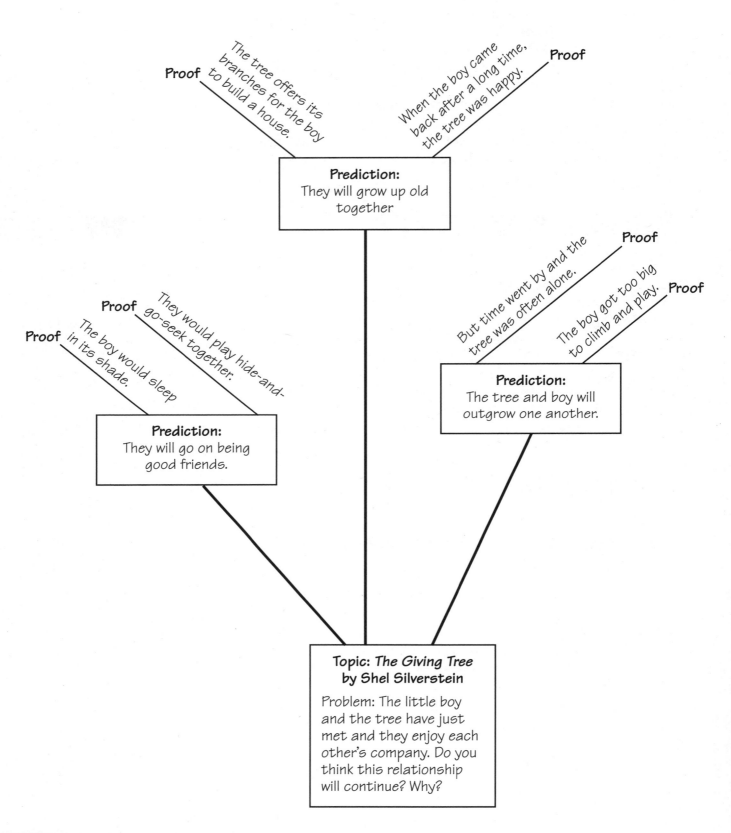

Proof

The tree offers its branches for the boy to build a house.

Proof

When the boy came back after a long time, the tree was happy.

**Prediction:**
They will grow up old together

Proof

But time went by and the tree was often alone.

Proof

The boy got too big to climb and play.

**Prediction:**
The tree and boy will outgrow one another.

Proof

They would play hide-and-go-seek together.

Proof

The boy would sleep in its shade.

**Prediction:**
They will go on being good friends.

**Topic: *The Giving Tree*
by Shel Silverstein**

Problem: The little boy and the tree have just met and they enjoy each other's company. Do you think this relationship will continue? Why?

# KWL Charts

This popular graphic organizer is used when the teacher wants the students to connect information they already know, information they want to know, and new information they have learned about a topic. Students use a sheet of paper divided into three columns with a "K" label in the first column, a "W" label in the second column, and a "L" label in the third column of the chart. They are then asked to record what they *know* about an assigned topic in the first column, what they *want* to know in the second column, and then, when they have completed their research, what they *learned* in the third column. An example of a KWL Chart for a study of Helen Keller is shown below.

## SAMPLE KWL CHART

**TOPIC:** *The Life of Helen Keller*

| KNOW | WANT TO KNOW | LEARNED |
|---|---|---|
| 1. Was blind, deaf, and dumb as a baby due to illness | 1. Who taught Helen how to read and write? | 1. Anne Sullivan, a teacher from Perkins School for Blind in Boston, tamed the "wild, young girl" named Helen. |
| 2. Born in U.S. in 1880 | 2. How did Helen learn these skills? | 2. Anne tapped out sign alphabet and names of objects with her hands for Helen. Helen learned to talk by touching Anne's throat and feeling her voice vibrate. She then imitated the vibrations on her own throat. |
| 3. Learned how to speak and write Braille | 3. Did she go to college? | 3. She went to college and spent her life helping the deaf and blind. |

# Data-Gathering Grids

Another graphic organizer, created by James Bellanca (1992), is called a Data-Gathering Grid. It can be used in any content area that requires classification skills or requires the student to make distinctions between facts and concepts that appear to be similar. This grid shows similarities and differences in a very structured format, and, according to Bellanca, it points out common elements and shows how each example might be slightly different in one or more attributes.

To use this organizer, the student first decides on an overall topic to explore. Then, in the center column of the grid, he or she lists factors to be addressed in the study. Next, the student selects specific items that will be examined in this study and writes them at the tops of the columns. Then, in the appropriate spaces in the columns, he or she writes the data gathered by research. Finally, the student analyzes the information recorded on the grid and organizes it for a comparison-and-contrast essay, report, or position paper. Refer to the following Data-Gathering Grid on "Clothing around the World" as an example.

## SAMPLE DATA-GATHERING GRID

**TOPIC:** Clothing Around the World

| ITEM 1: | ITEM 2: | CATEGORY | ITEM 3: | ITEM 4: |
|---|---|---|---|---|
| Greeks | American Indians | | Japanese | Africans |
| Cloth Wrappings | Headdress of Feathers | **HEADGEAR** | Combs | Turbans |
| Cloth Tunics and Togas | Leather Tunics | **DRESS** | Kimonos | Loincloths |
| Barefoot | Leather Moccasins | **FOOTWEAR** | Rope or Straw Sandals called Getas | Barefoot |
| Tapestries | Animal Skins, Horsehair, Buffalo Fat, Moose Hair | **FABRIC** | Silks | Cotton |
| Shawls, Masks | Beads, Leggings | **OTHER** | Sashes | Jewelry of Animal Bones and Ivory |

# Venn Diagrams

Most commonly used in mathematics, Venn Diagrams consist of sets of intersecting circles. These circles can be drawn to show the similarities and differences of related people, places, things, events, objects, or ideas. To use the Venn Diagram as a graphic organizer, decide on a topic for comparison and contrast. Research that topic and explore how pertinent information and ideas fall into subtopics that interrelate in various ways. In the diagram, draw circles that represent the subtopics. Show areas of commonality in the intersecting segment of the circles, and show differences in the appropriate non-intersecting portions of the circles. An example of a Venn Diagram for "Gliders, Parasails, and Hot Air Balloons" follows.

## SAMPLE VENN DIAGRAM ON GLIDERS, HOT AIR BALLOONS, AND PARASAILS

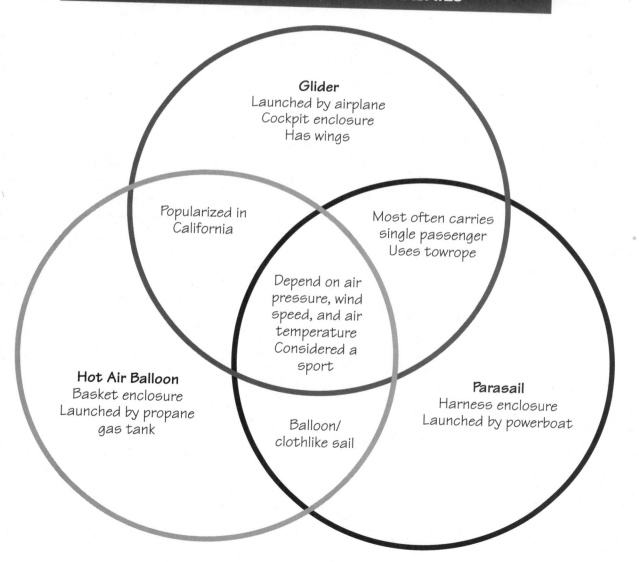

**Glider**
Launched by airplane
Cockpit enclosure
Has wings

Popularized in California

Most often carries single passenger
Uses towrope

Depend on air pressure, wind speed, and air temperature
Considered a sport

**Hot Air Balloon**
Basket enclosure
Launched by propane gas tank

Balloon/ clothlike sail

**Parasail**
Harness enclosure
Launched by powerboat

# Fish Bone Diagrams

The Fish Bone Diagram is an graphic organizer often used for problem solving in business. It is particularly helpful in analyzing changes, conflicts, and cause-and-effect situations. First, identify the effect to be studied and the related category names to be analyzed as part of that effect. The effect is written on the head of the fish and the category names serving as clues to the effect are written at the ends of each major bone. Students brainstorm and discuss ideas about the possible causes of the problem, and these are recorded on the smaller bones under the most appropriate category name. Students then deliberate the varied causes, order them by rank, and decide on the most rational conclusion. A Fish Bone Diagram for "Rising Crime Rate" is shown below as an example.

## SAMPLE FISH BONE MODEL ON RISING CRIME RATE

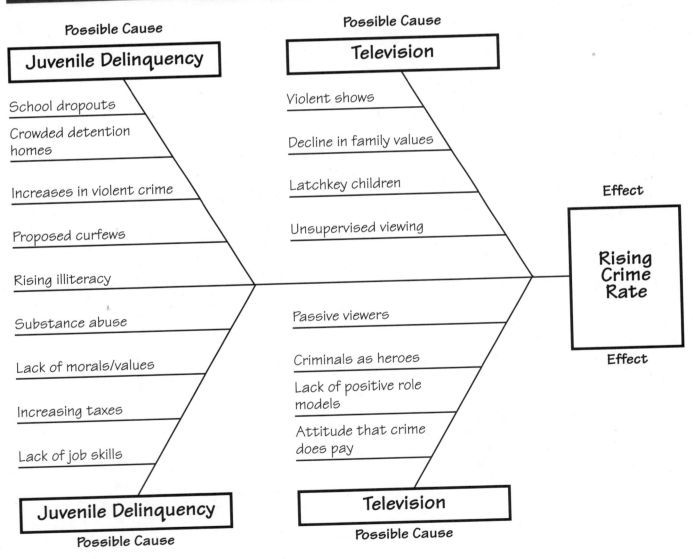

Possible Cause

**Juvenile Delinquency**

School dropouts

Crowded detention homes

Increases in violent crime

Proposed curfews

Rising illiteracy

Substance abuse

Lack of morals/values

Increasing taxes

Lack of job skills

Possible Cause

**Television**

Violent shows

Decline in family values

Latchkey children

Unsupervised viewing

Passive viewers

Criminals as heroes

Lack of positive role models

Attitude that crime does pay

Effect

**Rising Crime Rate**

Effect

**Juvenile Delinquency**

Possible Cause

**Television**

Possible Cause

# Web Diagrams

A Web Diagram is a tool for generating multiple ideas. To initiate the webbing process, draw a large circle in the middle of a page and write the name of a topic in the center of that circle. Draw straight lines out from the circle much like the spokes on a wheel. In boxes attached to the end of each line, write the large ideas related to the web's overall topic. Additional lines can then be added to these boxes extending in any direction. The pattern can be repeated again and again as long as the random ideas keep flowing in some direction that can be tied back to the original theme. For an example, see the following Web Diagram on "Time."

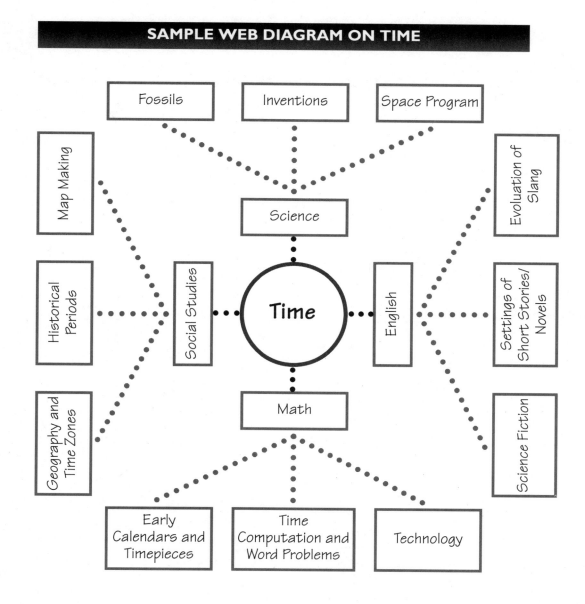

## SAMPLE WEB DIAGRAM ON TIME

# Flowcharts

Flowcharts are very helpful for representing sequences of events, actions, or decisions. Popular with computer programmers, Flowcharts allow the student to plan courses of action, to determine stages of development in a process, to depict cycles of change, to write directions for completing a task, and to picture the steps for solving complex problems. It is important to use the standard set of symbols when designing Flowcharts because they have a universal meaning for others who use them. To design a Flowchart, decide on a decision, action, or sequence of events to be pictured in the chart. The symbols should be arranged to depict the steps or decision points in the process, and open rectangles should be included for writing brief explanations for each of those major steps and/or decision points. See the following flowchart on "Creating a Book Project" for an example.

## SAMPLE FLOWCHART ON CREATING A BOOK PROJECT

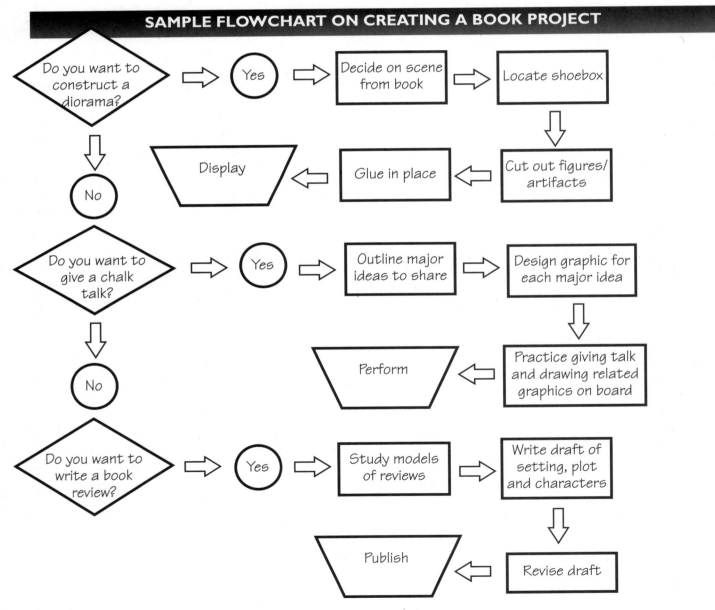

## Stepladder Diagrams

Stepladder Diagrams are simple but effective graphic organizers for determining the priority order of a given set of events, ideas, processes, steps, or tasks. The Stepladder is a visual tool for students to use to rank options according to given criteria. To use it, give students a problem or situation that has several possible outcomes. Have the students generate a list of relevant criteria to use in ordering these potential outcomes and record their choices on the steps of the ladder with the best solution on the top rung of the ladder and the weakest solution on the bottom rung. It is important that students be able to defend their first choice with three to five reasons why it is better than the others. A Stepladder Diagram on "Making Paper" is included in the side column as an example.

## 5Ws and How Charts

Based on the work of newspaper reporters, this popular organizer provides students with a six-question format that helps them summarize important information on a given topic by asking *Who? What? When? Where? Why?* and *How?* This strategy is most effective when the topic is narrow and specific. To use this advanced organizer, ask students to draw a seven-row chart with *Who?* at the left of the first row, *What?* at the left of the second, and so on. In the last row of the chart, have students write *Summary Statement*; this is where they will write a detailed statement summarizing the major points from the information listed in the chart. Give the students a topic to research by finding the appropriate responses to the 5Ws and How and summarizing their ideas in one comprehensive statement at the bottom. An example of a 5Ws and How Chart on "Peoples of the Sahara Desert" is included on the next page.

## ►SAMPLE STEPLADDER DIAGRAM ON MAKING PAPER IN FACTORIES CALLED PAPER MILLS

1. Logs are ground up and mixed with paper to make pulp.

2. Pulp is then bleached white and additives, like glue, are mixed in.

3. Next, pulp is spread out on a belt of wire mesh.

4. Water is sucked away through holes in mesh and pulp forms sheet of paper.

5. Paper goes through rollers to dry it and smooth its surface.

6. Different kinds of paper, like tissue paper, wallpaper, and writing paper are made with different kinds of pulp.

**TOPIC:** People Who Live in the Sahara Desert

**Who:** Three tribes live in the Sahara Desert: Moors live in the west, Tuaregs live in the central part, Tebus live in the east. Some are nomads.

**What:** Nomads travel to find food and water for their herds because animals quickly eat the few plants that exist in a desert pasture.

**When:** They keep traveling to find water. Sometimes they can find underground water called oases.

**Where:** The Sahara Desert is in Northern Africa. It is about the size of the U.S. and is very hot and dry.

**Why:** They must have water for themselves and their herds of animals, which are raised for meat and clothing.

**How:** Nomads carry their supplies on backs of camels because camels can carry heavy loads, can go without water for several days, and can live for long periods of time on fat stored in their humps. They also provide meat, milk, and hides for tents.

**Summary Statement:** Nomads live in the Sahara Desert and move from place to place to find water and food for themselves and their animals. They depend on the camel for transportation, food, and shelter.

# Compare and Contrast Diagram

Howard and Sandra Black (1990) developed the Compare and Contrast Diagram to help in clarifying and understanding important concepts. In their model, the comparison step—How alike?—encourages learners to relate a new concept to existing knowledge. According to the Blacks, "the more similarities the learner can identify, the more clearly the new concept will be understood and remembered. The contrast step—How different?—allows learners to distinguish the new concept from similar concepts. This promotes clear understanding and memory by eliminating confusion with related knowledge." To apply this model, have students write two concepts in blanks at the top of a page. Then ask them to write phrases that express similarities on each "How alike?" line; these phrases generally should begin with the word *both*. Next, have students write phrases that express differences on each "How different?" line. Each difference between the two concepts should relate to the same quality. It might be helpful to follow this pattern: "With regard to (quality), (concept one and its distinctions), but (concept two and its distinctions)." A Compare and Contrast Diagram showing how chimpanzees and humans are alike and different is included as an example on the next page.

**Concept 1** Chimpanzees

**Concept 2** Human

## HOW ALIKE?

Both are mammals.

Both can/do walk on two feet.

Both have no tail.

Both have their own language.

Both show many different emotions in faces.

Both get diseases like cancer and TB.

## HOW DIFFERENT?

## With Regard To

### CHIMPANZEE

Slender arms and legs

Hairy body

Limited to 20 different sounds for speaking

Walks around on two legs and all fours

Carries offspring on back

Limited diet and preferences for food

**Size**

**Body Cover**

**Language**

**Locomotion**

**Offspring**

**Nutrition**

### HUMAN

Larger arms/legs

Smooth body

Infinite sounds for speaking

Walks around on two legs only

Carries offspring in arms

Unlimited diet/preferences for food

# ► Where do we go for more information?

Bellanca, J. 1990. *The cooperative think tank: Practical techniques to teach thinking in the cooperative classroom.* Palatine, IL: Skylight Publishing, Inc.
Shows how to use graphic organizers in the middle school classroom. Includes copious examples of graphic organizers designed to help students see what they're thinking, sort out their thoughts, and expand their thinking on any topic. Also includes sample lessons, tests, and hints on appropriate uses.

Bellanca, J. 1992. *The cooperative think tank II: Graphic organizers to teach thinking in the cooperative classroom.* Palatine, IL: Skylight Publishing, Inc.
Continues like the volume described above, offering even more ideas for graphic organizers in the same format as the first.

Bellanca, J., and Fogarty, R. 1990. *Blueprints for thinking in the cooperative classroom.* Palatine, IL: Skylight Publishing, Inc.
Presents practical ideas and model lessons for encouraging cooperative learning in elementary, junior high and high school classrooms, including illustrations and samples. Tasks are designed with rigor and complexity. Presents the basics for forming a cooperative classroom.

Black, H., and Black, S. 1990. *Organizing thinking: Graphic organizers.* Bk. 2. Pacific Grove, CA: Critical Thinking.
Contains reproducible graphic organizers designed to integrate higher-order thinking skills across the curriculum. The book is easy to use, and everything is included: lesson plans, background information, graphic organizers, and suggested answers. The lessons cover all major areas of the curriculum: writing, math, science, language arts, social studies, enrichment, and personal problem solving.

## *References*

Bellanca, J. 1992. *The cooperative think tank II: Graphic organizers to teach thinking in the cooperative classroom.* Palatine, IL: Skylight Publishing, Inc.

Black, H., and Black, S. 1990. *Organizing thinking: Graphic organizers.* Bk. 2. Pacific Grove, CA: Critical Thinking.

## Prediction Tree Model

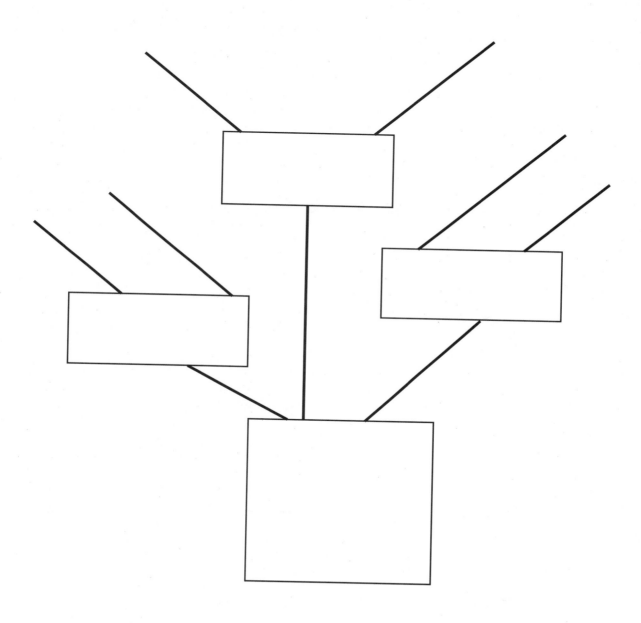

# KWL Model

TOPIC: _____

| Know | Want to know | Learned |
|---|---|---|
|  |  |  |

# Data-Gathering Grid

TOPIC: _____

| ITEM 1: | ITEM 2: | CATEGORY | ITEM 3: | ITEM 4: |
|---------|---------|----------|---------|---------|
|         |         |          |         |         |
|         |         |          |         |         |
|         |         |          |         |         |
|         |         |          |         |         |
|         |         |          |         |         |
|         |         |          |         |         |

# Venn Diagram

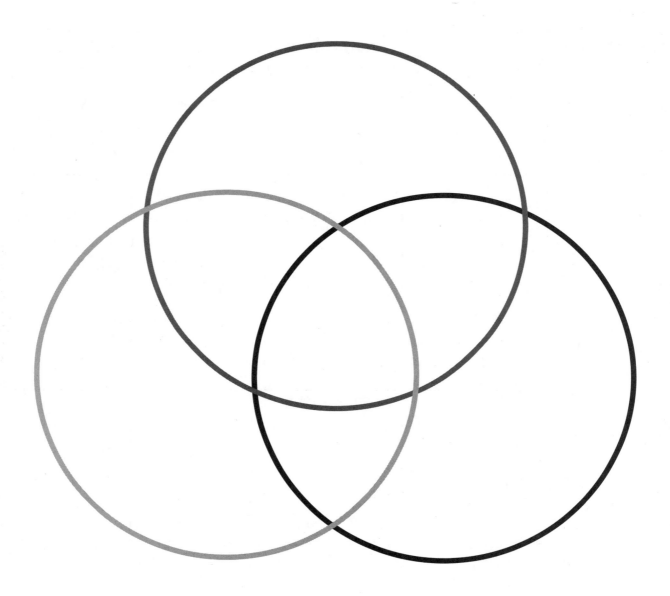

# Fish Bone Model

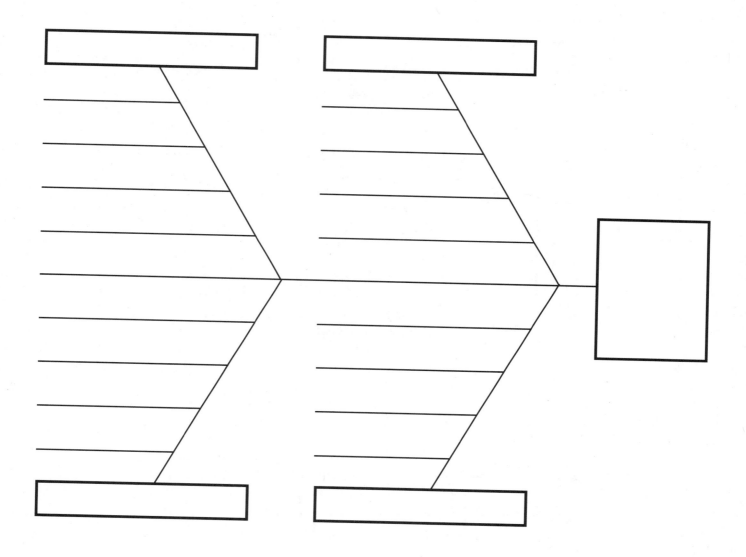

# Web Diagram

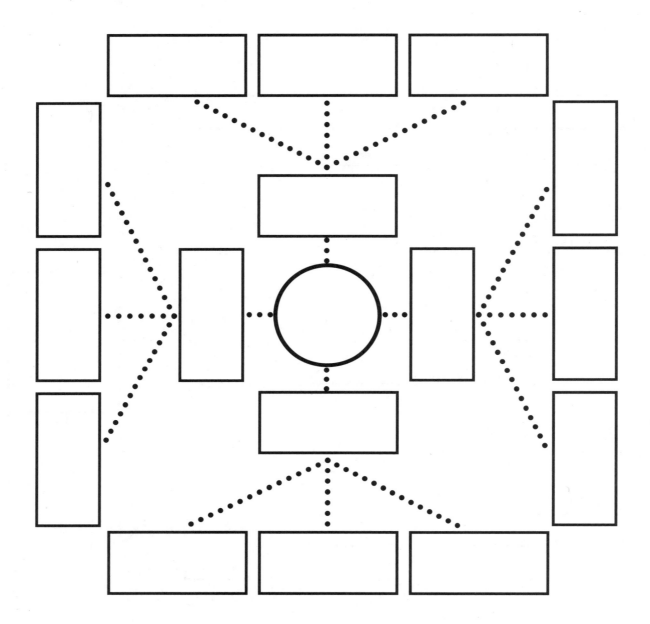

# Flowchart Model

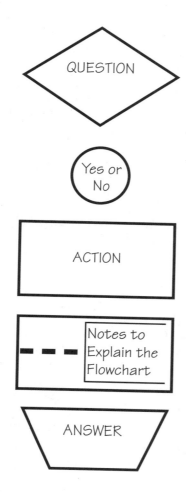

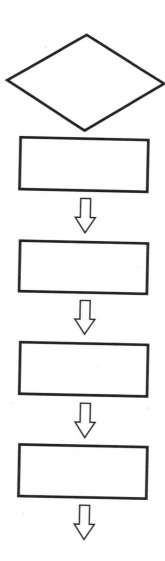

## Ladder Diagram

1.

2.

3.

4.

5.

6.

# 5W Model

TOPIC: _____

| | |
|---|---|
| **Who:** | |
| **What:** | |
| **When:** | |
| **Where:** | |
| **Why:** | |
| **How:** | |
| **Summary Statement:** | |

# Compare and Contrast Diagram

| Concept 1 _____ | | Concept 2_____ |

### HOW ALIKE?

```
_____
_____
_____
_____
_____
```

### HOW DIFFERENT?

### With Regard To

```
_____        _____
_____        _____
_____        _____
_____        _____
_____        _____
```

# ▶ What are they?

Reports are oral or written collections of information on a specific topic. Report writing should be interesting and challenging as well as a learning experience. From the first step of choosing a topic through gathering the information, writing the report, and citing the sources, the student becomes the active learner in the process. Some new and motivating types of reports are described below.

# ▶ How are they different?

A typical research report includes a title page, outline, introduction with thesis statement, body of information, conclusion, footnotes or references, and bibliography. The paper may be presented orally, often with some type of visual aid to add color and clarity. Three variations of the traditional research report are described here.

- The **magazine report** requires a minimum amount of writing. After reading and deciding on the facts to be contained in the report, the student takes notes and then rewrites them in complete sentences. The magazine report format includes a title page, ten pages with one fact and one picture on each page, and an "About the Author(s)" page.

- The **ABC report** is a vehicle for writing about people, places, or things. The student writes something about the topic on each of twenty-six pages; the focus of each page begins with a specific letter of the alphabet. This structure helps students recognize and organize specific information about the topic. Some type of illustration or example on each page is also required.

- Another creative reporting format is the **dodecahedron report.** A geometric solid with twelve faces is the basis for this report. The focus is on selecting the most important or most interesting pieces of information to share, writing that information (in sentences, not paragraphs) on each face of the dodecahedron, and then assembling the shape to display.

Alternative reporting and assessment formats help sustain middle level students' interest and keep them motivated to complete the assignment while they are learning about the topic. Teacher direction; specific requirements; and clear, understandable expectations are key elements for success in these endeavors.

# ▶ How do we get started?

## Magazine Report

**Step 1:** Students decide on a topic. Biographies and countries are appropriate, although almost any topic can be covered in this type of report. Share an example of a completed magazine report from a previous class. Explain how students' work will be evaluated.

**Step 2:** Have individuals or pairs of students select appropriate research materials. After reading the information on their topic, they list the ten most important facts or key ideas.

**Step 3:** Direct the students to arrange the listed facts in the order they will be covered in the report and to state each fact in a set of complete and original sentences.

**Step 4:** Ask students to show the completed sentences to you. At this point, check the order and grammar of the sentences.

**Step 5:** Allow students to search through magazines, newspapers, catalogs, and booklets to select at least one picture that illustrates each sentence. You also may allow them to illustrate with original drawings.

**Step 6:** Provide a supply of construction paper (12" x 18") from which students will select six sheets to fold in half to form the actual booklet.

**Step 7:** Show the students what is required on the title page (title, date, author[s] name, illustration). Have them create a title page for their report.

**Step 8:** Have students carefully print or write each set of sentences on the successive pages of the booklet and paste related illustrations on the appropriate pages.

**Step 9:** Instruct the students to create an "About the Author(s)" page to finish their magazine report. This should include name, age, hobby, hometown, and more if they wish.

**Step 10:** Have students sign up or draw numbers out of a hat to determine when they present their report orally to the class.

**Step 11:** After the presentations, assess students' reports. A sample evaluation form follows.

---

### SAMPLE MAGAZINE REPORT ASSESSMENT FORM

**POINTS**     **REQUIREMENTS**

_____ (5)    Title page, including title, author(s) name, date, illustration

_____ (40)   Format, including at least one picture and one fact per page

_____ (20)   Complete sentences, including correct capitalization and punctuation

_____ (20)   Correct spelling in all sections

_____ (10)   "About the Author(s)" page, including at least name, age, hometown, and hobby

_____ (5)    Overall neatness and appearance

_____        Total Points Earned

---

# ABC Report

**Step 1:** Decide whether students will work as individuals, in pairs, or in trios to complete their reports. Then, assign topics to the students. Information related to all disciplines can be covered in this type of report. Be sure to share an example of a completed ABC report with your students. Explain how their work will be evaluated.

**Step 2:** Instruct students to use research materials (at least three sources) to identify important subtopics that begin with each letter of the alphabet. It might be helpful to schedule at least two periods in the school media center for this process. Students must take notes and think about appropriate illustrations for each subtopic.

**Step 3:** Ask students to rewrite their notes in complete paragraphs addressing a subtopic for each letter of the alphabet. Each paragraph will occupy one page in the final report.

**Step 4:** Have students look through magazines, newspapers, booklets, and catalogs to find pictures to illustrate each subtopic. They also may include original drawings.

**Step 5:** Review the requirements for a title page (title, date, author[s] name, illustration) and have students design their own.

**Step 6:** Ask students to transfer their paragraphs and illustrations to the appropriate pages in their booklet. Stress the importance of neatness and accuracy.

**Step 7:** Have students include a page listing their resources in the format you provide.

**Step 8:** Suggest an "About the Author(s)" page to conclude the report. This should include name, age, hometown, and hobby.

**Step 9:** If you wish, have students present the reports orally (two to three minutes) before displaying them in the classroom, in a showcase, or in the school media center.

**Step 10:** Assess students' reports. A sample evaluation form follows.

---

### SAMPLE ABC REPORT ASSESSMENT FORM

| POINTS | | REQUIREMENTS |
|---|---|---|
| _____ | (5) | Title page, including title, name, date, illustration, teacher's name |
| _____ | (25) | All letters of the alphabet included with complete information |
| _____ | (25) | Illustrations, including at least one per page, directly related to the subtopic |
| _____ | (20) | Complete sentences and paragraphs, including correct capitalization, punctuation, and paragraphing |
| _____ | (10) | Correct spelling on all pages |
| _____ | (5) | Overall appearance and neatness |
| _____ | (10) | "About the Authors" page (optional), including name, age, hobby, hometown |
| _____ | | Total Points Earned |

---

## Dodecahedron Report

**Step 1:** Show a finished report of this type to your students to create interest and motivation. Then, assign the topics to be covered by individual students. This format works well for book reports, reports about a city or a country, and science reports. Explain how students' work will be evaluated.

**Step 2:** Allow time for the students to determine the eleven most important facts or key ideas about the assigned topic.

**Step 3:** Decide whether the information must be written in complete sentences. Students illustrate each fact in some way (pictures cut from magazines, etc., or original drawings).

**Step 4:** Provide multiple sheets of colored construction paper, and have students make the twelve circles using the pattern found at the end of this section.

**Step 5:** Show the students how to fold each circle (again, using the pattern) to create the shape necessary to form the dodecahedron.

**Step 6:** Have students decorate each face with one fact and one illustration. The twelfth face is for the title of the report, the date, the student's name, and an illustration.

**Step 7:** Have students glue together the folded edges to form a three-dimensional "ball."

**Step 8:** (optional) Ask students to share their reports orally with the class or team before suspending the dodecahedrons from the ceiling with string, yarn, or fishing line.

**Step 9:** Assess students' reports. A sample evaluation form follows.

### ◤ POINT TO PONDER

According to James and Barkin (1983), reading a book is not the only way to learn about your subject or topic. They suggest visiting a local museum, watching a television special, and interviewing someone who can provide firsthand information. Why would middle level students enjoy such alternative information-collecting activities?

---

### SAMPLE DODECAHEDRON REPORT ASSESSMENT FORM

| POINTS | | REQUIREMENTS |
|---|---|---|
| _____ | (10) | Overall appearance and neatness; holds shape |
| _____ | (55) | Five points for each of the eleven faces that includes one fact and one illustration |
| _____ | (5) | Personal title section (the twelfth face), including title, student name, date, and illustration. |
| _____ | (20) | Correct spelling on all faces |
| _____ | (10) | Complete sentences (if required, if not, reassign the 10 points) |
| _____ | | Total Points Earned |

# ▶ Where do we go for more information?

Larson, R. 1991. *How to write reports: A guide for grades 6–9*. Portland, ME: J. Weston Walch.
Includes a step-by-step teaching guide, answer key, a list of report topics, and reproducible exercises meant to motivate and interest the learner.

Meister, T. 1993. *Research skills through integrated themes*. Torrance, CA: Frank Schaffer Publications, Inc.
Presents a variety of integrated themes that lend themselves to active student research activities in all disciplines. The format is uniform: a section overview, a summary of information, research activities, application and synthesis of the research, "teacher talk," and more ideas and suggestions.

## *References*

James, E., and Barkin, C. 1983. *How to write a great school report*. New York: Lothrop, Lee and Shepard Books.

## Pattern for the Dodecahedron

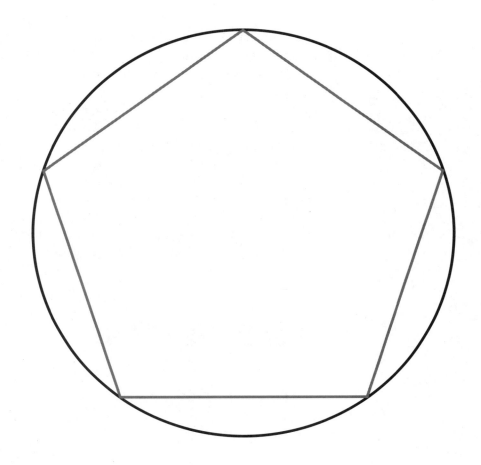

# Topic 15  INSTRUCTIONAL TECHNOLOGY

## ▶ What is it?

The Information Age is significantly affecting middle schools in a multitude of ways. More high-tech interdisciplinary teams are being formed than ever before, and technology is being used increasingly often to assist teaching and learning. When teams of teachers and students are equipped with the latest tools and technology, the focus of the classroom changes from a passive, subject-centered environment to an active, student-centered one because the focus changes from teaching to learning. Students, for example, become more responsible for their own learning as they plan and execute multimedia presentations, as they engage in computer simulations, as they research information through global networks, and as they correspond with students from other lands through telecommunications. In short, students gain a genuine electronic literacy that becomes a strong motivating force in their desire for independence and their thirst for knowledge.

## ▶ How is it different?

The role of the teacher in technology-rich classrooms changes dramatically from that in traditional classrooms. According to Collins (1991), major trends include these shifts: from whole-class to small-group instruction; from lecture and recitation to coaching; from assessment based on test performance to assessment based on products, progress, and effort; from a competitive to a cooperative school structure; from all students learning the same things to different students learning different things; and from the primacy of verbal thinking to the integration of visual and verbal thinking.

Technology accomplishes three major functions. It serves as a source of student information, replacing or enhancing both information dispensed by teachers and information from print sources. It also provides a means of simulating real-life performance situations, which give students the opportunity to use (and teachers the opportunity to assess) the higher-level skills of analysis, synthesis, and evaluation. And it assists in the monitoring of individual and school progress.

---

## Some Common Technology Terms

**authoring programs**—allow students and teachers to link text with video, audio, graphics, animation, and other digital data to create multimedia presentations (e.g., electronic slide shows, simulations)

**hardware**—the equipment used to run software; includes computers, monitors, printers, modems, videodisc players, CD-ROM drives, and other equipment

**interactive video**—a video format that provides the user with some control in the creation or the viewing of the production; promotes active learning

**LCD panel**—allows user to project computer screen through an overhead projector

---

Fitzpatrick (1993) cites the following additional contributions of technology to instruction:

**Simulations and Games** A growing number of computer simulations and games are available that provide students with first-hand experiences. Now students can work with others to build a city; grapple with environmental issues; face the dangers and pressures of everyday life in the past, present, or future; or, travel to all parts of the globe.

**Data and Research** Students can work with a variety of technologies (computer, CD-ROM, videodisc) to explore a vast array of information. Integrated computer programs allow students to search, collect, enter, and manage data while at the same time engaging them in the higher-order thinking skills of application, analysis, synthesis, and evaluation.

**Telecommunications** One way to gather data is to communicate with students from other schools, states, and countries. Learning crosses disciplines as students share ideas, information, and observations from a unique perspective based on their own culture and lifestyle.

**Multimedia** The power of multimedia to capture the interests and imaginations of students is unlimited. Multimedia is multisensory and accommodates diverse learning styles; empowers students to make their own project decisions; fosters an active, collaborative environment for the classroom; and, encourages communication at all levels, including student-to-student and student-to-teacher.

**Video Production** Video production is an integral part of the classroom technological movement. Using a video camera, students can make presentations and maintain video portfolios of their projects and work. Video production enhances student understanding, creativity, and technical prowess. A video camera with a tripod and a VCR are the main hardware necessities for this experience.

## MORE TECHNOLOGY TERMS

**modem**—connects the computer with other computers via telephone lines

**multimedia**—the integration of text, sound, graphics, animation, and movies on the computer screen

**network**—(most commonly a LAN, or local area network) a linkage of various pieces of hardware so they may have access to one another

**scanner**—allows the input of color or black-and-white art or text into the computer

**software**—programs that computers run to accomplish a specific purpose

**videodisc**—a platter that can provide up to one hour of high-quality video and stereo (or bilingual) audio on each side

**word processor**—software that allows students and teachers to type words, read them, and print them in a variety of styles, fonts, and sizes. Words can be manipulated, edited, and checked for spelling. Many word-processing programs contain a dictionary, a thesaurus, and a way to check for grammar and usage.

- Enter the classroom with the attitude that, as the availability and variety of technologies increase and change, they are capable of and committed to integrating new technologies into their classrooms

- Are aware that using technology in the classroom requires effort and planning

- Are concerned about legal and ethical responsibilities associated with the use of technology in the classroom and are aware of issues of equitable access to technology and technology training

- Believe that keeping abreast of new classroom technologies is as much a part of their professional development responsibilities as is keeping up with changes in their subject areas

- Know that they are in control of the technology, rather than vice versa

- Are willing to give both existing and future technologies a chance to make a difference in their classrooms

# How do we get started?

Before building a technology-rich classroom or team, elicit the support of people in the school—beginning with the principal and extending to the media specialist, the technology coordinator, the school technology committee, the district-level technology and media support group, and, if possible, a colleague to serve as a peer coach. Once support is in place, you are ready to begin.

**Step 1:** Read about new technology in professional journals. Most subject area professional journals have articles regarding the use of technology in the specific disciplines along with software and hardware reviews.

**Step 2:** Visit existing high-tech classrooms or teams. Plan to stay long enough to see students and teachers using the technology.

**Step 3:** Begin making key classroom changes even before you have the technology installed. You and your students should be comfortable with cooperative learning strategies. Workstations can be set up where students work at learning centers. If you haven't already done so, establish management techniques for working with learning stations.

**Step 4:** Enroll in technology training courses offered at the school, district site, or local professional development center. If you have a technology professional on staff, perhaps training sessions can be arranged for your team. There are also videotape and software packages that act as tutorial programs.

**Step 5:** Take the time to become comfortable with some basic software programs, but don't think you have to be an expert on every piece of equipment or new software program before you can begin to use technology. You will have several experienced, capable, and willing students or peers who will be glad to help you with the software and hardware options.

**Step 6:** Don't be afraid to seek help. Use colleagues, students, the computer coordinator, or the media specialist. Also, many hardware and software manufacturers have toll-free help lines you can contact.

**Step 7:** Be patient. Use technology when you are comfortable with it. Think big but start small.

**Step 8:** Decide how to set up your room. Access to electrical outlets and telephone jacks will be a determining factor. Decide which pieces of equipment will be used at each location.

**Step 9:** Obtain and organize the necessary furniture, materials, and equipment. Determine the number of students using each technology station at any given time. Complete the physical setup of the technology station as budget, time, and expertise allow.

**Step 10:** Determine a feasible management system. Who can use the equipment, and when can it be used? How will students' work be assessed?

**Step 11:** Conduct an orientation to the station and the equipment for all participating students, volunteers, and support staff. Make sure the students understand the objectives, procedures, and behavior standards. Inform everyone about the expectations and guidelines for functioning at the station.

# ▶ Where do we go for more information?

Bee, C. P. 1980. *Secondary learning centers: An innovative approach to individualized instruction.* Santa Monica, CA: Goodyear.
Provides a step-by-step guide to implementing, scheduling, keeping records of, and evaluating learning centers.

Dockterman, D. A. 1991. *Great teaching in the one computer classroom.* Cambridge, MA: Tom Snyder Productions.
Offers practical solutions for turning the computer into a valuable teacher tool both inside and outside the classroom. Includes anecdotes and personal experiences.

## VIDEOTAPE AND SOFTWARE PACKAGES THAT ACT AS TUTORIAL PROGRAMS

**MacAcademy**  477 S. Nova Rd., Ormond Beach, FL 32174 (800)-527-1914

**Professor Mac**  Individual Software, Incorporated

**Professor PC**  Individual Software, Incorporated

**Professor Windows**  Individual Software, Incorporated

**Introduction to Windows**  Mentor Notes

**Advanced Windows**  Mentor Notes

**Introduction to Word Perfect**  Mentor Notes

**Hypercard Projects for Teachers**  Ventura Education Systems

**Teacher in a Box Series**  American Education Corporation

**Teach Me Series**  American Training International

## References

Collins, A. 1991. The role of computer technology in restructuring schools. *Phi Delta Kappan* (September):28–36.

Fitzpatrick, C. 1993. Educational technology. In *Linking through diversity: Practical classroom activities for experiencing and understanding our cultures*, W. Enloe and K. Simon, eds. Tucson, AZ: Zephyr Press.

Rezabeck, L. L. 1993. *Florida Technology in Education Quarterly*, (Fall/Winter):47–55.

# Copy Form 20

The following products are good examples of existing software in each category.

## TELECOMMUNICATIONS
**America Online**
**K-12 Net**
**Global Village News**
**GEMNET**
**KIDSNET**
**AT&T Learning Network**

## AUTHORING PROGRAMS
**Multimedia Desktop** – Datalus
**Action** – MacroMedia
**MediaText** – Wings for Learning
**HyperCard 2.1** – Claris
**Persuasion** – Aldus
**Link Way Live!** – EduQuest
**Astound** – Good Disk
**Director** – MacroMedia

## SIMULATIONS AND GAMES
**Rice Farming** – Longman
**Sim City** – Maxis
**Sim City 2000** – Maxis
**Sim Life** – Maxis
**Sim Earth** – Maxis
**Balance of the Planet** – Mindscape
**Carmen Sandiego Series** – Broderbund
   **Where in Time Is Carmen Sandiego?**
   **Where in the USA Is Carmen Sandiego?**
   **Where in Europe Is Carmen Sandiego?**
   **Where in the World Is Carmen Sandiego?**
   **Where in America's Past Is Carmen Sandiego?**
   **Where in Space Is Carmen Sandiego?**
**Decisions, Decisions Series** – Tom Snyder
   Productions
   **Colonization**
   **Immigration**
   **Revolutionary Wars**
   **Urbanization**
   **American History Pack**
   **Substance Abuse**
   **The Environment**
   **Prejudice**
   **AIDS**
   **Balancing the Budget**

   **Foreign Policy**
   **Media Ethics**
   **The Campaign Trail**
   **The Government & Society Pack**
**InnerBodyWorks** – Tom Snyder Productions
**National Inspirer** – Tom Snyder Productions
**International Inspirer** – Tom Snyder Productions
**In the Days of Knights & Kings** – Entrex
**Eco-Adventures in the Oceans** – Chariot
   Software
**Eco-Adventures in the Rainforest** – Chariot
   Software
**Pilgrim Quest** – Decision Development Corp.
**Headline Harry & Great Paper Race** – Davidson
**Oregon Trail** – MECC
**Wagon Trail 1848** – MECC

## MULTIMEDIA
**Grolier's Multimedia Encyclopedia**
**Point of View** – Scholastic
**World Atlas 3.0 Multimedia** – Software
   Toolworks
**Voyage of the Mimi** – Sunburst Communications
**Visual Almanac** – Optical Data
**Composer Quest** – Dr. T's Music Software
**Guinness Disc of Records** – Unidisc, Inc.
**Destination Mars** – Compu Teach
**EarthQuest** – EarthQuest, Inc.
**Voyager II: The Dynamic Sky Simulator** – Carina
   Software
**Music Mentor** – Midisoft Corp.
**1994 Guinness Multimedia Disc of Records** –
   Grolier Electronic
**San Diego Zoo Presents: The Animals** –
   Software Toolworks
**Mammals: A Multimedia Encyclopedia** –
   Software Toolworks
**Oceans Below** – Software Toolworks
**From Alice to Ocean** – Claris Clear Choice
**The Big Green Disc: Interactive Guide to Saving
   the Planet** – Sony Electronics
**Exploring Ancient Architecture** – Medio
   Multimedia
**Dinosaurs! The Multimedia Encyclopedia** –
   Sony Electronics

*Great Wonders of the World* – InterOptica Publications
*Great Cities of the World* – InterOptica
*Great Solar System Rescue* – Tom Snyder Productions
*Great Ocean Rescue* – Tom Snyder Productions
*Time Traveller CD: A Multimedia Nigel's World* – Lawrence Productions
*Chronicle of History* – New Media Schoolhouse

## VIDEODISC

*The Holy Lands* – ABC News Interactive
*STV Rain Forests* – National Geographic
*STV Human Body Series* – National Geographic
*STV Restless Earth* – National Geographic
*STV Solar System* – National Geographic
*GTV Planetary Manager* – National Geographic
*GTV A Geographic Perspective on American History* – National Geographic
*The '88 Vote* – Optical Data
*Martin Luther King, Jr.* – Optical Data
*Salamander* – Voyager Company
*National Gallery of Art* – Videodisc Publishing
*Divided Union* – Public Media
*Presidents* – Data Disc International
*Desert Storm* – Warner News Media
*For All Mankind* – Voyager Company
*Great Quake of '89* – Voyager Company
*STS Science Forums I & II* – Videodiscovery
*Science Sleuths* – Videodiscovery
*Science Discovery Image & Activity Bank* – Videodiscovery
*Bio Sci II* – Videodiscovery
*Life Cycles* – Videodiscovery
*Physics at the Indy 500* – Videodiscovery
*Physics of Sports* – Videodiscovery
*Math Sleuths* – Videodiscovery
*Insects* – Smithsonian
*Flying Machines* – Smithsonian
*Dinosaurs* – Smithsonian
*National Zoo* – Smithsonian
*Gems and Rocks* – Smithsonian
*First Ladies* – Smithsonian
*Our Biosphere* – Smithsonian
*American History* – Instructional Resources
*Western Civilization* – Instructional Resources
*World History* – Instructional Resources
*Windows on Science* – Optical Data

## DATA & RESEARCH

*PC Globe* – PC Globe
*Microsoft Works* – Microsoft Corp.
*Atlas Graphing* – Strategic Mapping
*Sports Illustrated Almanac* – Warner
*North American Indians* – Compton's
*Street Atlas USA* – DeLorme Mapping
*Microsoft Excel* – Microsoft Corp.
*LogoWriter for Macintosh* – Logo Comp.
*Time Patterns Tool Kit* – Tom Snyder Productions
*Facts on File* – Systems, Inc.
*Multimedia World Fact Book* – Bureau
*NewsWorks* – Newsweek
*Culture 2.0* – Cultural Resources
*CIA World Fact Book* – Bureau Elect.
*Atlas Map Maker* – Strategic Mapping
*Hyperatlas* – Micro Maps Software, Inc.
*Social Studies Toolkit: Our World and Our Nation* – Tom Snyder Productions
*U.S. Presidents* – Quanta Press
*The American Journal Series* – K-12 Micromedia Publishing
   *Lewis and Clark*
   *Christopher Columbus*
   *The Alamo*
*Mathematicians I* – Ventura Educational
*Mathematicians II* – Ventura Educational
*TimeLiner* – Tom Snyder Productions
   *African American History*
   *American History*
   *Science & Technology*
   *Women in History*
   *World History*
   *A Day in the Life of Dinosaurs and Other Big Stuff*
   *Everything Is Relative*
   *Health*
   *The Arts*
   *Pre and Ancient History*

# Topic 16 TEACHING IN THE CULTURALLY DIVERSE MIDDLE SCHOOL CLASSROOM

## ▶ What is it?

**M**ulticultural education recognizes the diverse cultures that make up our schools, communities, nation, and world. Whether differences center on race, national origin, language, religious beliefs, age, gender, or disability, multicultural education recognizes the importance of understanding those aspects that make us who we are and define how we differ from one another. Multicultural education aims to restructure educational institutions so that all students will acquire the knowledge, skills, and attitudes needed to function effectively in a culturally diverse nation and world.

James Banks (1991) has described the following four approaches to moving a traditional curriculum toward multiculturalism.

■ The **Contributions Approach** involves adding to the traditional curriculum a mention of some of the heroes and social contributions of nondominant groups. These heroes and contributions are viewed strictly from the mainstream cultural perspective.

■ The **Additive Approach** involves adding nonmainstream "content, concepts, themes, and perspectives . . . to the curriculum without changing its basic structure, purpose, and characteristics." In this approach, despite more significant additions than under the Contributions Approach, the curriculum still "looks out" from a primarily mainstream perspective.

■ With the **Transformation Approach**, "the key curriculum issue involved . . . is not the addition of ethnic groups, heroes, and contributions, but the infusion of various perspectives, frames of reference, and content from different groups that will extend students' understandings of the nature, development, and complexity of the United States and the world." In contrast to the Additive Approach and the Contributions Approach, the Transformation Approach makes the mainstream perspective *only one* of several from which subject matter is viewed.

### GLOSSARY

*culture*—the traditions, customs, and social habits of a group based on an inherited set of beliefs or values

*disability*—under the Americans with Disabilities Act of 1990, a disability is defined as having a physical or mental impairment that substantially limits one or more of the major life activities of an individual

*discrimination*—treating people with partiality or prejudice based on their group affiliations, particularly their membership in racial, ethnic, religious, or cultural minorities

*diversity*—the range of ethnic, racial, and other categories that are perceived as dividing people into significant groups within a given society

*ethnicity*—affiliation with a group as distinguished by customs, language, and common history

*gender bias*—an unreasoned, personal judgment based on a person's gender

## GLOSSARY, CONTINUED

**multicultural awareness**—recognition of the contributions to a society by people of various cultures

**multicultural education**—educational experiences that consciously attempt to instill knowledge about and appreciation for cultural diversity

**prejudice**—an adverse judgment formed without adequate knowledge or reflection; also, an irrational attitude of hostility directed against an individual, group, or race

**racism**—any activity by individuals, groups, institutions, or society as a whole that treats people unjustly because of their race

**sexism**—any activity by individuals, groups, institutions, or society as a whole that treats people unjustly because of their gender

**stereotype**—an oversimplified opinion or unexamined judgment of a particular group

(Adapted from Garrett, Frey, Wetzler, & Phillips, 1993)

- Finally, the **Social Action Approach** extends the Transformation Approach by encouraging students to take social actions, within and outside the school, that are consonant with what they have learned through exposure to different perspectives.

# ▶ How is it different?

According to Tiedt (1990), the general outcomes expected from a multicultural program can be stated from many different perspectives. As a result of multicultural education, students should

- Display a positive feeling of self-esteem and be aware of the characteristics of their own individual cultures
- Extend this right to self-esteem to others and compare their individual culture to those of others
- Identify different cultural groups in their school, community, and nation and describe the similarities and differences of these groups
- Discuss stereotyped thinking and how it leads to prejudice. Students should apply critical skills to solve such problems in the school and community and consider how this process might be extended to solve worldwide conflicts of interest

## CHILDREN LEARN WHAT THEY LIVE

If a child lives with criticism,
He learns to condemn.

If a child lives with hostility,
He learns to fight.

If a child lives with ridicule,
He learns to be shy.

If a child lives with tolerance,
He learns to be patient.

If a child lives with encouragement,
He learns confidence.

If a child lives with praise,
He learns to appreciate.

If a child lives with fairness,
He learns justice.

If a child lives with security,
He learns to have faith.

If a child lives with approval,
He learns to like himself.

If a child lives with acceptance and friendship,
He learns to find love in the world.

(Tiedt, 1990)

# ► How do we get started?

**Step 1:** The multicultural classroom approaches the study of culture through the universal elements present in all cultures (Hoffman, 1993). Ask students to brainstorm a list of elements of culture they would expect to find if they were dropped into a village anywhere on the planet. Then, given a specific latitude and altitude, a specific climate (annual rainfall and seasonal temperature), and a specified type of vegetation, ask students to predict the following:

- What might the inhabitants eat?

- How might they dress?

- What might they use to build shelter?

- What might they do for work and recreation?

- What goods or materials might they need to import? What might they export?

- What might they use as a monetary system?

- What religious or belief system(s) might they have?

- How might they express themselves (art, music, literature)?

- What types of social or political systems might they have?

Through such inquiry, students can see why an igloo or a thatched-roof hut becomes a home; a seal fur coat or a sarong, logical clothing; whale blubber or coconuts, sensible food staples. Students begin to understand their world on a "personal to intercultural continuum" (Hoffman, 1993).

**Step 2:** Along with the basic human needs of water, food, shelter, and clothing are the needs for love and self-esteem. People everywhere strive to meet these needs. Many cultural groups define themselves according to the way they deal with such life experiences as birth, passage from puberty to adulthood, marriage, and death. Celebrating these traditions and customs helps different groups preserve their culture. If you have a culturally diverse classroom, ask the students to share

- How their families celebrate birthdays and weddings

- Which holidays are important to them and why

- How rights of passage are celebrated

- What specific rituals or traditions accompany death

> "The 'Multicultural Education' approach promotes cultural pluralism and social equality by reforming the school program for all students to make it reflect diversity. These reforms include school staffing patterns that reflect the pluralistic nature of American society; unbiased curricula that incorporate the contributions of different social groups, women, and the handicapped; the affirmation of the languages of non-English-speaking minorities; and instructional materials that are appropriate and relevant for the students and which are integrated rather than supplementary."
>
> (Sleeter & Grant, 1987)

**Step 3:** Expose students to a rich array of objects, folktales, lullabies, games, songs, foods, dances, and stories from various cultures. The following activities help to accomplish this goal:

- Compare and contrast children's artwork from the various cultures. Discuss how the artwork reflects their surroundings and daily lives.

- Create a class quilt. Each square can represent a different culture in some way.

- Invite a storyteller to tell folktales.

- Read folktales from other countries, and have students choose one to illustrate or dramatize.

- Create a "global connections" display of everyday things.

- Write and perform a play depicting life in another culture.

- Have groups of students work together to research games from different countries. Have each group teach their game to the rest of the class.

- Compile a class international cookbook containing recipes from different countries. Have a tasting party to try out some of the recipes.

- Expose students to music from around the world, starting with the cultures represented in your classroom.

- Invite guest speakers or performers that represent different cultures.

- Show films, videos, filmstrips, laser discs, and CD-ROMs that depict different cultures.

- Use telecommunications to correspond with students and teachers around the world.

**Step 4:** To truly understand multiculturalism, students need to view situations and events from a variety of perspectives. Simulations are excellent tools for putting students in "other people's shoes." Discussions and debates also foster an understanding of, and appreciation for, varied points of view. Looking at current events through the eyes of diversity (age, politics, gender, race, class, religion, disability) encourages students to look at issues from more than one perspective. Opposing views from history make good springboards, and the media are excellent sources of contemporary material including political cartoons, letters to the editor, and the news.

**Step 5:** Teach students the benefits of working cooperatively. Once students learn to work together, they are more likely to be tolerant of differences. Create positive, interdependent relationships "based on shared goals, a division of labor, complementary roles, and dependence on each other's resources" (Johnson & Johnson, 1991). Because interdependence and differing perspectives naturally create

> **"B**ehavior is a mirror, in which everyone shows his image.**"**
>
> Johann von Goethe
> (Tiedt, 1990)

conflicts of interest, teachers and students need to know how to negotiate so that differences can be resolved. According to Johnson and Johnson, there are five basic steps in negotiating a resolution to a conflict of interests. They are

1. Jointly defining the conflict

2. Exchanging reasons and the rationale for their positions

3. Reversing perspectives

4. Inventing options for mutual benefit

5. Reaching a wise agreement

**Step 6:** Build positive self-concepts through activities. Students who feel good about themselves are better equipped to deal with the diversity of others around them. Celebrate student differences. Sensitize students to the similarities and differences among people, helping them to see that people are more alike than different, but that differences are valuable (Forte & Schurr, 1991).

**Step 7:** Thread multicultural activities and themes throughout the curriculum. This might be accomplished by

- Developing a multicultural interdisciplinary unit

- Sponsoring a schoolwide international cultural fair

- Ensuring that posters and other visible graphics reflect race, gender, and disability diversity

- Selecting instructional, library, and other resource materials that depict diverse people in nonstereotypic manners

- Discovering stereotypes in popular media (magazines, newspapers, TV, videos, and music). Observe the extent to which the media reinforce unequal and exploitative gender, racial, and class relationships. Write letters to the editor, the station, or the program sponsor.

**Step 8:** Read aloud books, poems, and short stories reflecting diversity. Research shows that the single, most important activity for building success in reading is reading aloud to students. It makes sense to develop students' cultural literacy at the same time that we develop literacy.

**Step 9:** Build bridges to the curriculum to allow the exceptional and culturally different students to be successful in the mainstream classroom. Sometimes the bridges are temporary, sometimes long-term. According to Grant & Sleeter (1989), the bridges include the following:

- **Learning Styles.** These may show overlapping patterns for many, but not all, members of a cultural or gender group. Conduct learning style inventories and observations to identify your students' styles.

- **Curriculum Relevant to Students' Experiential Backgrounds.** Spend some time observing in the neighborhoods where your students live (geometric building design, plant life, stores, games children play, music). Identify topics of interest to students, and locate and use "curriculum materials that make the students want to learn."

- **Skill Levels.** These often vary widely within a class but can be successfully bridged using cooperative learning groups, peer tutors, adult volunteers, varied grouping patterns, and alternative resources representing a variety of levels and learning styles.

- **Language.** Language differences can be bridged successfully by supplying peer and adult tutors who speak both languages, consulting with teachers of English to speakers of other languages and bilingual teachers, and preparing home communications in other languages. English-speaking students who do not speak standard English need to be taught the differences between their dialect and the standard but not to be punished or criticized for using their home dialect. However, standard English should be expected to be used at school.

- **Cultural Capital and Expectations.** "Teachers should strive to guide exceptional and culturally different learners toward acquiring the knowledge that will help them the most later in life (competing for college entrance, jobs, scholarships)." Setting high expectations is the key.

- **Success Stories.** Incorporate all students into the American mainstream. Role models and mentors can help.

- **Connections with the Home and Community.** Spend time getting to know the community and the parents. Learn their expectations of schooling, help them develop a schooling support system at home, and invite them into your classroom.

**Step 10:** Eliminate stereotypes and stereotyping by actively engaging students in activities and situations that help them realize the inaccuracies of stereotypes. For example, have students create magazine collages showing men and women of all races, ages, and disabilities engaged in nurturing family situations and responsibilities or engaged in all kinds of jobs and professions. Invite guest speakers who counter stereotypical images.

# ► Where do we go for more information?

Grant, C. A., and Sleeter, C. E. 1989. *Turning on learning: Five approaches for multicultural teaching plans for race, class, gender, and disability.* Columbus, OH: Merrill Publishing Company.
Contains a wealth of curricular ideas and lesson plans for multicultural education in the middle school and high school. Lesson plans that vary in length from one class period to several days are suggested for all basic skill and curricular areas.

James, R. 1993. *Open circles: An anthology for personal and cultural awareness.* Portland, ME: J. Weston Walch.
The insightful stories, speeches, and true accounts in *Open Circles* expand students' understanding of racial, ethnic, and socioeconomic groups—theirs and others'. The nine selections encourage readers to examine how they view other cultures and help them develop pride in their own cultural heritage.

Lerner, E. 1986. *Cultural conflicts case studies in a world of change.* Portland, ME: J. Weston Welch.
Focuses on student role playing. The case studies set up students with background information, a scenario to stimulate discussion, and four to six conflicting parts to play.

## References

Banks, J. A. 1991. *Teaching strategies for ethnic studies.* 5th ed. Needham, MA: Allyn & Bacon.

Banks, J. A. 1993. *Multicultural education: Development, dimensions, and challenges.* Bloomington, IN: Phi Delta Kappan.

Forte, I., and Schurr, S. 1991. *Advisory: Middle grades advisor/advisee program.* Nashville, TN: Incentive Publications, Inc.

Garrett, S. D., Frey, J., Wetzler, J., and Phillips, P. B. 1993. *Celebrate diversity!* Newspaper Association of America Foundation, International Reading Association, National Council for the Social Studies.

Grant, C. A., and Sleeter, C. E. 1989. *Turning on learning: Five approaches for multicultural teaching plans for race, class, gender, and disability.* Columbus, OH: Merrill Publishing Company.

James, R. 1993. *Open circles: An anthology for personal and cultural awareness.* Portland, ME: J. Weston Walch.

Johnson, D. W., and Johnson, R. T. 1991. *Teaching students to be peacemakers.* Edina, MN: Interaction Book Company.

Hoffman, D. (1993). Creating the intercultural classroom. In *Linking through diversity: Practical classroom activities for experiencing and understanding our cultures,* W. Enloe and K. Simon, eds. Tuscon, AZ: Zephyr Press.

Sleeter, C. E., and Grant, C. A. 1987. An analysis of multicultural education in the United States. *Harvard Educational Review* (November):421–444.

Tiedt, P. L. 1990. *Multicultural teaching a handbook of activities, information, and resources.* Needham, MA: Allyn & Bacon.

Trelease, J. 1989. *The new read-aloud handbook.* New York: Penguin Books.

## SUGGESTED MULTICULTURAL READ-ALOUD BOOKS

Jim Trelease (1989) recommends the following books for reading aloud in the middle school multicultural classroom because their fast pace and high interest will keep students' attention.

*Where the Buffaloes Begin* by Olaf Baker

*Courage of Sarah Noble* by Alice Dalgliesh

*Indian in the Cupboard* by Lynne Reid Banks

*The Sign of the Beaver* by Elizabeth George Speare

*Sing Down the Moon* by Scott O'Dell

*Bridge to Terabithia* by Katherine Paterson

*Roll of Thunder, Hear My Cry* by Mildred Taylor

*The Friendship* by Mildred Taylor

*Marching to Freedom: Story of Martin Luther King, Jr.* by Joyce Milton

*The Hundred Dresses* by Eleanor Estes

*Words by Heart* by Ouida Sebestyen

*An American Slave* by Frederick Douglas

*Twenty and Ten* by Claire H. Bishop

*North to Freedom* by Anne Holm

*The Golem* by Isaac Bashevis Singer

*The Little Riders* by Margaretha Shemin

*Smoke and Ashes: The Story of the Holocaust* by Barbara Rogasky

*Snow Treasure* by Marie McSwigan

*Child of the Silent Night* by Edith Fisher Hunter

*Helen Keller: From Tragedy to Triumph* by Katherine Wilke

*The Man Who Sang in the Dark* by Eth Clifford

*In the Year of the Boar and Jackie Robinson* by Bette Bao Lord

*J.T.* by Jane Wagner

*Jump Ship to Freedom* by James and Christopher Collier

*War Comes to Willy Freeman* by James and Christopher Collier

*Who is Carrie?* by James and Christopher Collier

*The Long Journey* by Irene Hunt

*And Nobody Knew They Were There* by Irene Hunt

*No Promises in the Wind* by Irene Hunt

*Favorite Folktales from Around the World* edited by Jane Yolin

*The People Could Fly: American Black Folktales* by Virginia Hamilton

# Topic 17  ENGLISH AS A SECOND LANGUAGE

## ▶ What is it?

Although the United States has always been known as a nation of immigrants, it is only in recent years that the field of English as a Second Language (ESL) has emerged. As distinguished from English as a Foreign Language, ESL methodology is oriented toward students who live in a country where English is the dominant medium of communication. As might be expected, learners of a second language who live in the country in which that language is used face significant challenges to be fully functional within the larger community. ESL students in the middle school, for example, must continue to adjust to a language and culture that is not their own while at the same time coping with increasingly difficult course work and the myriad problems that adolescents in the United States typically encounter.

At the same time, most teachers of ESL students—whether in a class comprising only ESL students or in a mainstream class—face the challenge of dealing with a mix of students from several diverse cultural and linguistic backgrounds in the same classroom. Add to that the often vast differences in educational backgrounds of the students, and it becomes apparent that the teaching strategies, methods, and materials used in ESL must be adapted to suit particular teaching situations.

While some ESL methodologies have grown directly out of theoretical models about how second languages are best acquired, others have developed out of mainstream approaches to the teaching of language and literacy. Several of the more widely known methodologies have been presented as complete, systematic packages of materials that purport to take learners from the beginning stages of language learning through fluency.

Although there often has been little agreement among proponents of specific methodologies about how to teach ESL, there are two basic principles upon which most theorists and practitioners agree.

■ **Language develops best when students have multiple opportunities to *use* their new language.**

### KEY TO COMMON ABBREVIATIONS

**ESL**—English as a Second Language

**ESOL**—English for Speakers of Other Languages

**TESOL**—Teachers of English to Speakers of Other Languages (professional organization)

**EFL**—English as a Foreign Language

**ESP**—English for Specific Purposes (e.g., for science or business)

**EAP**—English for Academic Purposes

**LEP**—Limited English Proficient

- **Languages are learned most efficiently when students have an opportunity to practice communicating in a supportive environment.**

Current research in language teaching and learning suggests that a second language is best acquired when the learners are exposed to a steady flow of "comprehensible input." According to this principle, which is referred to as the "input hypothesis" (Krashen, 1982), we learn best when we understand the general meaning of what we hear and read, even though we may not comprehend it in full detail. Accordingly, the purpose of ESL methodology is to make language comprehensible to students through a variety of techniques and materials at increasingly challenging levels of complexity.

In light of current assumptions about how languages are learned, ESL teachers attempt to create supportive environments, stimulate meaningful communication, and expose students to increasingly difficult levels of authentic language.

Along with demographic changes have come new and difficult challenges for teachers. While many students whose primary language is not English arrive in the mainstream classroom academically prepared to learn new concepts in English, others do not for a variety of reasons. As a result, teachers are finding it necessary to implement changes that acknowledge and incorporate the second-language learning process.

In ideal situations, teachers team up with specially trained ESL professionals to design strategies and materials that complement their individual programs. Such changes are never easy to make because they affect the whole class and alter the roles of everyone in it. However, advocates for early mainstreaming of language-minority students argue that the successful inclusion of these students in the regular classroom not only accelerates language acquisition but can also benefit all students.

Because ESL students are rich sources of information on other languages and cultures (Rigg & Allen, 1989), their presence is an asset to the learning experience. In the words of Henry Trueba, Dean of the School of Education at the University of Wisconsin, the application of this principle to instructional practices is crucial because "the very existence of American democracy depends on the successful schooling of the ethnic, immigrant, and other 'minority' children who are indeed now becoming the majority" (introduction to Faltis, 1993).

> "We acquire . . . only when we understand language that contains structure that is 'a little beyond' where we are now. How is this possible? How can we understand language that contains structures that we have not yet acquired? The answer to this apparent paradox is that we use more than our linguistic competence to help us understand."
>
> (Krashen, 1982)

**DID YOU KNOW?**

According to U.S. Bureau of the Census figures, the number of speakers of languages other than English increased by 38.1 percent between 1980 and 1990. The bureau determined that 14 percent, or one person in seven, grew up or is growing up speaking English as a second or additional language.

# ► How is it different?

Approaches to teaching native speakers of English at the middle school level generally assume high levels of internalized English-language skills and knowledge of U.S. culture, which students who are acquiring English have not necessarily attained. Accordingly, ESL methodology makes these skills and this knowledge accessible to second-language students through a variety of techniques that provide students with multiple opportunities for repeated, meaningful communication.

Second-language students in the middle school mainstream class can benefit greatly from reading and discussing literature—a rich source of language and cultural knowledge. However, many such learners cannot accomplish these tasks on their own without considerable difficulty. ESL readers require considerably more contextualization of setting, story sequence, and theme than do first-language students.

Special attention to the building blocks of language and literacy benefits ESL students. Ongoing language support often consists of vocabulary-building activities, shared-reading techniques, and paraphrasing of complex or unusual language. In addition, tapping students' firsthand language experience and cultural knowledge can provide the native-English speakers in the class with valuable insights into stories and poems translated from other languages or written by recent immigrants.

ESL methodology also purposefully builds confidence in students by encouraging small-group interaction and extensive skills practice with partners or peer tutors. When placed in a lecture or large-group discussion setting, ESL students are often reluctant to participate for fear of drawing attention to their language errors. The small-group arrangement provides for a higher incidence of communicative exchanges in a supportive environment, thus enabling all students to express their knowledge under less threatening conditions.

> "*Instead of expecting second-language learners to adapt themselves as best they can to the new classroom cultural environment, it is necessary to adjust that environment to make connections . . . between their lives and experiences outside the classroom and the world within it, and then to facilitate students' continuing integration of these two realms of experience.*"
>
> (D. Scott Enright and Mary Lou McCloskey, 1988)

## ▶ ▶ ▶ Scenario

Amara is a seventh-grade student from a small village in Somalia. She is fourteen years old and has spent two years in an ESL program. Prior to arrival in the United States, Amara had attended primary school for four years—until she and her family had been forced to leave their village in search of food. She is minimally literate in the Somali language and had no experience with English before coming to the United States. Amara is strong in oral communication skills. Her current level of social English allows her to communicate freely with friends and understand most classroom instructions. However, her reading remains very slow, and she is unable to express herself in writing beyond the simple sentence level.

Sitting next to Amara is Sergei, a student from Ukraine who arrived just one year ago. Sergei's father is a civil engineer, and his mother is a teacher. He is twelve years old. Sergei attended school in his home country, where he excelled in science and math. He studied English as a foreign language for two years but had no experience in listening to or speaking English prior to his arrival in the United States. Sergei has excellent study skills and is highly motivated to improve his English. He gets help with his schoolwork from his mother, who has a reasonably good command of formal, written English. Sergei's spoken English is heavily accented, which remains a source of great embarrassment for him in the mainstream English classroom.

### Points to Consider

1. In what ways do Amara and Sergei remind you of any students in your classroom, past or present?

2. Try to describe other ways second-language students in your class have differed from each other.

3. How might your approach to teaching literature incorporate the needs of both Amara and Sergei?

> "*Second-language students need to be with first-language students. If they are isolated from native-English-speaking students, they cannot learn English from them, nor can they share any of the riches they have to offer. Classrooms should be organized so that small groups of first-language and second-language students work together on meaningful tasks.*"
>
> (Christian J. Faltis, 1993)

## QUESTIONS TO CONSIDER

1. Which programmatic approach do you feel best prepares ESL students for mainstream classrooms?

   a. Grade-level classes only (submersion)

   b. Grade-level classes plus an ESL class (ESL pullout)

   c. Native language instruction plus ESL class (transitional bilingual)

   d. Other _____

2. What criteria does your school use to decide when ESL students are ready for mainstream, all-English classrooms?

3. What is most difficult about having ESL students in your classroom?

4. Which of the following would be most helpful in dealing more effectively with the ESL students in your class? (Indicate order of preference.)

_____ Teamwork with ESL teachers

_____ More time to adapt lessons to ESL students' needs

_____ Training in ESL methodology and strategies

_____ Specific information about ESL students' cultures

# ▶ How do we get started?

**Step 1:** Get to know the ESL students in your class. One way to start is by making an introductory survey of languages and cultural backgrounds of all the students in your class. This can be accomplished by distributing a questionnaire (a sample is included as a reproducible page) or by asking the students in your class to interview each other and share the results. You will also want to look at English language proficiency test scores or review any other criteria used at your school to assess and place ESL students.

In addition, you may want to conduct your own informal assessment of students' language abilities. Consider using the following techniques:

- Invite all the students in your class to write a letter to you telling about their backgrounds and explaining their own objectives, strengths, and areas where they think they will need improvement in your class. Later, meet with ESL students individually or in small groups of three to four students.

- During an informal discussion, ask students about their language and cultural backgrounds, how long they have studied English, and what kinds of things they like to read in English and in their own language. Give students an opportunity to ask you about the class and express any doubts or concerns they might have.

- Ask the students to read a short sample text. Try to select a text that does not contain a lot of specific cultural references or other complicating factors such as dialog. Have students underline or list words and expressions that make them uncertain. Collect and review these lists as one indicator of your students' reading levels. This will help you determine the amount of time and effort students may need to spend on learning new vocabulary.

**Step 2:** Set up optimal conditions for second-language learning. Teachers with extensive experience working with multilingual classes report that setting up certain conditions for second-language learning promotes successful interaction between first and second language learners (Enright, McCloskey, and McCloskey 1988; Freeman and Freeman, 1989). Many of the following conditions are identical to those associated with **whole language teaching** and **cooperative learning arrangements**:

- Organize the classroom environment so that second-language students have a variety of opportunities for interaction with both the teacher and their English-speaking classmates.

- Create multiple learning areas so that a variety of learning activities can take place at the same time. For example, dedicate one area to readily accessible dictionaries and other reference works, another to audiotape listening, and a third to reading aloud. Arrange classroom furniture so that students can shift between small-group and whole-class activities.

- Promote a variety of possibilities for participation through talking, listening, writing, and multiple forms of collaborative tasks.

- Arrange learning equipment, tools, and materials according to the task at hand. Place special vocabulary learning supplements for ESL in a specified area, supplementary skill builders in another.

- Involve students in setting up a system of methods and criteria for evaluating their language progress. Team up with ESL teachers for suggestions on how to assess language development. Consider using portfolios.

- Establish an even balance among the three main configurations for classroom interaction (teacher-led large group, teacher-led small group, teacher-delegated small group).

- Work with students to establish classroom norms—stated in positive terms—for participation in whole-group and small-group activities.

**Step 3:** Use a variety of techniques to modify your own instructional approach and language. Strategies for making classroom language more comprehensible to second-language learners include the frequent use of visual supports, demonstrations, additional examples, and paraphrasing.

Especially at the beginning of ESL students' experience in a mainstream English class, it is vitally important that they gain confidence by understanding exactly what is expected of them. While it is important to avoid singling out second-language learners and talking down to them by oversimplifying instructions, it is useful to develop an awareness of students' comprehension levels by modifying complex language and building in frequent comprehension checks. Keep in mind that there are also major cultural differences in perceptions about ideal teacher-student and student-student interactions. These classroom interactions can be further complicated when gender issues come into play.

**Step 4:** Contextualize and clarify unfamiliar cultural references and historical information. Use a variety of discussion questions for previewing, employ visual aids, and engage in group interaction activities. In most cases, areas that require contextualization or comment are relatively easy for the teacher to anticipate. For example, recent immigrants are not likely to have background knowledge of such historical events as the California Gold Rush or the Great Depression. Conversely, students from other countries can provide valuable cultural background for stories and folktales from around the world. For example, Spanish-speaking students can become resources for explaining cultural background and Spanish terms in the stories of such writers as Gary Soto and Piri Thomas.

**Step 5:** Use frequent comprehension checks, graphic organizers, and other appropriate strategies to help students grasp the whole meaning of the literature they read. Second-language readers often lack the confidence and skills necessary to construct meaning without considerable help. Methods often used by ESL teachers include previewing key events or concepts, story retelling, story mapping, student construction of comprehension questions, and dramatic reading aloud.

**Step 6:** Assist students with critical thinking skills. Provide concrete examples and demonstrations that clearly explain concepts and critical thinking you wish to teach, such as cause and effect. Cultures differ significantly in their ways of viewing the world and explaining phenomena. In the classroom, this may mean that some ESL students will come up with explanations or rationales that differ significantly from the expected. Encourage all students to compare and contrast alternative explanations and points of view as a way of learning more about each other.

**Step 7:** Anticipate potentially difficult vocabulary items, and devise appropriate exercises. Such activities can be in the form of worksheets or group activities that foster increasingly sophisticated vocabulary-building skills. Encourage the ESL students in your class to build personal academic vocabularies for reading literature by keeping lists of new terms and idiomatic expressions in a separate notebook.

**Step 8:** Involve ESL students with first-language students as equal participants. Use cooperative learning activities, especially those that incorporate communicative interaction resulting in tangible products, reactions, or reports. For example, ESL students can both benefit from and contribute to simulations, noncompetitive language games, and small-group research or visual presentation projects. Faltis (1993) suggests that teachers can foster positive interdependence among their students by "structuring the activity so that the students cannot complete the task successfully without the active participation of all members of the group." When selecting cooperative learning activities for mixed first- and second-language students, the following steps can be helpful:

- Assign activities that have all the students in a group responsible for creating a written or visual product that they all sign before it is displayed.

- Make each step in the process dependent on a previous step to make the role of each student in the group equally important to completion of the task.

- Give the same reward to all members of each group. For example, let students know from the outset that a grade is going to be assigned to the outcome or product as a whole.

**Step 9:** Use peer tutors. Match up second-language students who are having difficulty in specific areas with English-proficient students—either native speakers or advanced second-language students—for peer-tutoring sessions. Tasks that are ideal for peer tutoring in a literature class include reading aloud, story-retelling activities, accessing resources for background information, clarifying vocabulary items, and composing written responses. Take care to limit the length of these sessions, and define the task clearly for both students. In some situations, it may be appropriate to reward peer tutors by assigning extra credit or official recognition. Some teachers find it helpful to hold group reflection sessions at which peer tutors can exchange ideas and experiences.

**Step 10:** Create opportunities for ESL students to reflect on their own learning and language acquisition processes. This can be accomplished through group discussions at the end of each unit, the completion of individual reflection sheets (such as the Copy Forms that follow), or student-teacher conferences. These opportunities help students review and accumulate what they have learned at regular intervals, develop critical thinking skills by evaluating the activities they have participated in, and gain new confidence by expressing their own ideas to a receptive audience.

# ► Where do we go for more information?

Alderson, J. C., Krahnke, K. J., and Stansfield, C. W. 1987. *Reviews of English language proficiency tests*. Alexandria, VA: Teachers of English to Speakers of Other Languages (TESOL) Publications. Provides a complete review of published ESL tests.

Cantoni-Harvey, G. 1987. *Content-area language instruction: Approaches and strategies*. Reading, MA: Addison-Wesley Publishing Co.

Collie, J., and Slater, S. 1989. *Literature in the language classroom: A resource book of ideas and activities*. New York: Cambridge University Press.

Fradd, S. H., and Weismantel, M. J., eds. 1987. *Meeting the needs of culturally and linguistically different students: A handbook for educators*. New York: Little, Brown.

Freeman, Y. S., and Freeman, D. E. 1989. Evaluation of second-language junior and senior high school students. In *The whole language evaluation book*, Goodman, Goodman, and Hood, eds. Portsmouth, NH: Heinemann Educational Books. Provides detailed suggestions on evaluating the progress of ESL students.

Maculaitis-Cooke and Scheraga, M. 1988. *The complete ESL/EFL cooperative and communicative activity book: Learner-directed activities for the classroom*. New York: Cambridge University Press.

Mohan, B. A. 1986. *Language and content*. Reading, MA: Addison-Wesley Publishing Co.

Nutall, C. 1982. *Teaching reading skills in a foreign language*. Portsmouth, NH: Heinemann Educational Books.

Omaggio, A. C. 1986. *Teaching language in context*. Boston, MA: Heinle & Heinle.

Ovando, C. J., and Collier, V. P. 1985. *Bilingual and ESL classrooms: Teaching in multicultural contexts*. New York: McGraw-Hill.

# References

Cummins, J. 1989. *Empowering minority students*. California Association for Bilingual Education.

Enright, D., McCloskey, S., and McCloskey, M. L. 1988. *Integrating English: Developing English language and literacy in the multilingual classroom*. Reading, MA: Addison-Wesley Publishing Co.

Faltis, C. J. 1993. *Joinfostering: Adapting teaching strategies for the multilingual classroom*. Columbus, OH: Merrill Publishing Company.

Freeman, Y. S., and Freeman, D. E. 1989. Evaluation of second-language junior and senior high school students. In *The whole language evaluation book*, Goodman, Goodman, and Hood, eds. Portsmouth, NH: Heinemann Educational Books.

Krashen, S. D. 1982. *Principles and practice in second language acquisition*. Tarrytown, NY: Pergamon Press.

Rigg, P., and Allen, V. G. 1989. *When they don't all speak English: Integrating the ESL student into the regular classroom*. Urbana, IL: National Council of Teachers of English.

# "Getting to Know You" Questionnaire

**Name** _____ **Date** _____

**Place of Birth** _____

**First Language** _____

1. What languages can you speak in addition to your first language?

   _____

2. How well can you read and write in your first language (check one):

   _____ very well

   _____ pretty well

   _____ not very well

   _____ not at all

3. Please give an example of writing in your first language here. (Write words or a sentence, or attach a short clipping from a newspaper or magazine here.)

4. Where do you use your first language now? _____

_____

_____

5. Who do you usually use your first language with? _____

_____

_____

6. When and where did you start to learn English? _____

_____

_____

7. Please explain how you learned English. Write one or two sentences.

_____

_____

_____

_____

8. What do you think you do best in English now? Put them in order (1, 2, 3, 4).

_____ speak

_____ listen

_____ read

_____ write

# "Language Points" Reflection Sheet

**Name** _____ **Date** _____

**Unit** _____

**Title of Story, Article, Poem, or Play**

_____

1. List three of the new words or expressions you learned as you read. Choose the ones you think you will see or use most often. Write a synonym, definition, or translation of each word.

   _____ - _____

   _____ - _____

   _____ - _____

2. What strategy did you use most often to figure out the meaning of new words? (studied clues from the sentence or paragraph, asked the teacher, asked a friend, looked it up in a dictionary)

   _____

   _____

3. Copy a whole sentence or line that was difficult for you to understand when you first read it.

   _____

   _____

4. What strategies did you use to figure out what the sentence means?

   _____

   _____

5. How difficult was the whole selection for you to understand? (Circle one.)

   **Easy  1    2    3    4    5    6    7    8    9  Difficult**

6. Which of your activities helped you understand it better?

   _____

   _____

7. Which activities were not very helpful?

   _____

   _____

8. What would you still like to be able to do better?

   _____

   _____

# 6 Assessment

A s the middle school movement has evolved over the past three decades, middle level educators have come to realize that assessment activities must be realigned with (1) the needs and characteristics of early adolescence, (2) the middle school organizational pattern of interdisciplinary teaming, and (3) the desired student outcomes of the middle grades curriculum. Rather than assessment driving what we teach and how we teach in the middle grades, the developmental needs of the student and the scope and sequence of the curriculum must drive assessment.

The trend today in middle school assessment is toward authentic types of measurement that focus less on recall of information than on processing of information. Product, portfolio, and performance tools and techniques, for example, reflect the mission of the middle school and its philosophy and components better than do their traditional counterparts of criterion- and norm-referenced tests.

Because it is important to view assessment as a collection of alternative methods for determining what a student knows or is able to do, this module presents a wide variety of formal and informal assessment ideas.

# Contents

## ▶ What is it?

Authentic assessment cannot be separated from authentic instruction. The goal of both is to ensure that students acquire new information and skills in a context that reflects the world outside the classroom. When you teach authentically, your objectives and methods of instruction, along with your tools for assessment, relate to real-world situations and out-of-school applications. Both authentic instruction and authentic assessment preclude isolated and artificial exercises and tests that do not represent the realities of the world students will face when they leave the classroom.

Student ownership is an important dimension of authentic instruction and assessment. When learning activities are truly authentic, students take an active part in the whole learning event; they help to choose materials, determine tasks and the time allocated to them, and establish the benchmarks of success.

While authentic assessment can take many forms, these forms share the following characteristics:

- They are public rather than private and involve an audience of some kind in addition to the teacher.
- They are not restricted by rigid time constraints.
- They offer questions or tasks that are already familiar to students or that students have been apprised of well in advance of the assessment occasion.
- They require some degree of collaboration.
- They involve the student's own research or application of knowledge.
- They are scored by a multifaceted system.
- They include self-assessment.
- They identify strengths as well as weaknesses.
- They allow for individual learning styles, aptitudes, and interests.
- They minimize needless and unfair comparisons.

(adapted from Wiggins, 1991)

---

## TIPS FOR TEAMS

- **Brainstorm ways to assess student achievement that are more authentic than those you currently employ.**

- **Explore how you might share the burden of developing and processing such assessments.**

**ANALYTIC RUBRIC** A set of criteria used to award points for each of several elements in a response (quantitative).

**ASSESSMENT** The testing or grading of students according to a given set of criteria.

**AUTHENTIC ASSESSMENT** Assessing student achievement or performance in situations that closely match the standards and the challenges of the world outside the classroom.

**EVALUATION** The process used to determine the general value or worth of practices, programs, or curricula.

**HOLISTIC RUBRIC** A set of criteria used to measure overall performance or response to a prompt (qualitative).

**MEASUREMENT** The assignment of a numerical quantity to a given assessment or evaluation procedure.

**METACOGNITION** The consciousness of one's own thinking processes.

**OUTCOME-BASED ASSESSMENT** Assessment in the context of outcome-based education. The learning outcomes and goals are those skills, experiences, and attitudes that will be useful to students outside the classroom in both their work and their personal lives.

**OUTCOME-BASED EDUCATION** Curricula, instruction, and measurement/assessment that focus on desired outcomes for the students—the knowledge, competencies, and qualities they should be able to demonstrate when they finish school.

**PRODUCT, PORTFOLIO, AND PERFORMANCE ASSESSMENT** Three forms of authentic assessment. **Product assessment** requires a concrete result such as a videotape, learning package, experiment, script, production, manual, or exhibit. **Portfolio assessment** is based on a meaningful collection of student work that exhibits the student's overall efforts, progress, and achievements in one or more areas. **Performance assessment** is based more on the processes the student uses than on the final product. It relies on the professional judgment of assessors who observe the student performing a predetermined task.

## ▶ How is it different?

The significant difference between traditional and authentic forms of assessment lies in the real-world orientation of authentic assessment and the integral relationship between authentic assessment and authentic learning. Teachers have often relied on materials and methods for both learning and assessment that distort some of the real purposes of education. Students have memorized lists, filled in blanks, answered questions by rote, scrutinized textbooks for simple facts, and computed math problems from predetermined formulas.

These techniques have their place and should not be arbitrarily excluded. However, the major role they have often played in the past must give way to strategies that account for process as well as for product, that consider not only the knowledge and skills students have acquired but how they have acquired them, and that evaluate students' ability to communicate and apply knowledge and skills. Differences in the assessment tasks themselves, in the degree of student involvement and independence, and in the methods of scoring and of reporting results are all discussed later in this module.

## ▶ How do we get started?

### Step 1: Set team goals.

Before you can embark on making alternative assessment measures an integral part of your middle school curriculum, you and your team members need to spend some time reviewing issues and setting goals. You may want to begin this process by using the copy form "How Do You and Your Team View Assessment?" at the end of this section. As you discuss how to implement the suggestions below, record your collaborative ideas on a planning worksheet and use them as your guide to changing your practices.

- Develop a mission statement on assessment by completing this sentence: *The desired outcomes for our assessment program are . . .*
- Arrive at a working definition of authentic assessment.
- Generate a list of ways you can make your assessment tasks and measures truly authentic and not merely authentic-looking.
- Create a plan for infusing higher-order thinking skills into all assessment tasks; utilize a range of thinking skill models and taxonomies.
- Explore ways to standardize criteria to support necessary student comparisons without sacrificing flexibility for individual students.
- Seek out quality staff development opportunities to improve your assessment skills; maintain a portfolio of your growth in this area.
- Find ways to utilize technology to make alternative assessment less labor intensive.

### Step 2: Engage your students in authentic instructional strategies.

Focus on helping students develop the ability to work independently of you and to become aware of their own learning styles and preferences. Gradually, they will display more initiative and empower themselves to take responsibility for what they do and how they do it. The Gradual Release of Responsibility Model of Instruction (GRR) (Pearson & Gallagher, 1983) provides a number of suggestions for generating lessons that will lead to higher levels of authenticity in the teaching and learning process.

- Provide students with multiple guided opportunities to use the new learning strategies.

- Continue to demonstrate, but encourage students gradually to take over. Emphasize the strategy of thinking aloud.

- Move to observing how students receive and give feedback as they become more independent. Offer help when needed, sometimes in the form of a question that directs them to observe something or predict what might come next.

- Structure opportunities for collaboration. After working with the whole class, have students form small groups and engage in exploratory talk. Gradually, this external talk among peers will be internalized to become a kind of inner speech that students can rely on when they work independently.

- Use self-assessment in examining your experience with the strategy.

- Provide a guide for students that contains information or a structure for the learning. Small groups may use it as they work together, and individuals may use it as a final support prior to independent work.

(adapted from Rhodes and Shanklin, 1993)

### Step 3: Develop a trial authentic assessment task.

The following plan is based on work by the Connecticut State Department of Education. It is appropriate for developing a range of assessment tasks. Modify the plan to suit your needs, keeping in mind both the content and the behaviors you want to evaluate. Be prepared to make changes or adjustments after looking at student work. It may surprise you!

- Start with an idea from
  - a book, newspaper, magazine, or catalog
  - a conversation or observation
  - a random thought or inspiration

- Begin converting the idea by determining
  - your objectives
  - how the idea fits into the curriculum
  - what the assessment can tell you about your students
  - what students will have to know to be successful
  - whether you will assess processes, products, or both

- Consider such response formats as
  - written exercises or reports
  - oral reports or performances
  - group discussions and activities
  - bulletin board displays

## POINT TO PONDER

How would you defend this statement?

" *The debate should not be about one measure over another, or new versus old. . . . No test, no matter how good it is, should be the sole criterion.* "

(Michael H. Kean, chairperson of the Test Committee of the Association of American Publishers, 1993)

- Proceed with your plan by
    - drafting a description of the task and stating the purpose and objectives
    - writing directions for students, including nondirective questions that nudge them to utilize their own strategies
    - describing for students the criteria for evaluation, including the attitudes and attributes you hope to see, such as group cooperation, persistence, and resourcefulness
- Develop supporting notes that indicate
    - what students need to know ahead of time
    - necessary materials and equipment
    - problems that may arise
    - the degree of guidance to be provided
- Determine how you will assess the task by
    - considering whether a holistic approach with anecdotal reports or an analytic point system is more appropriate
    - identifying which elements are most important to assess and whether "scores" should be weighted accordingly
    - defining levels of performance
- Try out the task by
    - having one or more colleagues review and critique the plan
    - administering the task in several classrooms
    - taking detailed notes on both what you see and what students say

(adapted from Stenmark, 1991)

### Step 4: Experiment with alternative assessment strategies.

At the end of this section, you will find seven alternative assessment strategies with sample tests. Try them with your students and keep notes on both the process and the results. When you have used several of the strategies, consider whether some types of students perform better on nontraditional assessment measures than on more traditional ones. Do certain testing tasks or formats tend to favor high achievers? low achievers? students from certain cultural backgrounds? students for whom English is a second language? creative students? males? females? students with particular learning styles? Discuss your conclusions with your team.

# ► Where do we go for more information?

Burke, K., ed. 1992. *Authentic assessment: A collection*. Palatine, IL: Skylight Publishing Co.
Covers the practical applications of authentic assessment in the context of authentic curriculum, methods, and outcomes.

Herman, J. L., Aschbacher, P. R., and Winters, L. *A practical guide to alternative assessment*. Alexandria, VA: ASCD.
Explains the details of setting assessment goals, selecting criteria, ensuring reliable scoring, and making decisions based on assessment.

Perrone, V., ed. 1991. *Expanding student assessment*. Alexandria, VA: ASCD.
Explores various issues in alternative assessments. See especially chapters by Edward Chittenden, Rieneke Zessoules, and Howard Gardner.

## References

Finney, S. 1991. Troubled waters. *Challenge* 45.

Kean, M. H. 1993. Getting it right: Authentic assessments and the true multiple-measures approach. *Education Week*, October 6: 13.

Pearson, P. D. and Gallagher, M. C. 1983. The instruction of reading comprehension. *Contemporary Educational Psychology* 8: 317–344.

Rhodes, L. K. and Shanklin, N. L. 1993. *Windows into literacy: Assessing learners, K-8*, pp. 75–76. Portsmouth, NH: Heinemann.

Schurr, S. L. 1992. *ABC's of evaluation: Twenty-six alternative ways to assess student progress*. Columbus, OH: National Middle School Association.

Stenmark, J. K., ed. 1991. *Mathematics assessment: Myths, models, good questions, and practical suggestions*, p. 17. Reston, VA: National Council of Teachers of Mathematics.

Wiggins, G. 1991 A response to Cizek. *Phi Delta Kappan*, 72(9) (May): 700–703.

# Strategy 1: Bloom-Constructed Test

Use Bloom's Taxonomy to construct a test of six questions, one for each level of the taxonomy, or a test of thirty-six questions, several for each level of the taxonomy. Assign points of differing values to each question or level of questions.

Explain to students that the lower-level questions will test their recall of information and therefore have specific right or wrong answers, while the higher-level questions will test their creative and critical thinking skills and therefore are open-ended with no predetermined right or wrong answers.

If you use a six-question test, students answer all questions. If you use a thirty-six-question test, they answer enough questions to create a total of 100 points. However, they must select questions from *each level* of the taxonomy to make up their 100-point total.

## Sample Bloom-Constructed Test: Fables

1. KNOWLEDGE (10 points): List the titles of five different fables that you read during our interdisciplinary unit on folklore.


2. COMPREHENSION (10 points): In your own words, describe the characteristics of a fable.


3. APPLICATION (15 points): Choose a fable and discuss the meaning of its moral.


4. ANALYSIS (15 points): Compare and contrast two fables. Consider origins, characters, settings, actions, and morals.


5. SYNTHESIS (25 points): Create an original fable of your own. Write it in three to five paragraphs.


6. EVALUATION (25 points): Rank the five fables you listed in Question 1 according to their appeal and relevance to the lives of middle level students. Your first choice (highest relevance) should be number 1 and your last choice, number 5. Give three reasons for your first and last choices.

*(adapted from Schurr, 1992)*

# Strategy 2: "Jeopardy"-Constructed Test

This answer-question format, based on the game of Jeopardy, can help wean students away from the "one right answer" syndrome. It can be a valuable tool for conducting a review or for demonstrating to students how subject areas overlap. This strategy is also useful in the context of an advisory program; students can use it to clarify their dreams, goals, and attitudes and to articulate personal experiences.

Provide a set of answers and ask students to generate relevant questions.

## Sample "Jeopardy"-Constructed Test: Punctuation

1. The ANSWER is <u>exclamation mark</u>. What is the QUESTION?

**Sample responses:**

   a. What form of punctuation appears at the end of a statement of surprise?

   b. What mark appears at the end of an exclamatory sentence?

   c. What is one of the three types of punctuation used at the end of a sentence?

2. The ANSWER is <u>comma</u>. What is the QUESTION?

**Sample responses:**

   a. What form of punctuation separates words in a series?

   b. What form of punctuation separates the city from the state in a written address?

   c. What punctuation mark is missing from this sentence: "John what are you doing up so late on a school night?"

3. The ANSWER is <u>noun</u>. What is the QUESTION?

**Sample responses:**

   a. What part of speech names a person, place, or thing?

   b. What part of speech is usually the subject of a sentence?

   c. What part of speech is the word <u>circus</u> in the sentence "We went to the circus"?

*(adapted from Schurr, 1992)*

# Strategy 3: Fact-Finding Test

Prepare a set of information cards on a selected topic, one card for each student in the class. Each card must contain a short paragraph describing an important item, concept, or issue. You can include key passages quoted directly from a textbook. You may want to create duplicate cards for concepts or passages that are especially difficult.

Each student in the class receives a different information card and reads it silently. Once students understand the information on their cards, they are ready to teach it to others. Students stand and circulate, pausing just long enough to share their information informally with another student or a small group. Students must restate the information in their own words. They may not read from their information cards but use them only as references. During this exchange, each student both teaches and learns new information.

After approximately 30 minutes, students sit and respond in writing to the five starter statements below. When students have finished, collect their response sheets and determine what they have learned through this activity and what you need to reteach.

## Sample Fact-Finding Test: Follow-up

1. The information from my card that I taught others was


2. Three new things I learned about the topic from other students are


3. Something about the topic that I already knew is


4. One part of the topic that I would like to know more about is


5. To me, the most interesting thing about this topic is


*(adapted from Schurr, 1992)*

# Strategy 4: Collaborative Test

Construct a set of items that require both individual and collaborative responses. Have students form into groups of three. Designate each student as team member 1, 2, or 3. Students then complete their own tests. Caution them to follow the directions carefully so that, either individually or as a team, they respond to the items exactly as the directions indicate.

## Sample Collaborative Test: The Digestive System

1. Write out your own definition of <u>digestion</u> by completing this starter statement:

   DIGESTION IS _____

   _____

   _____

   Share your definition with the other members of your team. Together, come up with a definition that includes ideas from all three of your individual responses.

   DIGESTION IS _____

   _____

   _____

2. By yourself, write down three functions of the digestive system.

   a. _____

   _____

   b. _____

   _____

   c. _____

   _____

   Share your ideas with the other two members of your team. Put a circle around the function your team decides is the most important.

3. Which of the following systems of the human body is most difficult for middle grade students to learn about and understand? Rank them from 1 to 5. Your first choice (most difficult) should be number 1 and your last choice, number 5. Do this first by yourself.

_____ Respiratory System
_____ Circulatory System
_____ Digestive System
_____ Skeletal System
_____ Nervous System

Now try to reach consensus with your team members. Change your ranking if necessary to reflect the decision of your team. On a separate piece of paper, write out three reasons for your team's first and last choices.

4. Work with the other two students on your team to record your individual responses to each of the questions below. You may discuss each topic with one another, but you should record only your specific answer.

Team Member 1: What is the most important idea you would want to teach someone about the role of the <u>mouth</u> in the digestive process?

_____

_____

Team Member 2: What is the most important idea you would want to teach someone about the role of the <u>digestive juices</u> in the digestive process?

_____

_____

Team Member 3: What is the most important idea you would want to teach someone about the role of the <u>small intestine</u> in the digestive process?

_____

_____

5. Does your team agree or disagree with this proverb: "The way to people's hearts is through their stomachs." Explain.

_____

_____

_____

*(adapted from Schurr, 1992)*

# Strategy 5: Kinesthetic-Constructed Test

This technique is excellent for assessing students' understanding of related concepts in a content area.

Identify nine important terms or concepts related to a specific topic. Give each student nine cards. Each student writes each of these terms/concepts on a card—one term or concept per card. The student shuffles the cards and lays them out with three cards across and three cards down. The student then writes a statement for each horizontal row (three statements), for each vertical row (three statements), and for each diagonal row (two statements). The statements should show how the three terms or concepts are related. The terms in the statement can appear in any order.

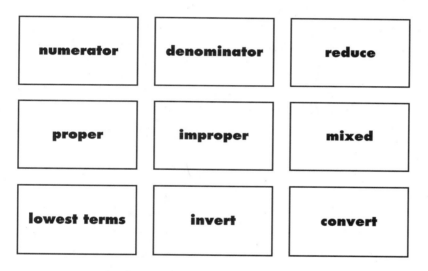

## Sample Kinesthetic-Constructed Test: Fractions

Fraction terms to use: *convert, denominator, improper, invert, lowest terms, mixed, numerator, proper,* and *reduce.*

**Sample statements:**

If the three concepts were *numerator, denominator,* and *reduce,* then you might write, "One cannot <u>reduce</u> a fraction to lowest terms if the <u>numerator</u> and <u>denominator</u> are not divisible by the same number."

If the three concepts were *proper, improper,* and *mixed,* then you might write, "There are three types of fractions: <u>proper</u> (such as 3/4), <u>improper</u> (such as 4/3), and <u>mixed</u> (such as 3 3/4)."

*(adapted from Schurr, 1992)*

# Strategy 6: Reasons-Constructed Test

Construct a test consisting of items that each require the student to generate a list of reasons. Encourage students to state reasons that reflect both creative and critical thinking.

## Sample Reasons-Constructed Test: Global Education

- Give five reasons why nations fight one another.


- Give three reasons for supporting the United Nations.


- Give six reasons why people should learn about cultures other than their own.


- Give seven reasons for learning more about Third World countries.


- Give eight reasons why a knowledge of languages is important.


- Give three reasons for studying geography in school.


- Give two reasons to support the statement "The world is getting smaller."

# Strategy 7: Perspective-Constructed Test

Construct a single-item test that presents students with a controversial situation and then requires them to view that situation from two or more different perspectives. Students write short dialogues between characters who represent these conflicting positions.

## Sample Perspective-Constructed Test: Troubled Waters

Oil spills and pollution from waste being dumped in rivers and in the oceans cause problems that find their way to the land. Polluted waters kill the animals that live in those waters, and waste deposited on the shores of our beaches creates situations that endanger wildlife and people.

Create a short dialogue between a politician interested in off-shore-oil drilling and a seabird. You are the seabird that wants to create an environment that is safe for you, and you are trying to convince the politician that oil and water do not mix.

Politician: _____

_____

Seabird: _____

_____

Politician: _____

_____

Seabird: _____

_____

Politician: _____

_____

Seabird: _____

_____

Did you change the politician's mind?

_____

_____

*(Finney, 1991)*

# How Do You and Your Team View Assessment?

**Directions:** Respond to these questions with your own thoughts, opinions, and experiences. There are no right or wrong answers. If possible, discuss your responses with members of your team. Look for common perceptions of what assessment should be like in the ideal middle school. After all, there is no purpose in looking at alternative methods for assessment if you and your colleagues are satisfied with the status quo!

1. What is the ultimate purpose or goal of testing in middle schools today? What should it be? Is there a discrepancy between what is and what should be?

   _____

   _____

   _____

   _____

2. What assessment measures do you or members of your interdisciplinary team use most frequently? Are they generally successful, informative, varied, and interfaced with the curriculum in meaningful ways?

   _____

   _____

   _____

   _____

3. How do you or your team members use test results for improving student performance? for delivery of instruction? for communicating with students, with parents, and with one another?

   _____

   _____

   _____

   _____

4. How do you or your team members prepare students to be "test-wise"? Do you include regular test and study skill sections as part of your interdisciplinary units? Are these issues discussed in your team handbook? in your team newsletters?

_____

_____

_____

_____

5. What are your team's current grading practices? Are they consistent with the middle school philosophy?

_____

_____

_____

_____

6. What would happen if all traditional paper-and-pencil tests were outlawed for three years at your middle school and replaced with student portfolios, product and performance assessment, and learning logs?

_____

_____

_____

_____

## Topic 2 — PRODUCT ASSESSMENT

### ▶ What is it?

In product-based assessment, formats created by students serve as concrete evidence that learning has occurred and a goal has been achieved. Many different types of products qualify as legitimate forms for authentic assessment. These include, but are not limited to, the following:

*essays, stories, novels, artwork, displays, lectures, sketches, plans, articles, books, compositions, experiments, models, games, designs, notebooks, study cards, flash cards, photographs, pictures, videotapes, charts, graphs, maps, diagrams, exhibits, audiotapes, plays, dances, scrapbooks, newspapers, diaries, transparencies, collections, letters, interviews, surveys, field trips, filmstrips, mobiles, artifacts, blueprints*

### ▶ How is it different?

Product-based assessment places less emphasis on the development process itself than on the outcome of that process. It requires a concrete, hands-on product as the end of the learning process. Furthermore, it requires that this product represent as nearly as possible a real-world application of specific learning.

### ▶ How do we get started?

**Step 1:** Analyze your curriculum topics, themes, or concepts to determine which areas could best be measured by assessing student products.

**Step 2:** Provide your students with a list of optional product formats. They should choose formats that are of real interest and relevance to them. This is an important step; unless directed otherwise, students tend to choose formats that are familiar to them from the elementary grades, such as mobiles, posters, and dioramas. The following chart indicates which of Bloom's categories is especially applicable to a given format and provides a list of formats to consider, along with a set of potential thinking skill objectives.

| BLOOM CATEGORY | OPTIONAL PRODUCT FORMAT | OPTIONAL THINKING SKILLS |
| --- | --- | --- |
| **KNOWLEDGE** | Flash cards, rebus story, scrapbook, drawing, puzzle, tape recording, mobile, collage | Define, draw, identify, label, list, locate, match, name, recite, select, state |
| **COMPREHENSION** | Puppet show, picture dictionary, pamphlet, news story/report, diagram, essay, bulletin board, diary, cumulative stories | Classify, demonstrate, describe, explain, generalize, give examples, group, paraphrase, put in order, retell, rewrite, show, summarize |
| **APPLICATION** | Chart/graph, model, peep show, display, interview, survey, experiment, magazine, directory, post cards, satire, documents | Apply, compare/contrast, construct, debate, diagram, draw conclusions, discover, examine, interview, investigate, keep records, make, predict, produce, prove, track, translate |
| **ANALYSIS** | Textbook, transparency, oral report, movie, scroll, collection, guest speaker, letter, data sheets | Analyze, compare/contrast, deduce, determine, examine, infer, relate, uncover |
| **SYNTHESIS** | Poem/song, game, speech, play, gallery/museum exhibit, choral reading, encyclopedia entries, monologue, puppet show, vignettes, spoofs | Combine, create, design, develop, imagine, invent, make up, perform, prepare, present (an original piece of work), produce, revise, tell, synthesize |
| **EVALUATION** | Written report, scroll, book cover, poster, project cube, photo/picture essay, advertisement, editorial, debate, persuasive letter, speech | Argue, award, choose, criticize, critique, defend, grade, judge, justify, rank, rate, recommend, support, test, validate |

# 10 REASONS WHY STUDENT PRODUCTS MAKE GOOD ASSESSMENT TOOLS

1. They can demonstrate originality.

2. They can demonstrate knowledge effectively and attractively.

3. They can reflect growth in social and academic skills and attitudes that are not reflected in paper-and-pencil tests.

4. They can engage students who are otherwise unenthusiastic about school.

5. They can bring education to life, making it memorable for students.

6. They can demonstrate to the community in concrete terms what students are achieving.

7. They allow for the integration of reading/writing/speaking skills with other subject areas.

8. They can give students flexible time to do thoughtful work.

9. They can permit students to work cooperatively with others.

10. They can encourage creativity.

(adapted from Stenmark, 1989)

**Step 3:** Have students develop a plan for creating their product. The plan should make the development process manageable and help to ensure that quality, and not quantity, becomes the focus. Students often try to put everything they know about a subject into a single product instead of covering some part of the subject in meaningful detail.

Two very different sample student plans appear at the end of this section. The first, for a multimedia product, puts the responsibility into the student's hands. The second represents a more directive approach.

**Step 4:** Provide your students in advance with a set of requirements: due dates, materials available, class time allocations for working on the product, and assessment criteria. Be sure to set aside sufficient class time for students to confer with you, to share ideas with one another, and to critique one another's products at various stages of development. You may even want to have the students give you brief progress reports on a daily basis. A sample progress report appears at the end of this section.

**Step 5:** When products are completed and ready for assessment, give students an opportunity to display their work and debrief one another (in a small or large group) on their product development process. The copy form "My Product: Personal Assessment" at the end of this section can serve as a basis for either self- or peer evaluation activities.

## References

Stenmark, J. 1989. *Assessment alternatives in mathematics: An overview of assessment techniques that promote learning.* Berkeley, CA: Equals and Assessment Committee of the California Mathematics Council, Regents University of California.

# Student Plan: Multimedia Product

1. I will choose a topic that is interesting, informative, and related to our study of _____.

2. I will choose the format for my multimedia presentation from these options: audiotape, videotape, filmstrip, slides, series of photographs, computer-generated segment.

3. I will list different ways to approach this topic, considering these and other possibilities: interview, demonstration, game show, documentary, panel discussion, reenactment, skit.

4. I will narrow the focus of my topic and then conduct research. I will take notes from my reading or interviews and keep records of my sources. I will write out a minimum of twenty note cards, using a minimum of five different sources.

5. I will organize my content so that I have no more than three main ideas. I will discuss these choices with my teacher and at least two peers.

6. I will decide on the sounds and/or images I will use to illustrate each of these main ideas.

7. I will create a storyboard that shows general information, narration, and graphics for each scene, shot, or segment.

8. I will then shoot the scenes, take or collect the photographs, or tape the sound.

9. I will edit my material and proofread my script.

10. I will give my product a title, introduction, and conclusion.

# Student Plan: Science ABC Book

**Directions:** Create an ABC Book on a science topic of your choice. To plan this product, select your topic and then write a concept, term, event, or person related to that topic next to each of the alphabet letters listed below.

Give your booklet a title page, a dedication page, a table of contents, and a bibliography. Treat one alphabet letter on each page. Each page should show something you have learned or know about that topic. Use graphics, symbols, charts, graphs, diagrams, or visual images to illustrate each of your pages.

**Topic for Science ABC Book:** _____

_____

**Date Science ABC Book is to be completed:** _____

**Ideas to write about:**

| | | | |
|---|---|---|---|
| **A** _____ | | **N** _____ | |
| **B** _____ | | **O** _____ | |
| **C** _____ | | **P** _____ | |
| **D** _____ | | **Q** _____ | |
| **E** _____ | | **R** _____ | |
| **F** _____ | | **S** _____ | |
| **G** _____ | | **T** _____ | |
| **H** _____ | | **U** _____ | |
| **I** _____ | | **V** _____ | |
| **J** _____ | | **W** _____ | |
| **K** _____ | | **X** _____ | |
| **L** _____ | | **Y** _____ | |
| **M** _____ | | **Z** _____ | |

# Mini Progress Report: Multimedia Product

| | |
|---|---|
| **Today I completed _____ note cards and wrote up _____ sources for my bibliography. The sources are** | **Today I spent _____ minutes doing my research to answer the question(s)** |
| **Today I took _____ photographs of** | **Today I collected _____ resources for my research. They are** |

# Evaluation Form: Science ABC Book

Parent's/Guardian's signature by assigned date (5)  _____

Used time well in media center and classroom (20)  _____

Table of contents completed (10)  _____

Title page, dedication page, and
bibliography included (10)  _____

Every letter in alphabet shown (10)  _____

Appropriate pages numbered (5)  _____

Required facts included (20)  _____

Completed entries (1 pt. ea. = 26)  _____

Illustration for each entry (1 pt. ea. = 26)  _____

Spelling/neatness (10)  _____

Creativity (15)  _____

Turned in on time (5)  _____

**Total** (162)  _____

Bonus—An entry for all 26 letters (5)  _____

**Comments:**

# My Product: Personal Assessment

**Please take a few minutes to think about how you went about planning, creating, and sharing your product over the last few days or weeks. Use these sentence stems to help you write down your thoughts.**

1. While developing this product I spent most of my time on

2. The best ideas I had for this product came from

3. A major problem I encountered while working on this product was

4. I believe that the greatest strength(s) of my product is

5. The major skills I used in developing this product were

6. When the teacher and others judge the quality of my product, I want them to consider

7. Something I will do differently next time I develop a product is

8. The most important concepts I learned from developing this product are

# Topic 3 · PORTFOLIO ASSESSMENT

## ▶ What is it?

**A** portfolio is a purposeful collection of student work that exhibits the student's overall efforts, progress, and achievements over time in one or more areas of the curriculum. The collection is usually arranged in some chronological order within a predetermined conceptual structure. Portfolios include a wide sampling of the student's work, along with the student's own reflection on and evaluation of the contents.

Portfolios may include a wide array of items: interest inventories, written assignments, reading records, performance plans and logs, journal entries, textbook tasks, reports and research findings, and even standardized and/or objective tests—whatever materials provide the best information about the student's development during a given reporting period. Because they involve students as active stakeholders in their own learning, portfolios have become one of the most popular and effective forms of authentic assessment.

### Eight Reasons to Acknowledge the Power of the Portfolio

1. Developing a portfolio offers the student an opportunity to learn about learning. Therefore, the end product must contain information that shows that a student has engaged in self-reflection.

2. The portfolio is something that is done *by* the student, not *to* the student. Portfolio assessment offers a concrete way for students to learn to value their own work and, by extension, to value themselves as learners. Therefore, the student must be involved in selecting the pieces to be included.

3. The portfolio is separate and different from the student's cumulative folder. Scores and other cumulative folder information that are held in central depositories should be included in a portfolio only if they take on new meaning within the context of the other exhibits found there.

4. The portfolio must convey explicitly or implicitly the student's activities, for example, the rationale (purpose for forming the portfolio), intents (its goals), contents (the actual displays), standards (what is good and not-so-good performance), and judgments (what the contents tell us).

5. The portfolio may serve a different purpose during the year from the purpose it serves at the end. Some material may be kept because it is instructional, for example, partially finished work on problem areas. At the end of the year, however, the portfolio may contain only that which the student is willing to make public.

6. A portfolio may have multiple purposes, but these must not conflict. A student's personal goals and interests are reflected in his or her selection of materials, but information included may also reflect the interests of teachers, parents, or the district. One universal purpose of student portfolios is to show a student's progress on the goals of the instructional program.

7. The portfolio should contain information that illustrates growth. There are many ways to demonstrate it. The most obvious is by including examples of actual school performances that show how the student's skills have improved. Changes observed on interest inventories, records of outside activities such as reading, or on attitude measures are other ways to illustrate a student's growth.

8. Finally, many of the skills and techniques that are involved in producing effective portfolios do not happen by themselves. To support them, students need models of portfolios and examples of how others develop and reflect upon portfolios.

(Paulson, Paulson, and Meyer, 1992)

# ▶ How is it different?

Portfolio assessment differs significantly from the traditional types of assessment. Testing and grading have tended to be quantitative, product-oriented, closed-ended, short-term, and limited in their application to life. Portfolio assessment, on the other hand, tends to be qualitative, process-oriented, open-ended, long-term, and unlimited in its application to real-life situations. Unlike traditional assessment products, portfolios accommodate the developmental stages of young adolescents and allow for individual differences in their growth patterns. Because the process of creating a portfolio is dependent upon self-discovering, self-motivating, and self-initiating behaviors, it demands far more critical and creative thinking from students than traditional assessments have elicited.

## POINTS TO PONDER

Spend some quality time with your team discussing these "portfolio points." Do you agree or disagree?

1. Portfolio contents must be selective and not a catch-all for student work.

2. The cornerstone of success for portfolio assessment is acceptance by all stakeholders.

3. Early implementation of portfolio assessment in any given instructional setting must be on a volunteer basis to avoid the inevitable resistance to an imposed system.

4. Portfolios are based on collaboration and mentoring between students and teachers.

5. Portfolios can be fit into current evaluation practices with very little disruption.

6. Because their primary purpose is to enhance learning, portfolios are an effective tool for instructional improvement.

7. The portfolio is an "imperfect system striving for perfection which is obtainable."

# ► How do we get started?

The first step in launching a portfolio assessment program at the classroom level is to make a series of key decisions. Remember, however, that portfolio assessment will be an ongoing, evolving process. You will revisit and modify your initial decisions as you and your team evaluate the results of your practices.

**Decision 1:** What is the purpose of the portfolio, and what contents will best reflect that purpose and represent the diverse abilities, interests, cultures, and work of your students?

**If the purpose is to promote and examine writing across the curriculum, portfolio contents might include**

- A "best" or "most representative" piece from each discipline

- A piece in which "you learned something you didn't know before"

- Different kinds of writing (e.g., oral histories, journals, diaries, autobiographical sketches, historical fiction, stories, lab reports, letters, scripts, etc.)

- Extended projects (e.g., newspapers, magazines, children's books, I-Search and research projects, pieces around a theme)

- Written reflection on writing to learn and on writing in different disciplines

**If the purpose is to examine the teaching and learning of writing as a process, portfolio contents might include**

- Process entries—all prewriting for, drafts of, and responses to each finished piece

- A written reflection on the process involved in writing each piece or collection of pieces and on the routines that help the student writer

- Work(s)-in-progress, with the author's written plans for revision

**If the purpose is to examine growth over time, contents might include**

- Several samples collected at regular intervals (e.g., personal experience papers collected each quarter)

- Initial products with revisions made later in the year

- Dated papers organized chronologically according to a particular principle or strategy (e.g., papers that demonstrate organization, use of detail, sentence variety, focus, persuasive evidence)

- A written reflection on the student's progress

- Student-constructed rankings of papers from least to most effective, with commentary

If the purpose is to focus students' attention on in-depth explorations and areas of concentration, contents might include

- A series of pieces around a theme, a genre, a particular purpose or audience

- Documentation of the evolution of an extended project (e.g., selected sketches and interviews for a biography)

- A written reflection on the organizing principle, the process, and the products

If the purpose is to help students prepare for a job search, contents might include

- An application letter and resumé

- An autobiographical piece or self-introduction

- Samples representing the range of the student's experiences and abilities, with commentary

(Murphy and Smith, 1991)

**Decision 2:** What should your students' portfolios look like? What format, structure, or organization schema will best fulfill the purpose you have identified?

**Decision 3:** How and when should your students select the items for their portfolios? Should you as a teacher be involved in the selection? If so, what is your role?

**Decision 4:** What time line, assignments, tasks, and products will ensure that your students' portfolios will effectively document their learning process and meet the requirements of your school or district?

**Decision 5:** How will you and your students evaluate their portfolios? What outcomes, performance standards, or criteria will you establish for judging their worth and effectiveness? Sample evaluation rubrics appear at the end of this section.

**Decision 6:** How will you pass on the portfolio from year to year? What methods, procedures, or guidelines will you establish in your class, school, or district for moving the portfolios, or portions of them, along with students through their careers?

## TIPS FOR TEAMS

- *Start small and emphasize quality, not quantity.* If your curriculum is organized around subject areas, start portfolios with samples from only one subject area. If you use an integrated or thematic curriculum, begin with samples that represent a particular type of classroom assignment, such as journal writing.

- *Use photographs, drawings, and reflective descriptions to document projects that don't fit inside the portfolio.* In their descriptions, students can explain why they chose the project, the steps they used to complete it, and any problems they encountered and how they resolved them.

- *Be sure students date their work.* Consider using date stamps and ink pads; six to eight stamps should suffice for twenty-five students.

- *Keep portfolios accessible to students.* I keep them in large files hung in a box, which sits on the classroom floor. Audiotapes are stored in pockets inside the portfolios; computer disks and videotapes are shelved near the portfolio box.

(Buschman, 1993)

# Portfolios: The SCRIPT Model

**Selective:** First and foremost, a good portfolio is a highly selective, not an exhaustive, collection.

**Connective:** A clear structure and logical organization should be immediately apparent to the reader.

**Reflective:** A portfolio should be more than a compilation of materials: work samples **plus reflection** are a powerful formula in this and every learning context.

**Illustrative:** The samples of student work are the heart of a portfolio—not teacher comments on students' learning but the artifacts themselves.

**Persuasive:** A portfolio is a careful, thoughtful gathering of documents and materials that make the best case for a student's learning.

**Transformative:** Portfolios have a special power to involve students in reflection on their own learning practices and how to improve them. Portfolios can be a path from the learning of the past to the learning of the future.

(adapted from Eison, 1993)

## Assessing Student Portfolios

The following chart can help you develop a customized rubric for assessing the quality of portfolios in your classroom. You can use these descriptors to develop either an analytic or a holistic rubric. While this chart focuses specifically on collections of student writing, it can be adapted to apply to portfolios that contain a broad range of content.

---

## MORE TIPS FOR TEAMS

- *Make sure each portfolio has a table of contents.* This is particularly important if some items aren't stored inside the portfolio itself.

- *Select a few work samples yourself.* For student-selected work, write "SS" in one corner; for teacher-selected work, "TS." If students are concerned about having all of their "prized papers" in the portfolio, use photocopies instead.

- *Give parents the opportunity to review their child's portfolio.* Since the whole process will probably be new to them, be patient. Their first reaction may be, "I don't have time to review all this. All I want to know is how my child is doing." But after they've seen the value of portfolios, you should hear comments like, "For the first time I can really see what my son can actually do, and how much progress he's made since the last conference."

(Buschman, 1993)

| STRONG PERFORMANCE | | NEEDS IMPROVEMENT |
|---|---|---|
| **VERSATILITY** | | |
| Collection shows wide variety of reading and writing across genres. | Collection shows some variety. | Collection shows little or no variety, little breadth or depth. |
| **PROCESS** | | |
| Samples reveal discoveries or pivotal learning experiences. | Process illustrated in inflexible or mechanistic ways. | Minimal use of process to reflect on achievements. |
| **RESPONSE** | | |
| Engaged with story. Discusses key issues. Evidence of critical questioning. | Personal reflection but focus is narrow. | Brief retelling of isolated events. |
| **SELF-EVALUATION** | | |
| Reflections are multidimensional with wide variety of observations. Meaningful goals are established. Improvement is noted. | Reflections show developing insights. Some specifics are noted. Goal setting is limited. Ideas of improvement are vague. | Reflections are single in focus or too global. Goal setting is too broad or nonexistent. |
| **TEXT CONTENT, STRUCTURE, AND SURFACE FEATURES** | | |
| Pieces show strong control of a variety of elements: organization, cohesion, surface features, etc. | Growing command is evidenced. Some flaws exist, but major ideas are clear. | Improvement is needed in sophistication of ideas, text features, and surface features. |
| **PROBLEM SOLVING** | | |
| Collection indicates that student wrestles with problems using various resources, enjoys problem solving and continues to learn new strategies. | Collection indicates limited use of resources. There is evidence that student wants quick fixes. | Collection shows evidence of student's sense of helplessness and frustration when faced with problems. |
| **PURPOSEFULNESS/USES** | | |
| Collection indicates that student uses reading and writing to satisfy various goals, including sharing with others. | Collection indicates that student uses reading and writing to meet goals set by others. | Collection indicates apathy and resistance. |

(adapted from Tierney, Carter, & Desai, 1991)

# ▶ Where do we go for more information?

Murphy, S. and Smith, M. A. 1991. *Writing portfolios: A bridge from teaching to assessment.* Markham, Ontario: Pippin.
Describes how to decide on purposes of portfolio assessment, determine what goes into portfolios, and develop evaluation criteria. Tells how students can learn from reflecting on their portfolios. Focuses on writing as a process and emphasizes the importance of encouraging students to become active partners in fostering their own growth as writers.

Rhodes, L. K. and Shanklin, N. L. 1993. *Windows into literacy: Assessing learners, K-8.* Portsmouth, NH: Heinemann.
Centers on the assessment of various aspects of students' reading and writing. Covers metacognition, attitudes and interests about reading and writing, how language systems and strategies are used in the reading and writing processes, comprehension and composition, and the development of emergent reading and writing.

Stenmark, J. K., ed. 1991. *Mathematics assessment: Myths, models, good questions, and practical suggestions.* Reston, VA: National Council of Teachers of Mathematics.
Discusses shifting assessment practices, including myths of teaching and the need for change. Examines performance assessment, along with observations, interviews, conferences, questions. Treats mathematics portfolios and implementing assessment models. Includes samples, tables, bibliography, and index.

Tierney, R. J., Carter, M. A., and Desai, L. E. 1991. *Portfolio assessment in the reading-writing classroom.* Norwood, MA: Christopher-Gordon.
Introduces the concept of portfolios, ways to begin using them in the classroom, the variety of uses, self-assessment, and ways to analyze and keep records on portfolios. Contains reproductions of materials (letters to parents, student handouts, checklists, etc.), examples of student portfolios, and research-based information for explaining portfolios to parents, the community, administrators, and others. Includes annotated bibliography.

# References

Arter, J. 1990. *Using portfolios in instruction and assessment,* pp. 4–5. Washington, D.C.: Office of Educational Research and Improvement.

Buschman, L. 1993. Portfolios: Windows on learning. *Learning* 21(5) (January): 22–25.

Eison, J. 1993. *Creating a teaching portfolio: The SCRIPT model.* Tampa, FL: University of South Florida, Center for Teaching Enhancement.

Forte, I. and Schurr, S. 1993. *The definitive middle school guide:* A *handbook for success.* Nashville, TN: Incentive Publications, Inc.

Maples, C. 1992. Presenting portfolios. *Learning* 21(3) (October): 41.

Murphy, S. and Smith, M. A. 1991. *Writing portfolios: A bridge from teaching to assessment,* pp. 28–29. Markham, Ontario: Pippin.

Paulson, F., Paulson, P., and Meyer, C. 1992. What makes a portfolio a portfolio? In *Performance assessment: Readings from educational leadership,* R. S. Brandt, ed., pp. 51–54. Alexandria, VA: Association for Supervision and Curriculum Development.

Schurr, S. L. 1992. *The ABC's of evaluation: Twenty-six alternative ways to assess student progress,* pp. 153–155. Columbus, OH: National Middle School Association.

Stenmark, J. K., ed. 1991. *Mathematics assessment: Myths, models, good questions, and practical suggestions.* Reston, VA: National Council of Teachers of Mathematics.

Tierney, R. J., Carter, M. A., and Desai, L. E. 1991. *Portfolio assessment in the reading-writing classroom,* pp. 133, 134. Norwood, MA: Christopher-Gordon.

# Portfolio Guide for Language Arts: Writing

**Directions:** During this school year, you will be developing a writing portfolio by collecting samples of your work. Please follow these guidelines.

1. Keep your writing samples in the file your teacher has given you for this purpose.

2. Organize your writing samples in chronological order. Make sure the date is on each item (include dates on drafts as well as on final copies).

3. Select samples that will best show your parents what you are doing during class writing time.

4. Try to include one writing sample for each week of the school year.

5. Once a month, include both the first draft and the final copy for one writing sample.

6. Include the types of writing listed in the chart; note the number of samples of each type to select.

7. Do not include any writing sample that you do not feel good about or that you do not feel is satisfactory. (Of course, the writing samples you select at the beginning of the year may not please you as much as those you choose at the end of the year, but keeping the early samples in your portfolio will show how your writing has improved.)

8. At the end of the school year, select your five best writing samples, and write statements explaining why you chose each piece.

## POETRY
(Include two writing samples from this group.)

_____ Haiku

_____ Limerick

_____ Free verse

_____ Diamante

_____ Tanka

_____ Other

## FOLKLORE
(Include two writing samples from this group.)

_____ Legend

_____ Tall tale

_____ Myth

_____ Fairy tale

_____ Fable

## MEDIA
(Include four writing samples from this group.)

_____ Editorial

_____ News story

_____ Book/movie review

_____ Letter to the editor

_____ Newspaper advertisement

_____ Television commercial

_____ Radio announcement

_____ Advice column

_____ Feature story

## HUMOR
(Include three samples from this group.)

_____ Original jokes

_____ Original riddles

_____ Editorial cartoon

_____ Comic strip

_____ Puns

_____ Tongue twisters

## FICTION
(Include three samples from this group.)

_____ Short story

_____ Bedtime story

_____ Character sketch

_____ Skit or play

_____ Fantasy story

_____ Science fiction story

## NONFICTION
(Include three samples from this group.)

_____ Autobiography

_____ Biography

_____ Character sketch

_____ Encyclopedia entry

_____ Interview

_____ Magazine article

## MISCELLANEOUS WRITING
(Include three samples from this group.)

_____ Pamphlet

_____ Travel brochure

_____ Critique

_____ Book jacket

_____ Record album cover

_____ Magazine advertisement

_____ Tribute

_(adapted from Schurr, 1992)_

# Parent Response Form: A Year of Work in Mathematics

**Student's name** _____

**Presented to** _____

**Date of presentation** _____

**Parent:** After your child has given the portfolio presentation, please take ten to fifteen minutes to fill out this form. We welcome any additional comments you'd like to make.

Please answer *Yes* or *No* to the following questions:

Did you see or hear any evidence of

_____ creativity

_____ growth in understanding over time (note dates)

_____ thinking skills

_____ problem-solving skills

_____ having worked in a group

_____ written reflections about math

_____ student organization

_____ explanations of processes (analysis)

_____ computation ability

_____ variety in activities

_____ use of technology (calculator, computer)

_____ positive attitude about math knowledge

_____ problems being revised (rough draft and final copy)

_____ explanations of why pieces were chosen

_____ other (please describe)

_____

_____

Communication is the key to understanding. How well do you feel your child presented his or her work from a year of mathematics class?

_____

_____

_____

**Student:** On the back of this form, please write your reactions to the presentation. List your strengths and weaknesses. Write what you learned by doing this. Be specific. Give examples.

*(Maples, 1992)*

# Portfolio Evaluation: Holistic Rubric

While this rubric focuses specifically on collections of student writing, it can be adapted to apply to portfolios that contain a broad range of content.

**Beginning:** Students may appear to be at beginning stages for a number of different reasons. They may be emerging learners or learners who are only partially engaged with the classroom community in this activity. They have yet to realize their full potential and may not be aware of their potential. Their portfolios exhibit

- Some or very little versatility, little risk taking in trying new forms, a preference for routine tasks over exploration

- Detachment from the portfolio process

- Unidimensional self-evaluations: either global statements or a focus on only one aspect of the work

- Inexperience with written organization, standard English conventions, and/or written development of ideas. Messages may be distorted due to surface-feature errors.

- Narrative pieces that include brief restatement of an incident but offer little evidence of personal stance or involvement

- Limited interest in or use of reading and writing beyond classroom requirements

- Either global or sketchy statements of ongoing goals and goal-setting processes

- Some improvement from piece to piece

- Few resources for problem solving: disengagement, lack of confidence, and/or lack of motivation

- Limited use of resources such as sharing or peer input

**Intermediate:** Developing learners exhibit strengths and independence in selected areas and potential in others. Their portfolios exhibit

- Expanding versatility

- A reasonable effort to compile the portfolio; some attention to detail, organization, and overall aesthetics

- Self-evaluations that may be multidimensional but lack specific details and/or breadth

- Individual pieces that falter on more than one feature. For example, papers may meander from the topic at times or contain significant spelling or punctuation errors. Papers may falter in development, structure, and/or sophistication of ideas but without distorting the central message.

- Narrative pieces that include comments about important incidents but show little development of incident or concept

- Some interest in using reading and writing beyond classroom assignments

- Goal setting that is restricted or does not grow or shift across time

- Repetitive use of problem-solving strategies

- Evidence that resources and support have been utilized only mechanically

**Advanced:** These learners are fully engaged and independent. Their portfolios exhibit

- Versatility in the variety of forms chosen

- Clear organization of contents

- Multidimensional self-evaluations that include reflections about both process and product: text features, surface features, voice, word choice, audience awareness, perspective, and purpose, for example.

- Individual pieces with a strong voice that stay on topic, are well organized, have well-formed sentences, and demonstrate effective word choice

- Narrative pieces that indicate strong engagement with and understanding of story elements and key issues

- Evidence that reading and writing are used for many different reasons and that the student is motivated to go beyond class assignments

- Expansive goal setting that shifts in relevant ways through time

- Problem solving that involves a variety of resources used meaningfully

- Flexible use of resources and support

*(adapted from Tierney, Carter, and Desai, 1991)*

# Portfolio Evaluation: Analytic Rubric

While this rubric focuses specifically on collections of student writing, it can be adapted to apply to portfolios that contain a broad range of content. Check the box that best reflects student performance. Use the space provided to comment.

| The Portfolio has these qualities | MOST OF THE TIME | SOMETIMES | SELDOM | NONE OF THE TIME |
|---|---|---|---|---|
| **Versatility and adaptability** | **4** | **3** | **2** | **1** |
| 1. Is there a variety of forms? | | | | |
| 2. Is there a variety of voices and purposes? | | | | |
| 3. Are there writings for a variety of audiences? | | | | |
| **Completeness of samples** | | | | |
| 4. Is there a sustained focus? | | | | |
| 5. Is there coherence? | | | | |
| 6. Is there appropriate balance of specificity and generality? | | | | |
| 7. Do the forms (letters, essays, research papers, etc.) have the characteristics of the genre? | | | | |
| **Carefulness in samples** | | | | |
| 8. Is there carefulness in grammar and mechanics? | | | | |
| **Beauty and power in samples** | | | | |
| 9. Is the wording precise? powerful? beautiful? | | | | |
| 10. Is the voice natural and effective? | | | | |
| 11. Are the arguments or images moving? | | | | |
| **Responsibility** | | | | |
| 12. Did the student select topics and forms? | | | | |
| 13. Did the student make choices based on comments of readers? | | | | |
| 14. Did the student revise? | | | | |
| 15. Did the student edit? | | | | |
| **TOTAL** | | | | |
| **General comments** | | | | |

# Self-Reflection: Portfolio

- Why did I select this piece for my portfolio?

- What was important to me about this piece?

- Where did I get the idea?

- How much time did I spend on this piece?

- What processes did I go through in creating this?

- What problems did I encounter? How did I work through them?

- What kind of revisions did I make?

- What points did the group raise about my work? What was/is my response to their points? How did their comments affect my revisions?

- What have I learned from working on this piece?

- If I could go on working on this piece, what would I do?

- What are its strengths?

- What points about it make me uneasy?

- What do I want you, the teacher, to look for in evaluating this piece?

- What questions do I have for you?

- What grade should I put on this piece and why?

- What have I learned about the subject of this course?

- How does this relate to what I already knew?

- What part of this subject do I feel most confident about?

- What kind of work would I like to do in the future?

*(adapted from Arter, 1990)*

# ▶ What is it?

Performance assessments evaluate student behaviors during a simulated or real-life problem-solving situation. Performance assessments can be formal and specific or informal and spontaneous. You can apply assessment criteria to a typical classroom event or design a task specifically for assessment. Performance assessment is based on observation of students' ability to apply higher-order thinking skills to a task rather than their ability to recall information and specific skills.

Researchers at the National Center for Research on Evaluation, Standards, and Student Testing (CRESST) are developing an expanded set of validity criteria for large-scale performance-based assessments. To date, they have identified eight criteria that performance-based assessments should meet.

## Criteria for Valid Performance-Based Assessments

**Consequences** Does using an assessment lead to the intended consequences or does it produce unintended consequences, such as teaching to the test? For example, minimum competency testing was intended to improve instruction and the quality of learning for students; however, its actual effects too often were otherwise (a shallow drill-and-kill curriculum for remedial students).

**Fairness** Does the assessment enable students from all cultural backgrounds to demonstrate their skills, or does it unfairly disadvantage some students?

**Transfer and generalizability** Do the results of the assessment generalize to other problems and other situations? Do they adequately represent students' performance in a given domain?

**Cognitive complexity** Do the assessments adequately assess higher levels of understanding and complex thinking? We cannot assume that performance-based assessments will test a higher level of student understanding just because they appear to do so. Such assumptions require empirical evidence.

**Content quality** Are the tasks selected to measure a given content area worth the time and effort of students and raters?

**Content coverage** Do the assessments enable adequate content coverage?

**Meaningfulness** Are the assessment tasks meaningful to students, and do they motivate them to perform their best?

**Cost and efficiency** Has attention been given to the efficiency of the data collection designs and scoring procedures? (Performance-based assessments are by nature labor intensive.)

(North Central Regional Educational Laboratory, 1991)

# ► How is it different?

Performance assessments have been used as far back as the 1930s, especially in the performing and studio arts, in athletics, and in vocational education. Unlike objective and standardized tests, they do not contain test items but rely totally on observation and professional judgment about student performance. Ratings of performance can include everything from formal scales and checklists to letter grades and anecdotal records of observations.

# ► How do we get started?

The following steps will help you design a performance test in any curriculum area:

**Step 1:** Identify the content area to be assessed and determine the level of factual and conceptual understanding you wish to measure.

**Step 2:** Identify the process/inquiry/thinking skills you wish to measure. (Do not develop a performance task for skills or concepts that can be better tested by paper-and-pencil items.)

**Step 3:** Write a description of the performance task.

**Step 4:** List the criteria you will use to evaluate the performance; this will help you focus on the targeted skills/concepts as well as establish scoring parameters.

**Step 5:** List the resources required for the task. These should be easily obtainable, inexpensive, safe to use, and similar to, if not regular, components of the program.

**Step 6:** Write directions for the students. Pay special attention to sequence; lead the student efficiently through the task. The vocabulary level of the directions should be one year below the grade level of the students being assessed, but at the same time, the language

Gather some examples of standardized or traditional single-answer tests—preferably any that are currently used in your school or district. Study them. How do these tests miss out on possible sources of feedback from students? Do they de-emphasize important objectives?

should be consistent with the content and processes of the curriculum. Use graphics where appropriate.

**Step 7:** Decide on how to interpret the results—comparison with other students, comparison with a preestablished standard of acceptable performance, or comparison with the student's own work.

**Step 8:** Develop scoring procedures that focus on performance, not content. Decide whether you will use a single holistic overall proficiency score, a set of analytic scores, or a combination of the two. Consider using a system that gives students a range of points for each task.

**Step 9:** Determine who will rate or evaluate the performance—teacher(s), peers, the students themselves, or a combination.

**Step 10:** Administer a trial test. Groups used in trial-testing situations should include students of different intellectual abilities, socioeconomic backgrounds, and ethnic and racial makeup; groups should be gender balanced.

(adapted from Doran and Hejaily, 1992; Stiggins, 1986)

# ► Where do we go for more information?

Brandt, R. S., ed. 1992. *Readings from educational leadership: Performance assessment.* Alexandria, VA: ASCD.
Examines important aspects of performance assessment: new forms of assessment, portfolios of student work as a means of assessment in different subjects, early childhood assessment, authentic and performance assessment issues, and standards and curriculum issues.

Kapinus, B. 1993. Investigating performance assessment. *Turning Points: State Network News* 3(3) (June): 1.
An interview with Barbara Kapinus on the implementation of performance assessment in middle schools in New York State. Concisely covers basic definitions of performance, performance assessment, and authentic assessment. Treats issues in grading, classroom teaching methods, interdisciplinary teaching, statewide performance assessments, and future developments.

Stiggins, R. J. 1986. *Evaluating students by classroom observation: Watching students grow.* Washington, D.C.: NEA.
A concise guide to performance assessments. Includes design guidelines, test blueprints, issues of quality and accountability in performance assessments, and a list of selected resources.

# 8 BASIC DESIGN CRITERIA FOR PERFORMANCE TESTS

1. Assessment tasks should be, whenever possible, authentic and meaningful.

2. The tasks should be a valid sample from which apt generalizations about overall performance of complex capacities can be made.

3. The scoring criteria should be authentic, with points awarded or taken off for successes and errors.

4. The performance standards that anchor the scoring should be genuine benchmarks, not arbitrary cut scores or provincial school norms.

5. The context of the problems should be rich, realistic, and enticing—within the inevitable constraints on time, resources, and advance knowledge of the tasks and standards appropriately minimized.

6. The tasks should be validated.

7. The scoring should be feasible and reliable.

8. Assessment results should be reported and used so that *all* customers for the data are appropriately informed.

*Brandt, 1992*

## References

Brandt, R. S., ed. 1992. *Readings from educational leadership: Performance assessment*, p. 117. Alexandria, VA: ASCD.

Doran, R. and Hejaily, N. 1992. Hands-on evaluation: A how-to guide. *Science Scope* 15(6) (March): 9–10.

North Central Regional Educational Laboratory. 1991. *Schools that work: The research advantage. Guidebook 4. Alternatives for measuring performance*, p. 9. Oak Brook, IL: North Central Regional Educational Laboratory.

Stiggins, R. J. 1986. *Evaluating students by classroom observation: Watching students grow*, 5. Washington, D.C.: NEA.

# Student Performance: "Teachers of the Day"

**Assignment:** Your cooperative learning group is to design and deliver a lesson plan. Your goal is to teach the other students in our science class about a special topic related to our unit on oceanography. Your lesson should

- be approximately 30 minutes long

- include a lesson plan

- involve all group members in both the planning and presentation process

Arrange with the teacher to videotape your presentation as a "dress rehearsal" before your group actually teaches the lesson.

## Criteria for Evaluating "Teachers of the Day"

Use the points below to plan your lesson presentation. These are the same points that will be used for evaluation.

### I. Planning notes                                    15 points

    A. Write the tasks to be performed.

    B. Note the roles of each team member.

    C. List materials you will need.

    D. Estimate time you will spend.

### II. Completeness of written lesson plan     35 points

    A. Write an introduction.

        1. Tell how you will get your classmates' attention and motivate them.

        2. Tell how you will focus attention on the subject.

            a. Remind classmates of what they already know.

            b. State objectives.

            c. Explain why the subject is important or valuable.

    B. Explain how you will present the content.

        1. Tell what you plan to teach and how.

        2. Include examples or applications.

        3. Include graphics and illustrations.

C. Explain your follow-up.

    1. Provide practice material—both guided and independent.

    2. Plan for assessment.

## III. Presentation of lesson          **35 points**

A. Follow the outline in written lesson plan.

B. Communicate ideas and directions clearly.

C. Display enthusiasm for subject.

D. Ask many and varied questions.

E. Involve all team members in instructional process.

F. Appear well prepared and well rehearsed.

## IV. Creativity          **15 points**

A. Make up creative titles for activities and activity sheets.

B. Include unusual, clever, varied, or original ideas and questions.

C. Use graphics, learning resources/references, or tasks creatively.

Finally, ask yourself

- What was the general goal of this lesson?
- What were the specific objectives of this lesson plan?
- Were they accomplished?

# RESPONSE JOURNALS AND LEARNING LOGS

## ► What are they?

A s more and more teachers are introducing journals into their classrooms, they are finding them to be versatile and valuable tools for both instruction and assessment. In a middle school classroom, the journal can serve as

- A convenient and flexible medium for exploring and reflecting on personal responses to independent reading and research, class discussions, television/film viewing, and other experiences

- A source book of ideas, thoughts, opinions, and first drafts that can be "mined" for later use in other contexts

- A place to record observations and questions prior to student-teacher conferences as well as a place to record comments and suggestions derived from the conferences

- A place to note, after a small-group discussion, students' own perspectives on what was discussed or their roles in the discussion

- A device for tracking what and how much students have read or researched

- A reference file to help both student and teacher monitor individual development and progress

- A way for individual students to "dialogue" in written form with their teachers, peers, or parents

(adapted from Parsons, 1990)

If you are trying response journals in your classroom for the first time, you may find it reassuring to have some idea of the types of responses you can expect. The examples below, which are excerpted from longer responses, are typical.

- Opinions about the plot and characters or about the information presented in a text. For example, Leanne's response:

  I think that the men, Sam and Lou were nice because they understood the kids wanting the meadow.

And Alonso's response:

> At the starting a guy throws something out of his car Leslie called out to him Litterbug and I agree with Leslie Litterbugs are destroying our environment. people who litter are stupid and dumb and I think there should be a penalty for litterbugs because our environment is in jeopardy because of these people.

- Expressions of enjoyment, boredom, compassion, or anger:

> I wish that I could stop the rain. I feel so sorry for Tucker and Chester. I also feel sad because they ran out of food.

> I couldn't believe how low down people can get like Ellie and Brenda to call Leslie a stick and not a girl.

- Comments on the language or literary techniques used, such as Samantha's observation:

> I think it is very realistic the way the author described how Tucker got all frantic.

- Comparisons of the text with the reader's life:

> In this chapter Jess and Leslie like to talk a lot during class, I know I talk in class but they talk on Leslie's father working with money and going to washington but one thing that Leslie talks a lot about is making a secret magic kingdom for themselves. I have conversations about what we are going to do at lunch time and stuff like that but they talk about totally different things.

- Predictions:

> When Tucker said "fascinating in fact" and so on I was sure he had a plan, I think he will tell in the next chapter.

- Articulation of expectations for a particular type of text. For example, Anthony's comment on what he expects in a fantasy adventure:

> This chapter needed more strength and more action.

- Reflections on the reading process. For example, Mira tells how she solved a comprehension problem:

> There's one part I don't understand is a sentence on page 6 where it says, You shouldn't ought to beat me in the head and went off obediently to fetch his T-shirt. After I read it over and over again I understood it.

> "*You can stop a lecture at a critical point and ask your students to make a short journal entry by defining a term, listing examples, or explaining in their own words something you have just demonstrated or discussed. You can also begin a class session by having students make a journal entry about materials covered in previous class meetings or at the end of the class summarizing an important thing learned.*"
>
> (Moss and Holder, 1988)

- Questions about vocabulary, language use, plot, information, characters' behavior, and the author:

> Then the next morning he eats a large breakfast but why?
> Mostly when somebody dies like a friend or family member
> you don't want to eat at all.

(excerpted from Wollman-Bonilla, 1991)

## ▶ How are they different?

Although journals can be powerful learning tools, they have sometimes been abused and misunderstood. Typically, teachers have asked students to record reflections, assignments, and work outlines in a given subject area (usually language arts) but have made few attempts to tie in other curriculum areas or to incorporate feedback from teachers or peers.

To use journals to their fullest capacity, extend the journal concept to include meaningful collections of spontaneous and informal writings as well as writing that is more closely connected to curriculum content. Have students use their journals as logs to record experiences involving out-of-school fieldwork and as notebooks for responding to readings, lectures, and other course activities. Suggest that students consider their journal writing as "thinking on paper"; their journals should become the "seedbeds" and sources for all the other writing students produce, from reports to stories.

## ▶ How do we get started?

**Step 1:** Begin keeping a response journal or a learning log of your own.

Reflect on your successful (or unsuccessful) lesson plans; describe personal interactions with students, parents, and colleagues; note ideas for creative classroom projects; react to professional journal articles; review educational materials; write reminders and notes to yourself about a new teaching technique or a staff development activity you have observed or participated in. Keeping your own journal will give you insight into the multiple roles that response journals can play in your classroom.

**Step 2:** Include your team members.

Discuss ways of using journals in various content areas. Do additional readings and research on the use of journals in the middle school classroom, and share your findings and your conclusions with your team.

## QUESTIONS TO CONSIDER

1. How can I fit response journals into my particular discipline and classroom schedule?

2. How do I know if response journals will work with my students or my subject area?

3. How can I coordinate response journals with my team members and their classes?

4. What materials will I need to begin the use of response journals?

5. How will I introduce the concept of response journals?

6. What kinds of reactions and responses can I expect from my students in their response journal entries?

7. How will I find time to reply to their response journals, and what kind of responses should I write?

8. How can I overcome student resistance or misunderstanding of the response journal concept?

9. How can I use response journals for assessment purposes, and what kinds of information am I likely to receive from them?

10. How often should I review or evaluate the response journals, and how will I keep track of this process?

**Step 3:** Introduce journals into your classroom or expand the ways students are currently using journals.

- Share with students some of the entries from your own journal.

- Discuss various formats, from commercial spiral-bound notebooks to hand-made scrapbook versions and decide which formats to use in your classroom.

- Provide students with an overview of journal-writing possibilities. Introduce them to the journal writing ideas on Copy Forms 7–10 at the end of this section. Encourage them to add their own ideas.

- Prepare a variety of daily journal-writing assignments for your students. Include a variety of types and lengths of entries so that students can experience both the range and the value of the journal as a meaningful instructional and assessment tool. Four examples of journal assignments appear at the end of this section.

# ▶ Where do we go for more information?

Carter, J. A. and Carter, D. E. 1994. *The write equation: Writing in the mathematics classroom*. Palo Alto, CA: Dale Seymour.
Journals, essays, and research projects for the mathematics classroom. Includes tips on starting a writing program, ideas for writing topics for middle school and high school, student writing samples, techniques for evaluating writing, ready-to-use checklists, and an example unit integrating writing with other teaching methods for complete learning and assessment.

Parsons, L. 1990. *Response journals*. Portsmouth, NH: Heinemann.
A handbook for implementing whole language programs based on student responses. Provides a step-by-step system and concrete examples based on classroom experience. Includes tips on using personal response. Suggests questions to cue responses to short stories, novels, readalouds, print advertising, rock videos, film, television, and newspapers. Provides guidance for small group discussions, criteria for evaluation, sample self-evaluation and summative evaluation sheets, help with student-teacher conferences, and extensive samples of student responses.

Wollman-Bonilla, J. 1991. *Response journals*. New York: Scholastic Professional Books.
Suggests strategies for getting started, encouraging timid writers, replying to student-written entries, assessing reading comprehension, and using response journals as the springboard for activities across the curriculum. Includes suggestions for further reading.

# References

Carter, J. A. and Carter, D. E. 1994. *The write equation: Writing in the mathematics classroom*, pp. 59–62. Palo Alto, CA: Dale Seymour.

Fogarty, R. 1990. *Inking our thinking*, pp. 10–11. Palatine, IL: Skylight Publishing Co. .

Moss, A. and Holder, C. 1988. *Improving student writing: A guidebook for faculty in all disciplines*. Dubuque, IA: Kendall/Hunt.

Parsons, L. 1990. *Response journals*. Portsmouth, NH: Heinemann.

*Reflections*. 1989. Burlington, WI: Write Source. iii–iv.

Scutt, E. 1992. Reader response journals. In *The whole language catalog supplement on authentic assessment*, p. 155, eds. Goodman, K. S., Bird, L. B., and Goodman, Y. M. New York: Macmillan/McGraw-Hill-American School Publishers.

Wollman-Bonilla, J. 1991. *Response journals*, pp. 24–25. New York: Scholastic Professional Books.

## Assignment 1: Responding to a Videotape or Movie

Think about the videotape you have just viewed. Focus on your reactions, feelings, and impressions as they relate to the video's content; don't focus on the information in the video. Use your journal to record your responses to the questions below.

1. What visual images impressed you in the telling of the story or the presenting of the ideas?

2. When you reflect on the purpose or main message of this video, what impressions immediately come to mind?

3. Did you see or hear anything in the video that made you feel frustrated, excited, surprised, or confused? Explain.

## Assignment 2: Responding to a Magazine

Browse through the magazine and try to get a sense of its overall format and of the audience it is intended for. Use your journal to record your responses to the questions below.

1. What immediately impresses you (either positively or negatively) about this magazine?

2. What type of reader would most like this magazine? What type of reader would not be interested in this magazine? Explain.

3. What types of features, articles, ads, or sections had personal appeal to you and for what reasons?

## Assignment 3: Responding to a Television News Show

Listen to a local thirty-minute television news broadcast. Pay more attention to the hidden messages you receive from the broadcast than to the actual facts stated by the commentators. Use your journal to record responses to the questions below.

1. How do these producers define *news* or what is newsworthy, judging from the segment you watched?

2. What personal attitudes or feelings did this news broadcast "trigger" in your mind?

3. Was anything you saw worth remembering or worth discussing with someone else? Give reasons for your answer.

# Letter to Parents: Reader Response Journals

Construct a parent letter like the one below, which one middle school teacher sends home to parents, explaining how his students utilize and learn from reader response journals.

*Dear Parent or Guardian,*

Recently we asked ourselves three questions about our work in our Reader Response Journals. Following are the results of our discussions around those questions. We'd like to share those results with you. Please talk to any one of us if you have any further questions.

## What kind of journal entries do we write?

- We discuss the *connections* between the story and our lives.
- We write about *characters*:
    our perceptions of various characters
    the empathy we have for, or the apathy we have toward, various characters
- We *compare* characters to
    ourselves and to other people we know
    other characters in other works of art
    other characters within the work of literature currently being studied
- We discuss the writer's *style*; for example, while studying *In Cold Blood,* several of us wrote about how Capote's style
    is descriptive and jumps from scene to scene
    is ironic
- We discuss *theme*:
    issues and questions about life
    our feelings of agreement or disagreement with the author's "message"
- We ask and answer *questions* about the text.
- We discuss, with specificity, our opinions about *how the reading is going.*

## How do we teach ourselves in our journals?

- We ask and answer our own *questions*.
- We *articulate* our thoughts about our reading experiences *for later reflection*.
- We generate our own *vocabulary studies*.

## How do we teach each other in our journals?

- We conduct *book talks*: writing to each other in our journals and discussing questions/characters/settings/connections/themes or ideas/writing styles
- We work together on *vocabulary studies*.
- We have *group discussions* based on the work in our journals, not on teacher-generated questions or topics.

*(Scutt, 1992)*

# Journal Jamboree!

- Make your journal a combination camera, clock, and tape recorder!

- Create visual photographs about timeless topics using recordings of your inner voice!

- Write    . . . descriptions of points that puzzle you

               . . . questions that don't have answers for you

               . . . reactions to ideas that confuse you

               . . . summaries of feelings that excite you

               . . . discussions of facts that intrigue you

               . . . explanations of things that make sense to you

               . . . comments about concepts that are difficult for you

               . . . paraphrases of definitions that are complex to you

# Stretch Your Mind!

Use these expressions to help you put your ideas on paper. They can help you reflect on your reading, your classroom discussions, the movies and television programs you watch, problems you need to solve, and decisions you have to make.

## ANALYZE!

Compared to . . .
The best part . . .
On the positive side . . .
An interesting part is . . .
Take a small part like . . .
A logical sequence seems to be . . .
On the negative side . . .
It's like . . .
In contrast . . .

## SYNTHESIZE!

Suppose that . . .
If you combined . . .
One possibility . . .
Imagine that . . .
If these were reversed . . .
What if . . .
I predict that . . .
How about . . .
I wonder . . .

## EVALUATE!

How . . .
Why . . .
It seems important that . . .
The best . . .
The worst . . .
If . . . then . . .
I hate . . .
One criticism I have is . . .

## APPLY!

Backtracking for a minute . . .
One way to . . .
I want to . . .
A connecting idea is . . .
A movie this reminds me of is . . . because . . .
If this were a book, I'd title it . . .
I think this applies to . . .
Does this mean . . .

## PROBLEM SOLVE!

I'm stuck on . . .
The best way to think about this is . . .
I conclude . . .
I'm lost without . . .
I understand, but . . .
I'm concerned about . . .
My problem is . . .
A question I have is . . .

## MAKE DECISIONS!

I disagree with . . . because . . .
I prefer . . . because . . .
If I had to choose . . .
I believe . . .
My goal is . . .
I can't decide whether . . .

*(adapted from Fogarty, 1990)*

# Idea Starters for Writing

**Do you have a case of writer's block? Get out your journal and try some of these ideas. Use them when you are**

- stuck for ideas
- have so many ideas you don't know which one to choose
- can't decide which writing prompt to use

**Cluster:** Begin a cluster with a "nucleus" word, a word that comes to mind when you think of a writing topic. Write down other words that occur to you when you think of the nucleus word. Don't pick and choose; record *every* word. Circle each word as you write it, and then draw a line connecting it to the closest "related" word.

After three or four minutes of clustering, you will probably be ready to write. Scan your cluster for a word or idea that will get you going, and write nonstop for about eight minutes.

**List:** Freely list ideas as they come to you. List ideas with a friend or classmate and work from each other's thoughts.

**Make up a dialogue:** Create an imaginary dialogue on your topic between you and someone else or between two strangers. Continue the dialogue as long as you can.

**Write a letter:** Draft a letter to anyone (friend, stranger, newspaper editor) about some idea or issue that comes to mind when you think about your topic.

**Be dramatic:** Develop a fictional scenario (plot). Write a very rough draft of a story based directly or indirectly on your writing idea. Consider writing it in the style of a movie or television program, complete with typical characters and clichés.

**Ask pointed questions:** Keep asking yourself WHY? WHY? WHY? as you write. Push the questions as far as you can. Sum up what you discover.

**Debate:** Try splitting your mind into two people. Have one person represent your thinking on an idea and have the other person disagree. Step in occasionally to point out a possible middle ground. Keep the debate going as long as you can.

**Twist it:** Write as though you were a different person or someone from a different time or place. Try writing in a style completely different from the way you usually write.

**Aim at an audience:** Address a specific audience. Consider a group of preschoolers, a live television audience, a panel of experts, or the local school board.

*(adapted from* Reflections, *1989)*

# Journal Writing Topics: Math

## Whole Numbers

- Which is easier for you—multiplication or division? Why do you think one is easier than the other?

## Decimals

- Describe situations in your life when you need to use decimals.

- Fred is very upset. He multiplies 5 by 3 and gets a greater number—15. But when he multiplies 0.5 by 0.3, he gets a number that is less than either one— 0.15. He has always thought that multiplying two numbers results in a number greater than either of the two factors. Explain to him why the results can be different when he multiplies decimals. In your explanation, include examples of when the product of the two decimals lies between the two factors and when the product is greater than each of the two factors.

## Metric Measurement

- Write a letter to the President of the United States, convincing him that the United States should or should not convert to the metric system.

- Research the origins of the metric system.

- Write a note to your mother, explaining why it would be better for her to spend $1.99 on a two-liter bottle of soda than on a six-pack of soda.

## Equations and Number Theory

- Explain the need for the order of operations. Give an example of how a calculation could have several different answers if the order of operations changes.

- Do you think there are a limited number of prime numbers or an infinite number? Explain your reasoning.

## Fractions

- Explain in three different ways what it means when fractions are equivalent.

- Why do you need a common denominator to add fractions?

## Introduction to Geometry

- Susie is the editor of the yearbook. She is working with a picture that covers 100 squares on her grid paper. She realizes that if she cuts each side in half, the picture will cover only 25 squares. This is a problem for her because she needs to cover 50 squares with this picture. She doesn't understand why this is happening, and she is becoming very frustrated. Write a note to her explaining why this is happening and give her some hints on how to solve her problem.

- Your parents have asked you to help redecorate your house. They want to put new carpeting in the living room, new wallpaper in the kitchen, and an in-ground pool in the yard. Determine the measurements they need and prepare a report for them on the anticipated cost of this project.

- You have been hired by the Johnsons to design a garden that contains 48 square feet of planting area. Give them examples of at least four different rectangular gardens. Include in each example the amount of fencing required to surround the garden and how you calculated the area.

- You have a piece of wrapping paper that measures 2 feet by 1 1/2 feet. Give the dimensions of three different boxes that could each be covered with this piece of paper with a minimum amount of waste.

## Ratio/Proportion/Percent

- If two boys drink six bottles of soda in two days, how can you determine the number of bottles ten boys will drink in eight days?

- Clearly explain how a city with 9.2 persons per square mile could have a smaller population than one with 5.6 persons per square mile.

- You open a music store, and you decide to reduce all of the prices in your store by 10 percent in order to attract customers. As a result, your sales increase. Now you decide to raise all the prices by 10 percent. Discuss whether raising the prices is a smart business move and why.

## Statistics and Probability

- Keep track of the progress of your favorite baseball team over the course of a month. Use that information to predict its performance for the rest of the year. Justify your prediction.

- You have a weekend curfew of 10:00 P.M. For twelve weekends in a row, you have come home by 10:00. However, on the Friday of the thirteenth week, you arrive home fifteen minutes late, and your parents ground you for the next two weekends because they think you will be late again. Write them a note in which you use your knowledge of statistics to convince them that it is not likely you will be late again.

## Integers

- Explain the multiplication rules for positive and negative numbers.

- When might you use negative numbers in your life?

*(Carter & Carter, 1994)*

# Topic 6  OBSERVATIONS AND INTERVIEWS

## ▶ What are they?

**O**bservations and interviews are valuable and authentic methods of assessing both achievement and behavior. Both are useful not only for assessment but for gaining feedback that will allow you to tailor instruction to the needs of particular students and classrooms.

Observations require the teacher/observer to record, comment on, and evaluate a student's performance in a way that provides a direct and concrete indication of how the student is functioning in the classroom setting. Observation tools range from standardized to personalized; they can be checklists, uniformly applied to all students, or open-ended, with provision for anecdotes or for student responses. Students themselves can develop observation tools as a part of the learning process.

Interviews are basically one-on-one meetings between teacher and student. The teacher asks a student a sequence of questions that require oral responses, and the teacher records the responses in some meaningful way. Unlike observers, interviewers can ask probing questions. Although interviews are time-consuming, they can be a rich source of information on students' thoughts, understandings, and feelings about a given subject area. They provide a basis for modifying the curriculum or for accommodating differences in students' progress. One valuable outcome of an interview can be clarification of ambiguous results obtained from other assessment sources. Since there are often patterns in students' thinking, interviewing even a sampling of students can provide valuable information about the teaching and learning processes in a given classroom setting.

# ► How are they different?

In addition to being more open-ended than traditional assessment tools, observations and interviews are more likely to stimulate creative thinking on the part of both teacher and student, more likely to encourage an exploration and application of knowledge, and more easily interfaced with the instructional processes.

They do, however, require more time to administer and score than traditional tests do, and objectivity is a critical issue. Setting criteria for evaluation and informing students of these criteria prior to the observation or interview can help ensure that these methods produce consistent results.

# ► How do we get started?

## Observations

Make certain that whichever type of observation technique you choose, you carry it out in an unobtrusive manner. As the observer, you should not interfere with normal routines or activities. Refrain insofar as possible from using either significant body language (facial expressions or posture clues) or any type of verbal exchange while you are conducting an observation.

**1.** Determine the purpose of your observation. Decide whether to observe students individually or as they work in groups. Keep in mind that observation is the best method of assessing some behavioral attributes, especially when they involve hands-on tasks or learning-by-doing assignments. Be selective in what you assess. Look for only a few aspects in a single observation.

**2.** If you are inexperienced as an observer, you might begin with quantitative observations, using a checklist of common behaviors or actions. This approach has the advantage of acquainting beginning evaluators with the observation method without requiring the degree of skill or training necessary for qualitative observations. Another advantage of quantitative over qualitative observations is the fact that they do not require as much follow-up time for interpreting findings.

The Observation Checklist (Sample Form 1) at the end of this section illustrates how a set of behaviors can be observed and rated with some degree of consistency.

## SOME EFFICIENT WAYS TO RECORD STUDENT BEHAVIOR

- A spiral notebook—one page per student

- A clipboard of staggered 4 x 8 file cards

- A card file of index cards arranged alphabetically

- A loose-leaf notebook—one or more pages per student

- A standard observation or interview form

- A gummed pad of checklists

- A sheet of notes that can be transferred later to more permanent records

**3.** If you are already an experienced observer, you will want to try a series of qualitative observations. They often bring about surprising results and creative ideas. First choose a specific skill to observe. Record your observations on an anecdotal record card similar to the one shown below. You may want to include a descriptive rating scale that assigns a numerical score to the student's application of the skill. One scale to consider: 5 Exemplary, 4 Competent, 3 Satisfactory, 2 Inadequate, 1 No attempt.

## Anecdotal Record Card

Student's Name _____

Date _____

Observation



Comments

**4.** In addition to documenting your own observations of students' performance, you may want students to observe and rate one another. They might assess one another's social behavior during a small-group learning activity or observe performances, products, and presentations that are part of a unit of study. In either case, provide specific directions for students to follow and adequate space for them to write or sketch their observations. Include a few reflective questions. A sample peer observation form appears as a copy form at the end of this section.

## Interviews

**1.** Before the interview, develop a comprehensive set of questions. The questions should give students the opportunity to display what they know and give you the option of probing for clarification or for evidence of a deeper understanding of a concept or skill. Keep your questions simple, to the point, and in the language of the student.

**2.** Begin the interview by putting the student at ease. Discuss something of personal interest and explain why you are doing the interview.

3. Throughout the interview, keep in mind that you are interested not only in what the student knows but also in how the student came to know it.

- Be flexible. The focus of the interview could shift to a new topic if something new surfaces during the interview.

- State all questions in a positive way, even when you might be asking for responses with a negative orientation.

- Encourage the student to respond fully and comprehensively to each question. Try using nonverbal cues and positive comments that encourage the expression of honest opinions and provide genuine feedback.

- Be sure to record all responses, even those that don't seem relevant. If possible, tape-record or videotape the interview so that you can give undivided attention to the student.

- Be a good listener and allow sufficient wait time. Silence is one of the most effective interviewing strategies, and you need to be comfortable with it. Keep in mind that the fewer comments you make the fewer clues you give as to the "correctness" of a response.

- Don't try to incorporate the reteaching of content during the interview; provide for reviews at another time.

- Avoid the temptation to do students' thinking for them or to supply the right answer when the student is demonstrating knowledge or applying a skill.

4. End the interview by reassuring the student that he/she did a good job. Show the student any written record of your observations to reduce apprehension about what took place and what was recorded. You can add evaluative comments at a later time.

## References

The Kids' Stuff. 1988. *Science yellow pages for students and teachers.* Nashville, TN: Incentive Publications, Inc.

Stiggins, R. J. 1986. *Evaluating students by classroom observation: Watching students grow.* Washington, D.C.: NEA.

# Observation Checklist: Science Experiment

**Name** _____

**Date** _____

| | POOR | | FAIR | | EXCELLENT |
|---|---|---|---|---|---|
| 1. Organizes equipment and materials for experimentation. | 1 | 2 | 3 | 4 | 5 |
| 2. Follows a scientific method and applies scientific process skills. | 1 | 2 | 3 | 4 | 5 |
| 3. Records data accurately. | 1 | 2 | 3 | 4 | 5 |
| 4. Demonstrates scientific curiosity. | 1 | 2 | 3 | 4 | 5 |
| 5. Predicts outcomes. | 1 | 2 | 3 | 4 | 5 |
| 6. Formulates reliable conclusions. | 1 | 2 | 3 | 4 | 5 |
| 7. Demonstrates effective use of time. | 1 | 2 | 3 | 4 | 5 |
| 8. Shows care and ability with equipment. | 1 | 2 | 3 | 4 | 5 |
| 9. Follows safety precautions. | 1 | 2 | 3 | 4 | 5 |
| 10. Shows care and ability in lab cleanup. | 1 | 2 | 3 | 4 | 5 |

*(The Kids' Stuff, 1988)*

# Peer Observation Form

**Directions:** After examining a product or viewing a presentation of another student or group in your class, take a few minutes to complete this evaluation and give feedback to your peers.

1. What was the theme, topic, or purpose of this product or presentation?

2. What two or three key ideas did you learn about the topic or theme from this product or presentation?

3. What part of the product or presentation did you think was the most creative, unusual, or unique and why?

4. What did the product developer(s) or presenter(s) do to capture the attention and interest of the audience?

5. What suggestions might you offer the product developer(s) or presenter(s) for improving and strengthening the work?

6. How would you rate the overall product or performance? Write your comments below. If you assign a letter grade or a rating from a scale, you must defend your position.

# Topic 7 SELF-ASSESSMENT TOOLS AND TECHNIQUES

## ▶ What are they?

**W**hen students assess themselves, they reflect on, make judgments about, and report on their own behavior and performance. In most cases, students respond to specific questions or statements designed to elicit feedback on aspects of their academic experiences, affective behaviors, or personal feelings. Teachers use these responses to assess students' individual performance and attitude. Self-assessments can take many forms:

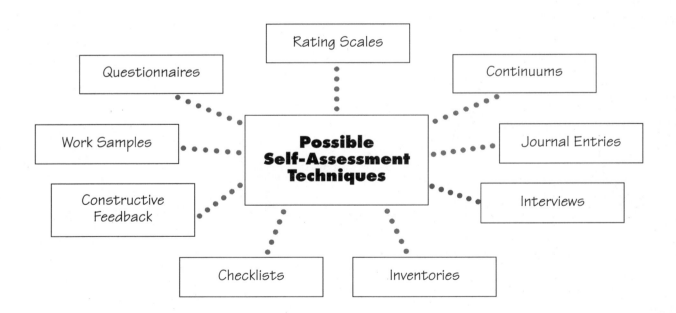

(Ann Arbor, 1993)

The advantages of self-assessment are many. It should be a significant component of any comprehensive student evaluation program. Following are two of the major purposes of self-assessments:

> First, they provide a way for the teacher to encourage the students to become responsible for what has been taught and what is expected of them as a result. Second, the students' responses provide rich data for the teacher in determining the next steps in instructional planning. They reveal students' understanding of what the teacher has taught and often provide hints about what else needs to be taught. (Rhodes, 1993)

Ten important benefits of self-assessment follow. Self-assessment:

1. Places the assessment burden on the students themselves

2. Can answer students' two most basic questions: "How am I doing?" and "Where do I go from here?"

3. Can provide a basis for agreement between you and your students on academic priorities

4. Can improve effectiveness, as opposed to efficiency, in the schooling process

5. Encourages students to analyze objectively their own attitudes and aptitudes

6. Relates progress to performance for both teachers and students by helping to answer such questions as "Are we doing the right things?" and "Are we doing the right things in the right way?"

7. Helps students prepare for added growth and responsibility

8. Promotes a feeling of personal accomplishment

9. Encourages individual goal setting

10. Acknowledges and accommodates differences in learning styles

(adapted from Forte and Schurr, 1993)

# ► How are they different?

Unlike more traditional types of measurement, student self-assessment reports allow you to view how students are understanding new material, internalizing unfamiliar concepts, and integrating new learning with previous knowledge. They give you, the instructor, an invaluable opportunity to intervene early in the learning process by correcting misinformation and clarifying misunderstandings as they occur.

Even more important, whereas traditional assessments provide you with the feedback that allows you to adjust your approaches and strategies, self-assessments give your *students* the information *they* need to make their own adjustments. Guided reflection and self-disclosure allow students to make discoveries about themselves as learners, and the qualitative measures they engage in metacognitively can result in their taking a more active part in their learning.

A sample student self-assessment checklist appears at the end of this section (Copy Form 12). The kind of questions it suggests can be adapted to many different learning situations and content areas.

## ▶ How do we get started?

**Step 1:** Establish a climate that encourages honest, thorough responses.

The usefulness of self-assessment data depends on how honestly students report their feelings, beliefs, intentions, and thinking processes. Brainstorm ways you and your team members can convey to students that self-analysis is an integral part of the teaching and learning process. Introduce a variety of reflective strategies—journal writing, conferences, personal inventories—to provide practice in self-assessment tasks.

**Step 2:** Introduce student contracts.

These are a valuable tool for making self-assessment an integral part of the classroom experience. With appropriate teacher input and approval, student contracts can provide an outline and a time line that describe what a student is accountable for. Contracts should include the metacognitive dimension that is an integral part of a self-assessment experience. A sample student contract appears at the end of this section (Copy Form 13).

**Step 3:** Model self-assessment strategies.

Students need role models to help them develop standards for their own performances. It is important, therefore, that you engage in many of the same self-assessment techniques you ask of your students. Keep a journal, complete an inventory, rate a lesson plan, maintain a portfolio. Share your own work and reflective feedback with your students at every opportunity. A sample self-assessment checklist appears at the end of this section (Copy Form 14). Although this checklist is specific to writing, it can serve as a guide for creating similar checklists in other curriculum areas.

**Step 4:** Become knowledgeable about what to look for in student self-assessment tasks and how to use the information from these tasks in meaningful ways.

■ Look for signs of change and growth in student attitudes, understandings, and achievement levels.

■ Look for alignment of students' beliefs about their performance with their actual performance.

■ Look for a match between your students' expectations and criteria for evaluation and your own.

■ Look for agreement between student self-assessments, student work, and your own assessments. Discuss agreements and disagreements, and negotiate any changes in students' assessments.

■ Document your observations, discussions, and findings.

■ Put self-assessments (dated of course) in student portfolios. Have students reflect on the changes in their work over time.

■ Encourage students to share their self-evaluations with both peers and parents.

(adapted from Stenmark, 1991)

**Step 5:** Conduct regular student-teacher conferences.

Use these as opportunities to review portfolios and self-assessment instruments, set short-term goals, provide feedback, and help students maintain a positive self-image. A sample conference form appears at the end of this section (Copy Form 15).

# ▶ Where do we go for more information?

Frank, M. 1979. *If you're trying to teach kids how to write, you've gotta have this book*. Nashville, TN: Incentive Publications, Inc.
A complete approach to understanding and working with the whole writing process. Provides at-your-fingertips sources for ideas on specific writing activities; a resource book to direct you to more sources of ideas and teaching aids; a ready-when-you're-in-need manual for solving writing problems; a private lesson for teachers on how and when and where to promote independent writing; and a personal propaganda notebook on the joys of teaching writing. Includes inventories, checklists, questions and answers, materials, and illustrations.

# References

Ann Arbor Public Schools. 1993. *Alternative assessment: Evaluating student performance in elementary mathematics.* Palo Alto, CA: Dale Seymour.

Forte, I. and Schurr, S. 1993. *The definitive middle school guide: A handbook for success*, p. 286. Nashville, TN: Incentive Publications, Inc.

Frank, M. 1979. *If you're trying to teach kids how to write, you've gotta have this book.* Nashville, TN: Incentive Publications, Inc.

Rhodes, L. K., ed. 1993. *Literacy assessment: A handbook of instruments*, p. 45. Portsmouth, NH: Heinemann.

Stenmark, J. K., ed. 1991. *Mathematics assessment: Myths, models, good questions, and practical suggestions.* Reston, VA: National Council of Teachers of Mathematics.

# Student Self-Assessment Checklist: Writing

**Name** _____

**Date** _____

**Directions:** For each statement below, answer *Yes*, *No*, or *Not Certain*, whichever seems to describe best how you feel about your own work in English. There is no right or wrong answer, so please be as honest as you can.

1. Sometimes I don't know what to do when I am given a writing assignment.

2. I like English because I like to "play with words."

3. I like to write stories, poems, reviews, essays, and mini-term-papers.

4. The more challenging the writing assignment, the better I like to work on it.

5. I usually give up when I can't think of a topic to write about.

6. There is more to writing than just getting something down on paper to fulfill the assignment.

7. I think writing is not really a useful tool to have in everyday living.

8. I would rather work alone on a writing project than with a group.

9. I like to do a lot of different types of writing rather than the same kind of writing again and again.

10. I enjoy writing tasks.

11. There's always a best way to start or finish a piece of writing.

12. I liked writing when I was younger, but now it's too hard.

## Put an "X" on this scale where you think you would belong.

| I am not good at writing | | | | I am O.K. at writing | | | | I am good at writing | |
|---|---|---|---|---|---|---|---|---|---|
| 1 | 2 | 3 | 4 | 5 | 6 | 7 | 8 | 9 | 10 |

*(adapted from Stenmark, 1991)*

# Contract for Learning

**Name** _____

**Date** _____

1. I will be starting my work on _____
   I will finish by _____

2. What I want to find out:

3. What I will be doing:

4. Resources I will need:

5. Places I will look for information:

6. Some problems I expect to encounter:

7. How I will share my findings:

8. Who will evaluate my work:

9. The criteria that will be used to evaluate my work:

10. The grade, score, or comments that I expect to receive:


**Student's Signature** _____

**Teacher's Signature** _____

# Teacher Self-Assessment: Writing

**Name** _____

**Date** _____

1. As a writer, I am

2. Three words that describe how I feel about teaching writing are

3. Three words to describe how I think my students feel about writing are

4. I believe writing lessons in the classroom are (*Circle one.*)

   *very important*      *of value, if there's time*      *not very important*

5. A classroom writing experience should involve

6. I spend approximately _____ each week on writing.
   *(time)*

7. The part of writing that I teach BEST is

8. One GOAL I have for writing in my classroom this year is

*(Frank, 1979)*

# Student-Teacher Conference Form

**Name** _____

**Date** _____

**Subject Area** _____

## STUDENT SELF-ASSESSMENT

What goals have you set for yourself since our last meeting?

In your opinion, how well have you met these goals?

How can you use these new skills and/or concepts to improve your understanding in the future?

What two new goals do you want to work toward during the next four to seven weeks?

## TEACHER ASSESSMENT

Comments on student responses to questions above:

# Topic 8  NORM-REFERENCED AND CRITERION-REFERENCED TESTS

## ▶ What are they?

*Standardized tests are norm-referenced—that is, the performance of sample populations has been established and serves as a basis for interpreting a student's test performance by comparing it with other students' performances.*          (Ornstein, 1992)

Standardization refers to the *sameness* of what is tested, how it is tested, and what the test scores mean. Norm-referenced tests tend to be both reliable and valid because the norms are based on large populations. These tests compare each individual student's score with a given set of peers; the score reports whether a student is above average, average, or below average in comparison to that group.

There are four basic types of norm-referenced tests:

1. Intelligence tests, which provide a general measure of a student's presumed potential learning ability or aptitude

2. Achievement tests, which measure the general and accumulated knowledge and skills of students in multiple subject areas

3. Aptitude tests, which predict achievement in areas often not formally taught in school

4. Personality tests, which can help diagnose some characteristics that affect students' learning

Criterion-referenced tests, by contrast, measure an individual student's level of mastery relative to specific criteria. They do not compare the performances of students with other students; rather, they determine what students know and are able to do at a specific point.

### POINTS TO PONDER

How compatible are norm-referenced tests and criterion-referenced tests with the middle school concept?

Is it wrong "to teach to the test"? Aren't tests supposed to reflect specifically what is taught?

| CHARACTERISTIC | NORM-REFERENCED TEST | CRITERION-REFERENCED TEST |
|---|---|---|
| **MAJOR EMPHASIS** | Measures individual's achievement (or performance) in relation to a similar group at a specific time | Measures individual's change in achievement (or performance) over an extended period of time |
| | Survey test, achievement test | Mastery test, performance test |
| **RELIABILITY** | High reliability; usually test items and scales are .90 or better | Usually unknown reliability; when test items are estimated, they are about .50 to .70 |
| **VALIDITY** | Content, construct, and criterion validity usually high | Content and curricular validity usually high if appropriate procedures are used |
| **USABILITY** | For diagnosing student difficulties; estimating student performance in a broad area; classifying students; and making decisions on how much a student has learned | For diagnosing student difficulties; estimating student performance in a specific area; certifying competency; and measuring what a student has learned |
| | Administration procedures are standardized and consistent from class to class | Administration procedures vary among teachers |
| | Large-group testing | Small-group, individual testing |
| **CONTENT COVERED** | Usually covers a broad area of content or skills | Typically emphasizes a limited area of content or skills |
| | School (or teacher) has no control over content being tested | School (or teacher) has no control over content being tested |
| | Linked to expert opinion | |
| **QUALITY OF TEST ITEMS** | Generally high | Varies, based on ability of test writer |
| | Test items written by experts, pilot tested, and revised prior to distribution; poor items omitted | Test items written by teachers (or publishers); test items are rarely pilot tested; poor items omitted after test has been used during second usage |

| | | |
|---|---|---|
| **ITEM SELECTION** | Test items discriminate among individuals to obtain variability of scores | Includes all items needed to assess performance; little or no attempt to deal with item difficulty |
| | Easy and confusing items usually omitted | Easy or confusing items are rarely omitted |
| **STUDENT PREPARATION** | Studying rarely helps students obtain a better score, although familiarity with the test seems to improve scores | Studying will help students obtain a better score |
| | Students are unable to obtain information from teachers about content covered | Students are able to obtain information from teachers about content |
| **STANDARDS** | Norms are used to establish a standard or to classify students | Performance levels are used to establish students' ability |
| | Intended outcomes are general, relative to performance of others | Intended outcomes are specific, relative to a specified level |
| | Score is determined by a ranking, average or stanine | Score is determined by an absolute number — i.e., 83 percent right |

(Ornstein, 1993)

# ▶ How are they different?

Although norm-referenced tests, criterion-referenced tests, and the types of authentic assessment discussed in this module are all designed to measure student achievement and attainment of skills, they go about it in very different ways. Standardized tests quantify the end result of the learning process through a series of simple, discrete items, while authentic measures focus on the process of learning through a series of complex, holistic activities. Authentic assessment places a high value on the student as an active participant in applying knowledge rather than as a passive receptacle who merely recalls information or knowledge.

Some *advantages* of norm-referenced and criterion-referenced tests:

- Standardized tests offer quick, easy scoring.
- Each student is judged against the same standard.
- Because of the number of items on an objective test, an extensive sample of a student's command of knowledge can be obtained.

- Consistency in scoring and extensiveness in sampling make objective tests more reliable than tests that require written responses.
- They recognize and reward high achievement.
- Standardized achievement tests can provide a good measure for assessing whole-school results.

(adapted from Ebel, 1977)

Some *disadvantages* of norm-referenced and criterion-referenced tests:

- Test results are often wrong. Because of inadequate reliability and validity, no test score is accurate enough to be used as the sole or primary basis for making decisions such as student placement or grade promotion.
- Many tests are biased.
- Tests are often improperly administered. Untrained test administrators; awkward seating; overheated, chilly, or noisy rooms can all produce lower scores.
- Test questions may be flawed. Sometimes a question will have more than one "correct" answer. Other times no choice may be completely right. Test writers may sometimes make mistakes. The machines that grade answer sheets can also make errors.
- Standardized tests discourage imagination and critical thinking. These exams reward students who quickly select the "best" answer without thinking too hard. Test-taking skills are the opposite of the good study habits our schools should teach. When the goal of schooling becomes high test scores, imagination and critical thinking get driven out of the classroom.
- Tests don't measure important thinking skills. Standardized multiple-choice tests don't deal with reasoning, problem-solving, or idea formation—the higher-order thinking skills. Instead they focus on simpler tasks like recognizing facts. Multiple-choice tests tell students what the problem is without making them figure it out. In no subject area can a multiple-choice test adequately evaluate higher-order thinking or the ability to use knowledge to solve real problems. Nor can any standardized test measure "people skills," imagination, creativity, determination, or leadership.
- Tests don't reflect how people actually learn. Psychologists now know that learning is active. People learn by connecting what they already know with what they are trying to learn. If students cannot actively make meaning out of what they are being taught, they are unlikely to learn or remember. When instruction is controlled by the tests, students become passive and unthinking. In the end, students forget most of what they "learned" because it had no meaning for them.

## CHALLENGE TO TEAM

Try constructing a test to measure your students' people skills, imagination, creativity, determination, or leadership. What would it look like?

- Standardized tests damage school quality. Increasingly, students' test scores are used to rate teachers, schools, and entire districts. This makes for "high-stakes" testing. When school officials and teachers feel pressure to improve test scores, they start to "teach the test." This means that classrooms are turned into test-coaching centers.

(National Center for Fair and Open Testing)

# ► How do we get started?

## 1. Inform yourself about the standardized tests in use in your school.

If your school or district requires norm-referenced testing, seek as much information as you can to clarify the selection purpose and process. Use the following five W's and the How to guide your investigation.

- WHAT standardized tests will I administer this academic year?
- WHO selected these tests and by what criteria?
- WHEN will I administer these tests to my students, and when will I receive the results?
- WHY are we administering these tests, and how will they serve my students?
- WHERE can I go for assistance to better understand the norms, content, and interpretation of test results so that I can use them as diagnostic tools to improve instruction for my students?
- HOW well do the test questions meet the curricular objectives for my students, grade level, and subject matter content?

## 2. Become knowledgeable about test-writing techniques.

Since criterion-referenced tests are usually teacher-created or tailored by teachers to meet their own content objectives, it is important for you to become "test-wise." Some general guidelines to follow when you are constructing criterion-referenced tests are

- Relate each test item to a specific content or skill (instructional) objective for the curriculum.
- Keep each item simple, clear, and well defined.
- Make sure that each item elicits information that is both relevant and useful to the student.
- Design each item to stand on its own, independent of all other items.
- Make each item a factual and objective statement rather than an opinion or subjective statement.

- Keep items free from textbook jargon or formal "teacher talk."
- Construct each item as a simple or compound sentence rather than a complex sentence whenever possible.
- Write each item in a style that matches the style of the desired response.
- Make certain that each item is age- and grade-appropriate.
- Double-check each item for any spelling, grammar, and typing errors.

A set of checklists for developing some of the most common types of teacher-created tests appears as a copy form at the end of this section.

## CRITERION-REFERENCED TESTS: SOME COMMON TYPES

| | ADVANTAGES | DISADVANTAGES |
|---|---|---|
| **SHORT-ANSWER AND FILL-IN TESTS** | Easy to score<br>Can provide comprehensive content sampling<br>Elicit direct recall of specific facts<br>Establish the presence of enabling knowledge | Usually don't sample content thoroughly<br>Test low-level cognition<br>Can unintentionally test reading comprehension |
| **RESPONSE-PROVIDED TESTS (TRUE/FALSE, MULTIPLE-CHOICE, MATCHING)** | Easy to score<br>Usually unambiguous<br>Less time-consuming<br>Formats familiar to students<br>Allow immediate feedback | Knowledge not always necessary for answers to be correct<br>Answers can be construed from phrasing of items<br>Often misused to test only low-level cognition |
| **ESSAY TESTS** | Flexible approach to topic<br>Comprehensive approach to topic | Require time to complete<br>Usually do not sample content thoroughly<br>Difficult to score consistently and fairly |

(adapted from Westgaard, 1993)

# ▶ Where do we go for more information?

Westgaard, O. 1993. *Good fair tests*. Amherst, MA: HRD Press, Inc. Provides everything necessary to create, customize, select, and administer superior tests. Designed for use in business and industry, but applicable also to schools. Covers types of tests and test items; measurement of competence, performance, and mastery; principal uses for tests; justifying, planning, and developing the test; formatting, producing, and administering the test; evaluating the test and evaluating the results; and ethics of test management. Includes references, testing terms, and sample tests.

## References

Carey, L. M. 1988. *Measuring and evaluating school learning*, pp. 128–129. Needham, MA: Allyn & Bacon.

Cashin, W. E. 1987, January. *Improving essay tests*. Idea Paper No. 17, Kansas State University, Center for Faculty Evaluation and Development.

Ebel, R. L. 1977. *The uses of standardized testing*, pp. 48–49. Bloomington, IN: Phi Delta Kappa Educational Foundation.

National Center for Fair and Open Testing. *Standardized tests and our children: A guide to testing*, pp. 11–17. FairTest.

Ornstein, A. C. 1993. Norm-referenced and criterion-referenced tests: An overview. *NASSP Bulletin* (October): 36–38.

Ornstein, A. C. 1992. *Secondary and middle school teaching methods*, p. 163. New York: Harper Collins.

Westgaard, O. 1993. *Good fair tests*, pp. 44–60. Amherst, MA: HRD Press, Inc.

# Test-Writing Guidelines

## TRUE/FALSE TEST

❑ Does each test item reflect only one major concept or idea?

❑ Is each item written with a positive rather than a negative focus?

❑ Does each item avoid trick or trivial statements?

❑ Is each item free of double negatives?

❑ Does each item avoid such words as *all, never, entirely, absolutely, only,* or *nothing*?

❑ Does each item, whether true or false, contain approximately the same number of words?

❑ Is each item totally true or totally false with no qualifications?

❑ Are there approximately equal numbers of true and false statements?

## MULTIPLE-CHOICE TEST

❑ Is the stem of each test item brief, concise, stated positively?

❑ Is each stem either a direct question or an incomplete statement?

❑ Does the stem include as much of the item as possible so that students can avoid reading the same information over and over as they are analyzing the alternatives?

❑ Have you included alternatives that would seem feasible to a student who is not prepared?

❑ Are the alternatives for a given stem of equal length?

❑ Are the alternatives sequenced in a random order?

❑ Are the alternatives free of such ambiguous options as "none of the above" or "all of the above"?

❑ Are grammar and punctuation between stems and alternatives correct?

## MATCHING TEST

❑ Are directions explicit, and are students told how often responses will be used?

❑ Is each set of stems and responses homogeneous?

❑ Are responses short and logically sequenced?

❑ To decrease guessing, have you included two or three extra responses?

## SHORT-ANSWER TEST

The following options can help you achieve variety in your short-answer items:

❏ Provide the definition of a concept. Students write the name of the concept defined.

❏ Name a concept. Students write a brief definition.

❏ Name a concept. Students list its unique characteristics.

❏ Provide a definition, rule, or principle. Students supply a missing word or words.

❏ Provide a resource paragraph. Students recall specific details, punctuate the paragraph correctly, reorder the information, or edit it.

❏ Provide an incomplete paragraph. Students write an introductory or concluding sentence for it.

❏ Provide passages. Students analyze them, list the main ideas, or discuss the relationships among them.

❏ Exhibit a product. Students list its qualities, including any inadequacies.

❏ Provide a series of exhibits such as slides or specimens set up at different test stations. Pose questions about each exhibit. Students circulate and write short answers.

*(adapted from Carey, 1988)*

## ESSAY TEST

❏ Do test items require higher-level thinking skills rather than simple recall of factual information? Do they elicit creative thought and problem-solving skills?

❏ Do items outline a specific task or set of tasks?

❏ Does each item specify the amount of time to be spent on it as well as the points to be awarded?

❏ Do items cover the key concepts of the course content, and are they designed so that students can write quality responses in a single sitting?

❏ Do items require responses that are specific enough that evaluators can agree on what constitutes an acceptable response?

❏ Does each item include a checklist of information or ideas that should appear in a satisfactory response?

❏ Are tests free from optional questions or opinion-based questions that can detract from the overall mission of the test, fragment the student's thinking, and hamper your ability to assess students consistently?

# It's Your Turn

Try this "essay test" on essay questions. HINT: You may want to take this test after you have read the entire module.

**1. Knowledge (10 points):** List some advantages and disadvantages of using essay test items with students.

**2. Comprehension (10 points):** Give two reasons why students might prefer essay test items to objective test items.

**3. Application (15 points):** Create a well-constructed essay question based on the material in this section.

**4. Analysis (15 points):** In the context of the subject area you teach, identify five essential characteristics of a well-written response to an essay question; then prepare a set of essay test instructions to guide your students to produce skillfully crafted responses.

**5. Synthesis (25 points):** Outline a five-minute presentation, based upon recent writing and research on essay tests, describing how middle school teachers should and should not approach grading a large stack of essay exams.

**6. Evaluation (25 points):** Under what classroom testing conditions do you think essay tests are most useful and under what classroom testing conditions do you think multiple-choice tests are most useful?

# ▶ What is it?

**W**hile achievement means many things to many people, there has long been an assumption among educators that achievement is synonymous with accomplishment and that it can be measured by degrees of accomplishment referred to as "grades." Most teachers establish a preset standard that their students must meet in order to receive a particular grade or mark, and many schools or districts adopt an official grading scale.

Grading scales have serious limitations; they are at variance with both the philosophy of the middle school and the unique needs and characteristics of ten-to-fourteen-year-olds. While many good middle schools do value grades as a viable method for measuring student achievement, they also recognize the importance of supplementing these with more authentic means of measuring student progress. Some of the limitations of the traditional grading system are outlined below and on the chart on the following page.

- Grades rarely convey a realistic picture of a student's achievement or progress. They provide limited information and are often inconsistent from grade to grade, teacher to teacher, school to school, and district to district.

- Grades are often dependent upon a teacher's ability to develop valid, reliable tests and evaluation criteria.

- Grades do not allow for individual differences in aptitudes, abilities, learning styles, and backgrounds.

- Grades create winners and losers; grading curves, norms, and quotas often force students to compete in no-win situations.

- Grades do not correlate with later achievement in the workplace; increasingly, employers prefer to see concrete evidence of a student's work rather than a transcript of grade point averages.

- Grades often motivate students for superficial and extrinsic reasons rather than for meaningful and intrinsic reasons. Grading can lead to an overemphasis on marks rather than learning for learning's sake and can motivate students to cheat, cram, or even drop out.

- Grades don't encompass all dimensions of an education; they place far more emphasis on test results than on behavioral attributes.

**T**O DEFINE

Determining student grades on the basis of predetermined standards is referred to as criterion-referenced grading. Norm-referenced grading, on the other hand, is based on the relative accomplishment of individuals within the group by comparing and ranking students within the group, which is most often known as grading on the curve.

(Kellough, Kellough, and Hough, 1993)

## ADVANTAGES

1. Is fair and objective. The teacher is not apt to be swayed by subjective factors, and the need for interpretation is minimized.

2. Is quantifiable, explicit, and precise. Students and teachers know exactly what the numbers are and what they stand for.

3. Minimizes conflict over what grade a student should receive.

4. Facilitates the weighting of tests and class activities. For example, a teacher may choose 5 points for each quiz, 25 points for a special project, and 25 points each for the midterm and final.

5. Is cumulative. The final grade can be determined by a single computation at the end of the grading period.

6. Facilitates grading by establishing clear distinctions. Once categories are weighted and points totaled, assigning the grade for each student is a straight-forward task.

## DISADVANTAGES

1. Emphasizes objectivity of scoring, not learning. Conveys the message that learning is equivalent to the accumulation of points, not the acquisition of skills and knowledge.

2. Presents an illusion of objectivity. Every test and assignment results from a series of subjective decisions by the teacher—what areas to cover, how to weigh particular answers or aspects of performance, and so forth.

3. Reduces impact of teacher's judgment. A point system minimizes the teacher's professional judgment and results in a somewhat inflexible grading system.

4. Hides importance of patterns. Average or total scores at any point, rather than improvement or decline, are emphasized.

5. Gives undue weight to fine distinctions. A single point difference, which may represent only a small difference in learning, may be the difference between a B- and a C+.

6. Leads to cumulative errors. A particular test score or classroom activity may not truly reflect the student's abilities or learning. The final total represents the sum of all such errors.

7. Is subject to misinterpretation. Without norms it is false to assume that a certain range (90 to 100) or number (93) represents a valid indicator (e.g., an A) of performance or that categories (breakpoints) can be decided in advance.

(Madgic, 1988)

# ► How is it different?

In effective middle level schools, report cards and grades are balanced using other data-gathering and reporting tools such as letters to parents, parent conferences, supplementary reports, self-assessment tools, collaborative tests, portfolios, product development, performance opportunities, observations, and learning logs or response journals. These alternative assessment methods help to offset the limitations and disadvantages of letter grades and point systems.

# ► How do we get started?

## 1. Establish a grading policy.

Since grades are an integral part of any instructional program, it is important that you and your team members agree on an approach to grading. Your policy should take the form of a clearly written statement of your team goals, policies, procedures, and standards regarding the assessment process. The policy should be included in your team handbook and should be accessible to both students and their parents. Some ideas for you to consider in developing your grading policy follow:

- Design a master plan for assessment that includes a variety of tools, techniques, and sources.

- Set standards for grades and mark each student in relation to those standards so that you come as close as possible to an absolute system of grading that incorporates your team's judgment of students' progress.

- Base grades on the degree of progress made by students; take into account both their achievement and their attitudinal levels.

- Avoid using grades as a threat, and avoid changing grades except in cases of an obvious error in calculation.

- Keep students informed of their standing and progress. This involves everything from returning tests to students on time to the distribution of interim reports, especially when problem situations occur.

- Involve students whenever possible in setting up criteria for grades and grading practices. The more input they can have into the system, the more ownership they will display when grades are awarded or distributed.

## Do YOUR METHODS MEASURE UP?

Do your grading methods

- Empower students?

- Involve students in self-evaluation?

- Give you, the students, or their parents enough information about student needs, interests, growth areas, and achievement levels?

- Connect directly to what you are teaching and what students are learning?

- Integrate well with classroom assignments, activities, and delivery systems?

- Provide evidence of students' development of desired skills and behaviors?

■ Maintain accurate records of all test results and other assessment measures. Be able to defend your grading practices at all times to all people.

■ Incorporate ongoing assessment measures into your daily classroom activities so that your students perceive them as an integral part of the teaching and learning process.

## 2. When traditional grading methods are necessary, adapt them to your beliefs and needs.

You can integrate alternative practices into traditional systems and at the same time reduce the time you spend on grading and record keeping.

■ Ask students to discuss completed assignments with a partner or small group. They can read their work to the group or make copies of their work for other students to read. The group comments on each student's work. In some classrooms, each student in the group makes a specific suggestion for improvement.

■ Randomly select students to work out problems or homework items at the blackboard. Discuss the work as a class. You can include the class in evaluation or use the opportunity to make your own evaluation notes.

■ Ask two or three students each week to act as teacher-helpers, checking class homework or using your test key to grade quizzes. Periodically check the helpers' work to ensure accuracy and honesty.

■ If you assign a list of questions to be answered, have students discuss each question on a separate sheet of paper. Select only one question for assessment.

■ Post answers to selected questions or problems on a bulletin board. Students can check their own work for the posted items, and you can collect and check the remainder.

■ Use the following technique to have students grade one another's homework or quizzes. One student assesses another student's paper and notes a proposed grade on an index card. Another student then assesses the same paper, notes a grade on a separate index card, and checks to see if the grades match. If they do, the paper is returned to the student whose work it is. If they do not match, then the student graders meet to work out the discrepancy. If you use this strategy, make sure that you provide students with specific criteria for their assessment.

■ Grade only one major paper or homework assignment per class per week.

■ Grade only every other, or every third or fourth, item in a series.

- Carry a clipboard or record book (use graph paper for easy observation and note taking) around the room as you monitor the work students perform in class. At the end of the grading period, include these classwork grades (perhaps 20 percent of the total grade).

- Assign self-correcting or programmed worksheets for homework. The value of this is that students become responsible for their own learning—and pace of learning. However, this kind of assignment should always be discussed in small groups.

- Grade only one major paper or activity for every two or three that you assign. Do not announce which you will grade until the day of submission. Have students review the other papers or activities in pairs, small groups, or in a whole-class discussion with feedback provided by both you and students.

(adapted from Ornstein, 1992)

### 3. As a team, conduct both student and parent conferences on a regular and consistent basis throughout the school year.

In some of these conferences, the entire team of teachers should meet with the student and parent or guardian to combine their input and collaboratively report on the student's progress.

## GUIDELINES FOR CONFERENCES

1. Try to arrange a group conference that includes all stakeholders interested and involved with the conference's desired outcomes. Consider inviting
   - All staff members of the interdisciplinary team
   - Other appropriate staff members such as guidance counselor, principal, etc.
   - The student
   - Parents/guardians if available

2. Plan for the conference in advance. Consider preparing
   - A student self-assessment sheet with a series of unfinished statements for the student to complete and share at the conference:

     My easiest subject is . . .

     My hardest subject is . . .

     I want my mom/dad to know about . . .

     I have trouble in school when . . .

     Something I want to discuss is . . .

# 10 QUESTIONS TO ANSWER FOR STUDENTS BEFORE YOU GIVE A TEST

1. Is it going to be a quiz or a test?

2. How much will it count?

3. What form will it take (multiple-choice, essay, fill-in-the-blank, vocabulary, open-book, true/false, short-answer, oral)?

4. How many questions will there be?

5. Will all questions be equal in value?

6. How much time will be allowed for it?

7. Will there be a review session?

8. What class material will it cover: notes? lecture? outside readings?

9. Should the answers be complete sentences?

10. Can I hand in the test/quiz as soon as I finish? (Teachers: set a minimum number of minutes before you will accept the test. Requiring students to keep it for a specified time encourages them to take their time, go back over it, and proofread it.)

– A conference record sheet that includes
   Conference date, time, place, and persons in attendance
   Purpose of conference
   Summary of problem, information, or data to be shared
   Outline of action to be taken by teachers, parents/guardians, and student
   Follow-up tasks to be completed by teachers, parents/guardians, and student
   A place for signatures of all conference participants

3. Conduct the conference in an open and positive manner by
   – Beginning with a positive statement about the student
   – Stating the purpose and/or problem in specific terms
   – Offering assistance and/or solutions to parents/guardians
   – Addressing the parents/guardians by name throughout the conference
   – Summarizing the conversation and decisions at the end of the conference
   – Ending the conference on a positive and optimistic note
   – Following up the conference with a telephone call or letter

4. **Try out one or more of these innovative practices for reporting student performance in your classroom.**

- Consider giving more than a single grade. Develop a progress report for each activity, detailing specific tasks and expected student performance.

- Include more than cognitive development and specific content knowledge in your grading. Note social, psychological, and psychomotor behaviors and creative, aesthetic, and artistic learning, as well as scientific and technical abilities.

- Develop report cards specifically suited to particular grade levels rather than using one form for the entire school.

- Grade students on the basis of both an absolute standard and a relative standard.

- Report each student's progress (based on the student's own ability plus a comparison with peers).

- Introduce new categories instead of, or in addition to, standard letter grades or categories; write individual statements such as "needs more time to develop" or "shows progress."

- Stress strengths of the student. Limit the weaknesses or problem areas to two or three and specify ways for improving them.

- Replace or supplement the standard card with a larger, more detailed folder that contains explanations for students and parents.

- Provide space for comments by both teachers and parents, not just for their signatures.

- Provide space for requests by both parents and teachers for parent-teacher conferences.

- Organize committees of students, teachers, and parents to meet periodically (every three or four years) to improve the school district's standard report card.

- Supplement report cards with frequent informal letters to parents, parent-teacher conferences, and student-teacher conferences.

(adapted from Ornstein, 1992)

# References

Cashin, W. E. 1987, January. *Improving essay tests*. Idea Paper No. 17, Kansas State University, Center for Faculty Evaluation and Development.

Kellough, R. D., Kellough, N. G., and Hough, D. L. 1993. *Middle school teaching: Methods and resources*. New York: Macmillan.

Madgic, R. F. 1988. The point system of grading: A critical appraisal. *NASSP Bulletin*, April: 29–34.

Ornstein, A. C. 1992. *Secondary and middle school teaching methods*, p. 235. New York: Harper Collins.

## Tips for Scoring Essay Tests

- **Outline the response BEFORE reading the essays.**
- **Choose the scoring method best suited to the question type.**
- **Use point values that are easy to assign and manipulate.**
- **Decide beforehand how you will handle grammar, spelling, handwriting, etc.**
- **Grade each test without knowing whose it is.**
- **Grade only those qualities relevant to course goals.**
- **Ensure that the question has been adequately answered.**
- **Be prepared to deal with "creative" responses.**
- **Grade the tests in a "question-by-question" rather than a "student-by-student" sequence.**
- **Shuffle the tests after scoring an item when there are several test items.**
- **Resist mid stream changes in grading.**
- **Maximize the specific feedback (both cognitive and affective) you provide.**
- **Provide extensive comments.**
- **When feasible, use multiple readings and/or readers.**
- **Consider keeping a test file on your essay questions.**

(adapted from Cashin, 1993)

# Grades—and You: Idea Starters

1. How many ways can you think of to improve your grades?

2. How, where, and when do you get the best grades? Are there any patterns?

3. List reasons why you want to make good grades.

4. How can you predict what grade a teacher is going to give you on a project, presentation, test, or report card?

5. What do you think would happen if all grades in the world were abandoned?

6. What would the notes you take in class say to a friend, teacher, or parent?

7. List your strengths and weaknesses as a student.

8. Design an ideal grading system for you and the students on your team.

9. What makes a grade fair?

10. Which is heavier—an A or an F—and why?

11. Invent a new technique for grading student work.

12. Classify ways students deal with academic failure.

13. Survey twenty people to get immediate reactions to the word *grades*. Interpret the results.

14. What rewards would you give yourself and others for getting good grades?

15. Create a model report card format for you and your peers.

# Acknowledgments

*Grateful acknowledgment is made for permission to reprint the following copyrighted material:*

**Page 74:** Alexander, W. M. and Mc Ewin, C. K. *Schools in the Middle: Status and Progress.* Copyright © 1989. Columbus, OH: National Middle School Association. **121:** Jacobs, H. H. "Planning for Curriculum Integration." *Educational Leadership,* 49: 27–28. Copyright © 1991. **129:** Palmer, J. M. "Plannning Wheels Turn Curriculum Around." *Educational Leadership,* 49: 61–65. Copyright © 1991. **129:** Beane, J. A. *A Middle School Curriculum: From Rhetoric to Reality* (2d ed.). Copyright © 1993. Columbus, OH: National Middle School Association. **148:** Glatthorn, A. and Baron, J. "The Good Thinker." In *Developing Minds: A Resource Book for Teaching Thinking,* ed. A. Costa. Copyright © 1985. Alexandria, VA: Association for Supervision and Curriculum Development. **149:** Lipman, M. "Critical Thinking—What Can It Be?" *Educational Leadership,* 46: 1, 38–43. Copyright © 1988. **152:** Beyer, B. K. *Developing a Thinking Skills Program.* Copyright © 1988. Needham, MA: Allyn and Bacon. **157:** Winocur, S. Lee. "Project IMPACT." In *Developing Minds: A Resource Book for Teaching Thinking,* ed. A. Costa. Copyright © 1985. Alexandria, VA: Association for Supervision and Curriculum Development. **166:** O'Shea, L. J. and O'Shea, D. J. "What Research in Special Education Says to Reading Teachers." Copyright © 1994. In *Teaching Reading to At-Risk Learners,* eds. K. D. Wood and B. Algozzine. Needham, MA: Allyn and Bacon. **196:** Campbell, B., Campbell, L., and Dickinson, D. *Teaching and Learning Through Multiple Intelligences.* Copyright © 1992. Seattle, WA: New Horizons for Learning. **197:** Johnson, D. W., Johnson, R. T., and Holubec, E. J. *Circles of Learning: Cooperation in the Classroom.* Copyright © 1991 Edina, MN: Interaction Book Company. **201:** Kagan, S. *Cooperative Learning.* Copyright © 1992. San Juan Capistrano, CA: Resources for Teachers, Inc. **259:** Fogarty, R. *How to Integrate the Curricula.* Copyright © 1991. Palatine, IL: Skylight Publishing, Inc. **263:** George, P. and Lawrence, G. *Handbook for Middle School Teaching.* Copyright © 1982. Glenview, IL: Scott, Foresman and Company. **271/274:** Bellanca, J. *The Cooperative Think Tank II: Graphic Organizers to Teach Thinking in the Cooperative Classroom.* Copyright © 1992. Palatine, IL: Skylight Publishing, Inc. **280:** Black, H. and Black, S. *Organizing Thinking: Graphic Organizers.* Book 2. Copyright © 1990. Pacific Grove, CA: Critical Thinking. **301:** Fitzpatrick, C. "Educational Technology." In *Linking Through Diversity: Practical Classroom Activities for Experiencing and Understanding Our Cultures,* eds. W. Enloe and K. Simon. Tucson, AZ: Zephyr Press. **358:** Paulson, F., Paulson, P., and Meyer C. "What Makes a Portfolio a Portfolio?" In *Performance Assessment: Readings from Educational Leadership,* ed. R. S. Brandt. Copyright © 1992. Alexandria. VA: Association for Supervision and Curriculum Development. **360:** Murphy, S. and Smith., M. A. *Writing Portfolios: A Bridge from Teaching to Assessment.* Copyright © 1991. Markham, Ontario: Pippin. **361:** Buschman, L. "Portfolios: Windows on Learning." *Learning,* January 1993: 21(5), 22-25. **368:** Maples, C. "Presenting Portfolios." *Learning.* October 1992: 21(3), 41. **373:** North Central Regional Educational Laboratory. *Schools That Work: The Research Advantage. Guidebook 4. Alternatives for Measuring Performance,* p. 9. Copyright © 1991. Oak Brook, IL: North Central Regional Educational Laboratory. **376:** Brandt, R. S. ed., *Readings from Educational Leadership: Performance Assessment,* p.117. Copyright © 1992. Alexandria, VA: Association for Supervision and Curriculum Development. **379:** Wollman-Bonilla, J. *Response Journals,* pp. 24–25. Copyright © 1991. New York: Scholastic-Professional Books. **385:** Scutt, E. "Reader Response Journals," p. 155. In *The Whole Language Catalog Supplement on Authentic Assessment,* eds. Goodman, K. S., Bird, L. B., and Goodman, Y. M. Copyright © 1992. New York: Macmillan/McGraw-Hill-American School Publishers. **390:** Carter, J. A. and Carter, D. E. *The Write Equation: Writing in the Mathematics Classroom,* pp. 59–62. Copyright © 1994. Palo Alto, CA: Dale Seymour. **396:** *The Kids Stuff.* "Science Yellow Pages for Students and Teachers." Copyright © 1988. Nashville, TN: Incentive Publications, Inc. **405:** Frank, M. *If You're Trying to Teach Kids How to Write, You've Gotta Have This Book.* Copyright © 1979. Nashville, TN: Incentive Publications, Inc. **408:** Ornstein, A. C. "Norm-Referenced and Criterion-Referenced Tests: An Overview." *NASSP Bulletin.* October 1993: 36–38. **409:** National Center for Fair and Open Testing. *Standardized Tests and Our Children: A Guide to Testing,* pp. 11–17. Fair Test. **418:** Madgic, R. F. "The Point System of Grading: A Critical Appraisal." *NASSP Bulletin.* April 1988: 29–34.

## PHOTOGRAPHS
**Cover:** (top) David Wolff-Young/Photo Edit (bottom) Will and Demi McIntyre/Photo Researchers, Inc. **page 1:** Nita Winter/The Image Works **31/ 65:** Mary Kate Denny/Photo Edit **115/177:** Joel Gordon **331:** Spencer Grant/Photo Researchers, Inc.

**Cover Design:** Robin Herr
**Book Design:** Bonnie Chayes Yousefian
**Technical Production:** David Reiffel

# Index

434